The Teachings of Mary

The pilgrimage route of the Virgin Mary

The Teachings
of Mary

The pilgrimage route of the Virgin Mary

Hans Lyngsgaard

AXIS MUNDI
BOOKS

Winchester, UK
Washington, USA

First published by Axis Mundi Books, 2012
Axis Mundi Books is an imprint of John Hunt Publishing Ltd., Laurel House, Station Approach,
Alresford, Hants, SO24 9JH, UK
office1@o-books.net
www.o-books.com

For distributor details and how to order please visit the 'Ordering' section on our website.

Text and drawings copyright: Hans Lyngsgaard 2011

ISBN: 978 1 84694 916 6

A CIP catalogue record for this book is available from the British Library.

Design: Lee Nash

Translation: Tove Angus

Printed and bound by CPI Group (UK) Ltd, Croydon, CR0 4YY

CONTENTS

Preface

Dear reader:

With this book I invite you on a journey into beautiful landscapes, historical events, and a spiritual world where I quite freely consort with angels and divine beings. It is a pilgrimage of a couple of thousand kilometers from Bingen in Germany to Ephesus in Turkey.

This is a personal journey which has grown out of the depth of my soul. But also a journey with the Virgin Mary as my companion and guide, where places and events on the way open one door after another into a world of wisdom and loving guidance. To what I allow myself to call 'The Teachings of Mary'.

All the incidents on the journey have deep meaning for me and are as tangible as the rest of my reality. In my culture, one normally keeps such experiences to oneself, and I am crossing my own threshold of modesty by publishing them. I presume to believe, however, that they can be of significance to others, and so I have chosen to present them more or less as they came and as I wrote about them in my diaries.

I have my limitations. My own framework of understanding and degree of openness dictate what I can receive. And even though I try to be clear, my ego cannot be prevented from peeping out and blurring the picture.

I ask you to make allowances for this and to try and sense whether something deep within you is touched. If this should be the case, it is not me but the Virgin Mary who has come through to you.

Welcome to the pilgrimage of the Virgin Mary.

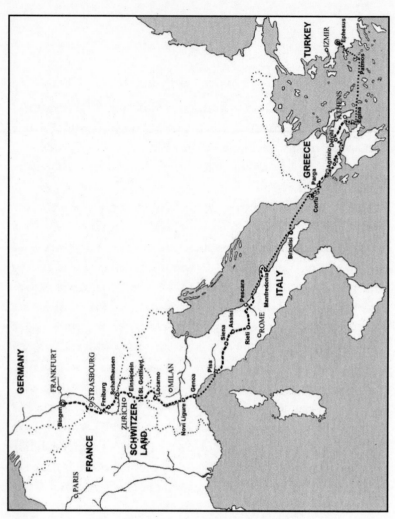

The pilgrimage route of the Virgin Mary

Introduction

Prelude

A large pile of floorboards lies in front of me. Everything is ready for the floor to be laid. I look across the attic which I am converting into a meeting room. The old floorboards have been taken out, so now I have to jump from one joist to another. I have just nailed in wedges to ensure that the new floor will be quite level. Now all I have to do is to lay the boards. I reach out for the first board, but stop in mid-air. I have seen something out of the corner of my eye. There is a figure standing behind me at the other end of the attic. I turn. Time stands still. Even before I have turned right round, I know quite unerringly that the figure is the Virgin Mary. When I look up I see – nothing. I am astonished. Nothing there; and yet something has taken place. I sense it powerfully and irrefutably.

That was the first time the Virgin Mary came to me. In 1997.

* * *

Now I was not brought up on the Virgin Mary. She actually played a very minor part in the Lutheran Christianity of my childhood. She was the mother of Jesus and quite central in the Nativity, but that was about it. Nor do I remember any pictures of her in our churches.

To be quite honest, I had never really switched on to Christianity. I found learning by rote difficult, so I hated all the memorizing of hymns that constituted the main part of our religious education at school. The one time I remember giving any particular thought to Christianity was at primary school.

One day, being a little sleepy, I had dozed off during a Religion lesson – growing up on a farm I had to get up early to muck out the pigs before cycling to school. I was suddenly disturbed by my teacher asking me a question. I promptly answered with a loud 'Yes' without knowing what he had asked. My teacher found this intriguing and asked me to elaborate, but my mouth was firmly closed as I had no idea what we were talking about. Afterwards I asked the boy beside me what the question had been and he repeated it for me: 'Some people think that Jesus was the first socialist. Do you agree? Hans?' I hardly knew what a socialist was; but the fact that I had now acquired an opinion about Jesus started me thinking.

Nothing came of it though, and through most of my adult life neither Christianity nor any other religion has held much interest for me.

In the last 20 years or so, however, my interest in spiritual matters has been aroused. Not through religion but through repeatedly experiencing spirituality in nature. Experiencing that there is an opening to something divine through the strange and wonderful world of nature.

Thus I also began to take an interest in primitive Christianity and visited both Mount Sinai and the Virgin Mary's house in Ephesus.

The second time the Virgin Mary appeared to me was on the shortest day of the year 2000. When you learn to identify with the cycle of the year and of nature, the winter solstice takes on a special importance, marking the retreat of darkness, the strengthening of light and the lengthening of days. As midnight passes on this the darkest night, at the darkest time of the year, it is wondrous to sit outside and be aware of the rebirth of light. And so I sat in the year 2000, meditating in the moonlight and the biting cold.

Suddenly a voice comes through to me and somehow I just know it is the Virgin Mary. Simply and clearly she asks, 'Will you rediscover my pilgrimage route?' Rather taken aback, I try to consider the request. Not that I doubt that it is Mary asking, but I sense that if I agree, I will be taking on a great task. Am I ready for this? Her pilgrimage route could be anywhere in the world.

To refuse, however, would be like refusing life itself. Something inside me overcomes any doubt and I give her my answer: Yes.

* * *

That night the door to a great adventure was opened. It began with three and a half years of research.

Something made me take an interest in Lake Constance in southern Germany. That first summer I managed to lure my wife (Kirstin Pinstrup Thomsen) on a camping holiday in that area. In a previous meditation, I had been told that it would be expedient to make a stop at the convent of Hildegard of Bingen, west of Frankfurt. Here I somehow expected to be given a hint about where in southern Germany we might find traces of the route. So I sat down in the church of the convent to 'tune in' to Mary. It was actually just like turning the knob on an old radio to try to find a station on a certain frequency. Great was my surprise when Mary came through quite clearly and said, *'The route starts here!'* She later added that our course was to be *'30 kilometers south and then turn right'*. We drove approximately 30 kilometers south and turned right. Here we were given new directions: *'30 kilometers south-west, over a bridge and turn left'*. We carried on, crossed a bridge and immediately saw a signpost to the ruined convent of Disibodenberg. Was this a coincidence? This was where Hildegard had spent 37 years of her life. Hildegard – one of the most significant religious figures of the Middle Ages. I was given further instructions, but at some stage we lost the thread and ended up at Lake Constance. Here, however, I did not sense any of the special 'Mary-energy' and received no confirmation.

After a couple of days' holiday by the Rhine, Kirstin and I went to see the Rhine Falls. Here I found the energy again. I sensed Mary's presence and was overwhelmed by the impressive waterfall. This place was clearly on the route, and at the time, I understood it to be the end goal of the pilgrimage.

Driving home, I was given directions for the route up across Schwarzwald.

In the summer of 2002 I walked the 420 kilometers from Bingen to the Rhine Falls, quite convinced that the route ended there. But on my arrival, sitting in the church by the waterfall, I felt no release and I received no confirmation from Mary. I found this very harsh after all the hardships of my trek, and my tears flowed freely. I was very frustrated and needed help to carry on. Later, by a lucky coincidence, I happened to meet a clear-sighted woman, Grethe Toftlund Nielsen, who was able to help me by mediating a communication with Mary for me. Grethe is able to facilitate a connection with spiritual levels without personally coloring the contact. I have since used Grethe whenever I have been in doubt. My driving force and guide throughout the journey has been my direct contact with Mary, and the experiences I have had in the landscape. But during my search there have been things I could not understand and here I have looked to Grethe for explanation. Mary has, however, only given me directions through Grethe if my own search and experiences had brought me to the point where the answer was just below the surface. Throughout the book I have been careful to state when contact has been via Grethe.

Through Grethe, Mary told me that the pilgrimage route went on from the Rhine Falls to her house in Ephesus – the site near Izmir on the west coast of Turkey where Mary is said to have spent the last years of her life, and which is now a place of pilgrimage. In Mary's time Ephesus was a great city with more than 200,000 inhabitants – a cosmopolitan port and the gateway to 'Asia', busy with shipping bound for the rest of the Roman Empire. In the mountains south of the town lies 'Mary's House' and this was apparently where her pilgrimage really ended.

It took me a couple of days to absorb this information. The

challenge was much greater than I had expected. Would I be physically able to walk so far – and was I prepared to do it? Had I the right to be absent from my duties at home for so long? From the running of my architect's office and our farm? My legs might not last out the whole walk.

I decided that I could at least try to determine the key locations of the route.

Even on the 420 kilometers of my first journey, I had found it difficult to believe that Mary herself had walked so far. Though she had told me several times that this was the case, I found it simply too unlikely. But when she now repeated this yet again through Grethe, I had to give in.

I had to now think of the route as a road that could have been walked nearly 2000 years ago.

In 2003 and early in 2004 Kirstin and I spent our holidays in Italy and Greece to try and find the key locations of the route: towns or holy places where I – after some training – could sense and recognize Mary's energy. As if she had left a special scent in her footprints.

Slowly the general outline of the route was beginning to take shape. I now hoped to have a chance to make the actual journey in the not-too-distant future. Based on my first walk, I calculated that it would take nearly four months to do the whole pilgrimage, which I judged to be between 2,000 and 2,500 kilometers. I thought I would have to wait several years and perhaps even until I retired. For many years I have run my own architect's practice where I design and oversee the construction of a wide variety of buildings. There has always been more than enough to do, and I could hardly imagine having the time to take such a long holiday. But in 2004, by a very strange coincidence, I suddenly had a four-month break between two jobs. Very odd, seeing as how there had been so much to do over the last two years that I had almost had to work double time. On the other hand I had now saved up just what was needed for the journey –

and suddenly I had the time. Once again my wife Kirstin supported me. She promised to see to my duties at home. The impossible had come to pass, everything was arranged, and I could start out on the walk of my life.

PART I

TO BE CREATED

Germany, France, Switzerland

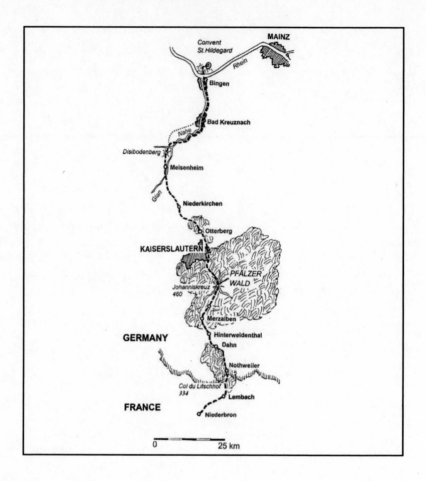

I

The Journey Opens

Hildegard – Temples in the landscape – Pfalz

It is drizzling and I am wearing my waterproofs. With my rucksack on my back, I pass through grapevines along a narrow lane parallel to the Rhine. The beauty of the landscape unfolds before me despite the wet weather. Mountains rise up in the north, sometimes towering towards the river, sometimes retreating and sending inviting, lush runnels down to the river bank. The green vineyards cling like a wet vest to the mountain sides. The rain blots out all colors, turning the river water grey. It flows along perfectly peacefully. Here the Rhine is wide and in the broad riverbed it does not reveal its enormous power. Further down is Rüdesheim and, on the opposite bank, Bingen.

I am on my way to the convent of Hildegard of Bingen. I climb a small hill, and the twin towers of the convent come into sight across the vineyards. I am glad to see it again and quite excited too. In that church, in a very short time, I shall begin my pilgrimage.

I take a deep breath and enter the church. The nave is dark. A single lamp casts a feeble light over the front pews. From a large mosaic in the apse Jesus looks down over the nave, and on the tall wall to the left Hildegard greets me from a large painting.

At the back of the church I put down my rucksack and light a candle in front of a small statue of the Virgin. I walk up the aisle to the altar rails. I am anxious, for I know that the beginning is important. This is where the door of the tour will be opened.

I have brought small gifts as tangible tokens of my gratitude for being allowed to make this journey in the company of the Virgin Mary. I sense that I am to place the gifts on the broad cover-stone of the rails. Gifts are important. I would have liked to have picked a rose for Mary myself. There was no time for that, and instead I have brought flowers which my wife and good neighbors have given me. A pink rose, variously colored tulip petals, and a heart-shaped stone. After carefully arranging my gifts, I sit down and let calm and quiet fill my body and soul. I say a short prayer, in which I contact the Virgin Mary and tell her I am ready to travel her pilgrimage route. I ask for help to be obedient and to trust in her instructions as I make the journey. I conclude by asking for her protection.

As if with a voice from within me, Mary answers that my gifts are accepted. The heart-shaped stone from me, the rose from my wife, and the tulip petals from my neighbors. *'The rose and the tulip petals show that you are rooted in the place where you live. That is good.'*

For a fleeting moment I feel ashamed. My hastiness with the gifts cannot be hidden from Mary.

Convent of St. Hildegard

I have started journeys here in this church twice before and, each time, a ceremony seems to play itself out in my mind's eye. In front of me I see not only the Virgin Mary but also the archangel, St. Michael. They ask me to accompany them up to the altar. Physically I remain seated, but it is as if the figure of my soul steps out of my body and goes with them. I walk up to the altar with Mary and Michael on each side of me. We bow, turn and approach an imaginary christening font. Here they sprinkle me with water, and explain that this is a purification. We return to the altar and Mary and Michael address themselves to God. They say I am ready. We are answered that the road is open for me. *'You will meet three challenges on your way: endurance, fervor and joy.'* For a while we remain standing there, and to my great surprise, an imaginary dove suddenly flies down and lands on my head. I can hardly believe it. This is the very symbol of the Holy Ghost. *'Not only have you been blessed, the embodiment of my blessing has been sent to go with you. On this journey you are granted the power to give blessing.'*

The ceremony at the altar is over. I am asked to physically approach the rails. Mary, the figure of my soul and Michael come down from the altar. They pass through me, turn and enter into me. I am ready. I give thanks and we leave the church. The journey can commence.

* * *

Before me lies the outline of a route that winds its way down through Germany, France, Switzerland, Italy and Greece, ending in Ephesus on the west coast of Turkey. Unlike the pilgrimage routes to Santiago de Compostella which are dedicated to the disciple James, this route is dedicated to the Virgin Mary. The remains of the house where she is thought to have lived out the last years of her life were discovered at Ephesus in the 1800s, through a vision. The vision was supported by archaeological findings, and for nearly a hundred years now the Roman Catholic Church has recognized the site as 'The House of the Virgin Mary'.

Unlike the James Way, there are no hostels along Mary's pilgrimage route and it is not mapped or signposted. Maybe the route was well known in former times, but today there are no details to be found.

However unlikely it may seem, Mary is said to have walked the route herself, shortly after the death of Christ. I have been told this over and over again. This puzzles me. Why in the world would Mary start a pilgrimage from here? She must somehow or other have come to Europe and then turned back here, the return journey becoming her pilgrimage route. Hildegard's convent was originally on the other side of the Rhine, in Bingen, but has recently been reconstructed where it stands today. Mary was somewhere in the vicinity, but she seems to have chosen the convent as the starting point for my journey due to the fact that it is today a fully operating and lively place – and because of Hildegard, a woman who was a significant female figure in medieval religious life.

HILDEGARD VON BINGEN

Hildegard lived from 1098 to 1179 and was known by her contemporaries as 'The Sibyl of the Rhine'. At the oracle of Delphi, the Greek Sibyl put into words the gods' answers to people's questions. Hildegard, however, received divine visions of impressive magnitude. Visions about the whole of Creation and its mysteries. About Jesus and the redemption of Man through him, in which Mary and the feminine aspect played a part. About cosmic man, the Holy Spirit, angels and much else. She wrote works on herbal medicines based on her own experiences and findings. She understood that man and nature were organically connected, and saw this as the explanation of nature's healing power. In addition to this she wrote liturgical songs.

Hildegard was acknowledged by the Pope, and her advice was sought on theological, medical and political matters. Her answers were often very blunt and direct.

Hildegard's manifestation of femininity shone in an otherwise totally male-dominated world.

Now I take my first steps. I leave the convent and walk downhill, down to Rüdesheim. Then I sail over to Bingen on a little passenger ferry.

The sun has not broken through the mist yet. The air is cool and refreshing. The other seven or eight passengers are sitting inside. I have taken a seat right up front in the bows where I can feel the spray of the water on my face. I feel as though I am being cleansed and baptized in the waters of the Great Mother. After all, the Rhine is one of Europe's major mother rivers – life-giver to great areas of land. We put in at Bingen. There is no gangway so we jump from the boat up onto the jetty. This is where the pilgrimage has its beginning – its root. Today Bingen is an industrial town full of large companies and with a busy railway. I slip over to the west bank of the River Nahe to the ruins of the Rupertsberg convent which Hildegard founded in 1150. The convent no longer exists. There are only a few meager remains.

I have been very much in doubt as to whether the Virgin Mary really had been this far up in Europe, so it is important for me to determine whether it was actually possible to walk here 2000 years ago. Determine whether there is any archaeological evidence of paths and roads dating back to the first half of the first century.

Sources do in fact show that Drusus, stepson of Caesar Augustus, built a river fortress, 'Castellum Bingium', at this location in the year 11 BC. The fortress stood until 355 AD. Archaeologists have even shown that during the first decade AD a wooden bridge was built across the River Nahe. It wasn't destroyed until 70 AD, so in Mary's time there was a good bridge here.

Hildegard and Mary presumably both followed the west bank southwards, each in their own time. Today the road is a very busy highway, so I choose to follow the beautiful cycle path on the east bank instead, the Nahe Radwanderweg. Germany is blessed with an extremely well-developed network of cycle roads on which traffic is sparse and one is free to concentrate on one's thoughts and surroundings. The path winds across flat fields and through small towns.

It is my first day, and I have to get into my stride. My shoelaces need retying. The straps of my rucksack need adjusting. My body needs adjusting too. After a few kilometers my limbs loosen up and I get into a good rhythm. It feels good to be underway. I fill my lungs with fresh air. Happily greet the few cyclists I meet.

At intervals I try to concentrate on my inner thoughts – seek inwards – but am interrupted by a ringing bicycle bell, a tractor in a field, a low-flying heron, a stinking manure heap outside a village. I drink it all in. Am so absorbed in everything that I even lose my way once or twice. So I have to consult the map and find my way back onto the route. I am well stocked with maps. Hiking maps for the first 1,000 kilometers. They weigh over a kilo. I have altogether more weight on my back than I had planned. I had aimed at keeping it down to 10 kilos. Everything was meticulously weighed and, except for a single change of clothing, I am wearing practically all I have brought. Lightweight trousers, lightweight shirts, lightweight sleeping bag, waterproofs and a good fleece. I have not brought a tent as campsites are few and far between, and because I prefer to have a shower after the sweat of the day. After having packed my rucksack, I was still within my weight limit but had forgotten my collection of maps, a liter of water and fruit for lunch. On top of all that, I ended up adding a pile of brochures and booklets about the places I visited. The whole thing quickly shot up to 14–15 kilos. It took some getting used to.

After nearly 30 kilometers I reach Bad Kreuznach, a town which has sprouted along the banks of the River Nahe. Today it is a well-known spa town, which may also have been the case in Mary's day.

The Romans set great store by the mild climate and life-giving waters of this valley, and archaeologists tell of a flourishing

Roman culture here in the centuries around the birth of Christ. Once in Bad Kreuznach, I am set on getting to the hostel where I have made a reservation. The hostel turns out to be at the opposite end of the town – a long walk and uphill all the way. I suddenly sense that Mary is becoming distant. Going up here is not what she has chosen for me. She accepts it reluctantly because I have a reservation, but she would rather I had stayed down in the town where she herself had spent the night. I resolve not to make any more reservations.

I have not listened to Mary's instructions properly and have gone astray. She suggests that we accept my straying as beginner's error and try to do things differently from now on.

I promise to do better, but I might as well admit now that this becomes a recurring theme of the journey.

I am a rational person, and like to be in control of myself and my situation. I like looking at maps and having some idea of where I am going. I don't dare to surrender myself to my intuition and to trust unquestioningly the inner voice which I ascribe to Mary. For how do I know when it isn't just my imagination playing tricks on me?

Sometimes I can guess Mary's probable route. But often the road takes unexpected turns, and if I am not paying proper attention to Mary I end up on the wrong track. At every crossroads, I have to ask her which way she went and trust to my intuition for the answer. If I do go the wrong way I usually realize my mistake when I sense her absence or when I land in some tiresome situation: heavy traffic, detours over steep hills or the lack of a certain special warmth in the landscape. Luckily I have had the opportunity to practice communicating on my earlier journeys, but it is not easy having to concentrate non-stop.

I usually find Mary speaks to me in my right ear, as if she is walking – or gliding – right next to me. I hear an inner voice and as a rule I answer with my own inner voice. At times, though, the situation seems so real that I catch myself speaking aloud.

When I need to choose which path to take, it happens that Mary expresses herself in words, but often I cannot grasp the words, and instead have to try and envisage which way she turns.

Through wordless conversation, Mary and I now agree on clearer signals:

- If she spreads out her arms, opening her cloak, it means: Here I have rested. You are on the route.
- If she raises only one arm, it means that I am to go in the direction her arm indicates.
- If she draws the cloak tightly around her, it is a sign that the place is not on the route.

From Bad Kreuznach Mary took a road going west, out of the town and up over the highlands. I am allowed to choose freely whether to take this road or to follow the valley. I decide to continue on the cycle path along the River Nahe. The beautiful undisturbed cycle path affords me the peace and quiet to turn my concentration inwards. Long unbroken stretches are best for this purpose. I practice being present on an inner spiritual level while at the same time being completely aware of the surrounding nature. It is quite fantastic to walk at the edge of a wood with all its scents, birdsong and traversing animals, and happy are the moments when I perceive the supernatural tones with which the soul of the wood seems to make itself known.

When I arrive at the junction where the cycle path meets up with the old road, it is as if Hildegard joins us. As if she has accompanied us from Bingen. I am happy. We join up and, however strange it may sound, it is as if there are three of us walking and talking together, despite there being a thousand years between each of our lives.

My work as an architect is all about building things. Solid objects and very concrete discussions with workmen. I am a practical person and enjoy physical labor. My wife and I have a smallholding with some land attached to it. There are incessant jobs to be done and a constant effort to make ends meet. One would think this down-to-earth side of me would be a stark contrast to supersensory experiences. But I have learnt to trust my intuition, to sort out the worst self-asserting experiences, to trust my first impulses and especially to trust sensations which take me by surprise. To me, walking and talking with Mary, as if she were right beside me in the flesh, is entirely real.

I am told that the journey from Bingen to Disibodenberg is a pilgrimage in itself. An illustration of the main pilgrimage. I have been in Disibodenberg several times, and each time has been an enormous experience. So I look forward to the visit.

Hildegard is obviously pleased to see Disibodenberg. She says it is the most beautiful place on earth.

She lived here from when she was 14 years old till she was 52. The mountain – or hill – is named after an Irish monk, Disibod, who settled here as a hermit in the 7th century. Before then, the place had been a site of both Celtic and Roman cult worship.

The remains of the abbey lie on a wooded hill in the middle of the valley. The ground between the trees and the many remains is carpeted in grass. The large church and extensive buildings bear witness to an impressive abbey which in its day housed a great number of monks and nuns.

Disibodenberg

Last time I was here, Hildegard led me up to the ruined church and to my surprise she asked me to kneel before the altar. There I felt a divine presence and heard it speak to me: *'I am pleased with what you are doing. There is something I want you to do: bless the route where you walk.'* I objected: 'How am I able to bless? I cannot do this.' *'Yes, you can. I authorize you to give blessing in my name.'*

On my present journey I have again been granted permission to give blessings; so, with much assistance, I formulate a blessing: 'In the name of God I bless this place as being a part of the Virgin Mary's pilgrimage. May this be revealed to all who come here, and may they be blessed.'

I bless all the significant places on my journey, and each time, the statement of the blessing somehow seems to physically settle there. Like lighting a candle to mark the route.

So here I am again at Disibodenberg, as full of anticipation as last time. After 'finding the frequency' – tuning in to the energy of the place – we walk up towards the old abbey gateway. I realize at once that we are processing. Hildegard, Mary and I, side by side. Slowly and in a stately manner. Through the gateway, into the abbey grounds, down along the old south wall of the church, through the entrance at the west end of the nave and into the aisle.

Here stands an enormous oak tree divided at its foot into three great trunks. There is strong symbolism in this division. I position myself between the trunks, attempting to sense whether they represent the Holy Trinity. It is as if the tree answers *'Yes: The Father, the Son and the Holy Spirit.'* 'Is it not: The Father, the Son and the Mother?' I ask. *'No,'* comes the answer, *'I abide by the interpretation of the church!'* And I must admit this is very loyal, seeing as how we are inside what used to be a church.

The remains of the old walls are all that is left to give an impression of the contours of the church. Yet it is as if the old church rises up out of the turf, forming invisible arches. We proceed up the aisle. There seem to be hundreds of monks on either side of us. They are all pleased to see Hildegard and Mary, and to my surprise they also seem to be looking at me with admiration. I try to ignore them. Mary and Hildegard lead me up through the nave to the heart of the church. They stop, and it becomes clear that I am supposed to say something. I pull myself together and make a little speech about my journey, concluding by donating a malachite stone to the church. Stand a while with Mary and Hildegard. Am then told to go up and sit on the chancel steps.

I inadvertently sit down with my back to the altar. Somehow this seems odd – but that is apparently the way it is meant to be. Sit for a while and study the dancing butterflies. Suddenly sense two dark figures approaching from behind to place a crown on my head. They come from the direction of the altar so for a moment I very nearly accept their actions, but then I feel the dove on my head trapped inside the crown. I stand up abruptly, throw away the crown and say angrily: 'No one shall trap the dove of the Holy Spirit inside a crown!'

The situation is tense, but seems to relax and I am asked to approach the altar itself. I am surprised that I do not, as before, sense a sublime, divine power. On the contrary I am encircled by abbots bowing and scraping to me. 'Stop it!' I say. 'You must praise the spiritual impulse I represent, not me.' Again the situation becomes tense, almost threatening. I turn sharply and go down to the center of the transept, the heart of the church. Mary and Hildegard follow me. First, following Mary's directions, we walk along the southern transept and turn to face the assembly in the side aisle and chapel. Then walk across and do the same thing in the northern transept. Return to the heart and pace down through the nave. Everything is done firmly and with steady steps, as if we are defying the assembly. Finally I climb up between the three trunks of the oak tree. Thank the tree for its years of contribution and establish the fact that a new impulse is now needed. I then leave the church with Mary and Hildegard the same way we came in. Mary hurries me on. There are clearly other powers at work here – dark powers. We aim for the new chapel where we have arranged to say our goodbyes to Hildegard, but first we stop just outside the church and turn to confront the dark powers behind us. I see immediately that I am up against something far greater than I can deal with and that I need help. I invoke St. Michael. At the opening of my journey, in the convent of Hildegard of Bingen, I had been granted St. Michael's help if ever I should need it. He appears now with his shining sword and enters the church. We wait. *'The dragon awakes,'* says Mary. *'We do not have much time.'* Shortly afterwards Michael comes out again. The dark powers are pacified but something is still rumbling. Mary hurries me on again and we make haste to the new chapel. Michael remains outside while Mary and I go in and take our leave of Hildegard. Again Mary hurries me on, saying that we must cross the river before four o'clock. I judge that we should be able to make it easily in the 20-odd minutes we have, and take time to say goodbye properly.

Then, swiftly, we leave the chapel and the hill of ruins. I find my rucksack and we hasten, half running, down to the road and on southwards, down to the town. Despite sensing that I must not focus my attention on the abbey – not look up there – I send Hildegard a final greeting and take a quick glimpse back at the chapel. Immediately register a searching stare from the church. We hurry across the river, and make it over just before four o'clock. Greatly relieved, I continue along the cycle path towards Meisenheim.

A kilometer later, Mary says we can relax and talk. She asks me what I thought about the episode in the church.

'It was a test,' I answer. 'My ego thrived on their admiration and that brought on the test. I feel that I handled the situation responsibly, but I was very much in doubt as to the deeper meaning of it.'

'Yes, you passed the test,' says Mary, *'but everything that happens*

on this journey happens on two levels. There is a personal level and a deeper, spiritual level.' I ask why we had to leave in such a hurry. Mary answers: *'There is no reason to stay standing at the edge of an erupting volcano.'* She continues, telling me that many dark powers have been building up underground and that the bubble was about to burst as a result of my rejection of the crown and my establishing that the era of the oak tree was ended. St. Michael pricked the bubble, causing it to explode. During such an explosion the dark powers – or lost souls – have a few minutes to attach themselves onto something before being pulled away, their first goal being whatever caused the explosion. *'And if you had still been on that side of the river, they would have clung to you. It was for your sake we had to hurry, and it worked. You acted well. You did and said the right thing.'* Mary ends: *'On this basis I look forward to the rest of the journey.'*

* * *

In Meisenheim the next morning I do not get properly tuned in. The churches are closed and I set off without being certain of my way.

Mary tells me that I must start by focusing my attention on her and make a point of consciously picking up the thread from the day before. Otherwise she will spend ages struggling to catch up before we can make contact.

She informs me that the challenge of the day is endurance, and she is right. My body is tired and wants to stop, but this is only day three and it is much too early for self-pity. I spend large parts of the day on a very busy road to Otterberg with the occasional relief of an alternative cycle path. On one such path I pass right by some ruins.

ROMAN COURTYARD

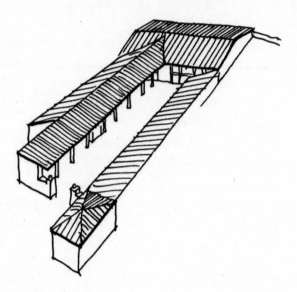

'The buildings (34x16 meters) stood around a square yard. The west and north wings were residential and bath houses.

The construction shows a functionally planned court-yard, with decorative ressauts and door frames in a repre-sentative frontage. The south-western remains are from a farm building ...

The site is on an unfavorably low-lying protrusion in the bottom of a valley. The construction was originally erected in the 1st century AD, as a half-timbered building. Shortly afterwards it was extended in stone. The extremely damp subsoil called for extensive groundwork and the use of large foundation plates.

The place apparently fell into disuse in the 3rd century'

Signboard at the ruin

However insignificant this ruin may seem, it is important for the pilgrimage route. A representational Roman farm with bathing facilities in such a low-lying situation would hardly have been any ordinary farm. On the other hand the stretch of meadowland between the farm and the stream would have been excellent grazing and so I presume that at this farm one could find a bed, a bath and overnight grazing for one's horses and draught animals. That is to say, a hostel. In other words an important road must have passed this way in Mary's time, important enough to have hostels. More proof that it was possible to walk this way 2000 years ago.

An old highway

A bypass has been built around Otterberg so I turn onto a gravel road. Uphill and into a forest. By the roadside I find a milestone from the year 1613 telling me I have found the original main road to Otterberg. Most old main roads from before 1700 are assumed to have been used as major thoroughfares since ancient times, for methods of transport did not change significantly and there was therefore no call to change the roads. One traveled on foot, by

horse or in carts drawn by horses or oxen. Not until the introduction of royal and imperial stagecoaches did the road patterns
change. A milestone from 1613 could even be a mark of a
thoroughfare a thousand years old.

The forest stretches right in to the center of Otterberg. My
road comes out onto a high ridge from where I can see the great
church of the monastery towering up at the center of the
medieval town.

Medieval travelers must have been met by the same sight and
for an instant the ages merge. I might just as easily have been a
pilgrim in the 14th century.

CISTERCIAN CHURCH IN OTTERBERG

The magnificent church in Otterberg was built between
1168 and 1254. In the early days it was part of a large
Cistercian monastery which flourished in the 1300s. Today
the church is used by both Catholic and Protestant congregations. Central to the church is a very powerful large
modern wooden sculpture of Mary.

I stay at the hotel next door to the church. I find out that there
happens to be an opera performance in the church that evening.
Rappresentatione di Anima e di Corpo, composed by Emilio de
Cavalieri in the year 1600. The music surges through the church,
thrown back and forth back by the great arches. Here, opera
comes into its own. Moreover the plot is remarkably relevant to
me. The play between the body (*Corpo*) and the soul (*Anima*). The
body is personified in a depraved male figure and the soul in a
pure female figure. After a series of interludes the body realizes
that it loves the soul and it all ends happily with a warm union
between them.

The next day Mary leads me out of Otterberg by a back road.

We pass south-east of the center of Kaiserlautern and reach Pfälzer Wald – the Palatinate Forest. A colossal forest area I need to cross. I try to follow the signposted paths. Get lost at first, and when I do that, I tend to be impetuous and act rashly. Luckily I recognize the signs and instead sit down and eat my lunch. I study my compass and see that the route I had picked first had actually been the right one. Enjoy walking for hours under shady, leafy treetops or between majestic fir trees. The air is fresh and very pure. My lungs almost gulp it in, letting it flow in to their farthest corners.

Later that afternoon I reach my goal in the middle of the forest, Johanniskreuz. An old and significant crossroads set at the highest point in the area. There are two hotels offering cheap accommodation here. The place does not distinguish itself with a vantage point or dramatic rocks. It is more a large clearing fringed with old deciduous trees. At first sight it is not particularly notable. But all the same something grand and somehow raw shines here. There are a couple of forest restaurants full of people. Men and women in black leather stand around impressive and highly polished motorbikes. The place is swarming with motorcyclists. Several larger roads meet here and traffic is intense. The revving up of the motorbikes especially paints a raw sound-picture. Even so, on special occasions, open-air worship is held at the edge of the forest. There is a small church here. Quite new. It is dedicated to both John the Baptist and John the Disciple. Perhaps the origins of the name Johanniskreuz (John's Cross) are uncertain and so it has been decided to take both Johns. I allow myself to believe that the name has its earliest origins in the disciple John of whom it is told that he was loved by Jesus and of whom Jesus required that he be like a son to Mary. It is also said that he then stayed at Mary's side for the rest of her life. I remember that even on my first visit to Johanniskreuz I got the feeling that he had accompanied Mary here.

Mary later confirmed this, and Grethe elaborated:

'That which my son spoke of on the cross was done. John became my new son. He became the one who, at a worldly level, dealt with the loving contact with Jesus that I had lost.

'I just want to tell you that even though a lot is written about the resurrection, Jesus did not live on in an actual physical form. He lived on in spiritual form. But those who knew his spirit had no difficulty in recognizing him. He was capable of recreating his form in a spiritual – almost tangible – body. It was tangible! This lasted until his ascension. I knew that Jesus would only be able to wear his spiritual body for a limited time.

'I mention this here to draw attention to the fact that John now became my companion and that he was my companion on my journey. At times he stayed a little longer somewhere, while I went on alone. But he had dedicated his life to taking care of me. So he was always somewhere close by. Therefore you will be able to sense his presence also.

'It could be quite dangerous for a woman of my stature and delicacy to travel such a long way alone, so he was there to protect me. One might assume that I was protected by God. And so I was. But even though one is protected by God, there can still be dangers lurking along your way.'

Here at Johanniskreuz it feels as though John and Mary crossed their own tracks. The first time I was here I was confused by all the tracks I sensed. As if they went north and south as well as east and west. Later I realized that Mary and John originally seem to have come from France and crossed through here going east. On their way home from Bingen they seem – like now – to have come from the north on their way south. It becomes more and more clear to me that John is to play an important role in a new, modern understanding of Christianity. Perhaps ancient stories of John crossing his own track through here sowed the idea of the name Johanniskreuz.

* * *

Next day I manage to tune in properly. In the thicket outside the hotel I pick up the threads of the route. I review the journey so far, and add to it the stage for today. As I am setting out from the highest point of the forest, the trail is now downhill. Down along the same stream for over 11 kilometers without meeting a soul. In the quiet of the forest and by the gurgling stream I ponder the question of whether I am doing this journey for my own sake, or whether there is some higher purpose. Basically I am doing it for myself. Deep down inside I want to know whether I am capable of carrying through what I have taken on. Whether I am still, at the age of 54, physically able to do it. But I also want to know whether I am capable of following a deep inner impulse, not knowing where it will take me. An impulse which nevertheless seems to concerns the very meaning of life.

Maybe it is my soul I am listening to. Perhaps walking 'Mary's Way' means that I am to work on my inner feminine aspects. I suppose I am also hoping to become a more whole person. After Disibodenberg, Mary told me the journey is taking place on two levels, and I am certainly not blind to the fact that there is some higher purpose too. That I am serving the Virgin Mary, and I am involved in accomplishing something very specific. Nonetheless, in the course of our conversations, Mary tells me repeatedly that it is my own personal journey, a journey to teach me to trust my feminine side. Though she also says that I will find I am doing it for other people's sake too.

It is clear that I must be careful not to turn the whole thing into some great missionary expedition for something outside myself.

A statue of the Virgin Mary

In the oldest church in Merzalben there is an interesting statue of Mother Mary standing atop a globe with her right foot on a snake which is winding itself around the earth. She has her left foot on the moon. Mary explains that the symbolism is correct. She elaborates on this, saying she is neither the mother of the earth nor the queen of the earth.

We pass through a beautiful valley, Waschtal, where a small waterfall cascades down into a lake. We come across a tall tree, full of buds, which puts me in mind of the sculptures of Aphrodite with her multitude of breasts. A wondrous little valley – feminine, I am tempted to say. Just before I got here, I had been given a telling-off. We had come to a small mountain, which bothered me. According to the map, my path went up over the mountain and, in my mind, the mountain became quite insurmountable. The railway ran straight through it, and I considered taking the train this short distance. I asked Mary if this would be alright. She told me off. *'If you are well and fit, you can manage the walk. If you cannot manage it you are weak and should perhaps not have ventured out on a journey such as this. For all you know, your greatest experience may await you on this very stretch?'*

I refrained from taking the train and found a path round the mountain which brought me to this lovely valley. The highlight of the day.

Yesterday's journey took me through a forest, and so far today has again been a forest walk. Now, the sky opens up in front of me once more as I come out of the trees into this long valley, ringed with remarkable stone formations. I have arrived at Felsland and stay the night at a youth hostel in Dahn.

* * *

Further down the valley I find a steep path leading up to a little airfield. Here, high above the lowland is a horizontal plateau, an enormous field of grass used as a runway for small private planes.

I get caught in a heavy shower and take shelter in an open-sided shed. Sitting there under cover and enjoying the view, I experience an almost solemn atmosphere about the place. Sense that the landscape has some quite special quality about it. As if Heaven is especially close to Earth here.

Whereas in Bingen I sensed I was at the root of the stage, this place seems to be the peak – the crowning glory.

For several years I have been part of a group who, with the guidance of the Englishman Peter Dawkins, have studied natural landscapes that seem almost to form temples. As in the human body, there are areas in the landscape that show all the chakras and they have an energy structure similar to that underlying the physical body. In the East one finds comprehensive definitions of the human energy centers – chakras. Each chakra can be seen as the life-energy that regulates and functions within a certain area of the body. Chakras are a sort of focal point – whorls or wheels of energy.

With time I have learnt to accept and apply Eastern terminology for energy, and it is now a long time since I learnt that there are seven major chakras, which together make up a unified system.

In the same way, it is possible to find certain landscapes that make up a unified energy structure, comprising the same energy points as the human body. In the case of human beings one could say that the energy of one's personality is absorbed into physical form – the skeletal structure of the body. We do not think of landscapes as having personality. Nonetheless, many landscapes do seem to have a similar quality.

Looking back on this stage of my journey, I can see the pattern:

The Root chakra is in Bingen. With its manufacturing industries and lively exchange of goods, the town has strong, worldly roots. Providing for daily needs.

The next chakra is known by its Japanese name Hara or the English term Sacral. Water is central to the Sacral chakra. And like water, this energy seems rather to flow, dance and merge. Bad Kreuznach is the water town. The river running through it, the spa baths and the parks with dance and music pavilions bear witness to sacral energy.

The symbol of the Solar Plexus chakra is fire. In the human body, fire is associated with the burning of energy and with purification processes. We also associate emotion with fire, and my test at Disibodenberg was definitely emotional.

The Heart chakra is of course in the chest. The heart is surrounded by the lung system so the element of the Heart chakra is air. Air can symbolize that energy is no longer bound to something physical but can appear in a free form and be seen, for example, as spirit or wisdom. Johanneskreuz is situated on high terrain in the midst of a large forest – like an enormous ribcage. It is a popular recreational venue. I see it as a Heart chakra.

The narrow valley around Dahn resembles a throat. Sound, which characterizes various forms of communication, is formed in the Throat chakra. Sound is the symbolic element for this chakra and in nature it often calls forth echo and song.

Often the Throat chakra in nature is cut off from the areas of the heart by a valley or a lake.

The Brow or Third Eye chakra of the body is placed just over or between the eyebrows. This chakra deals with intuition, spiritual impulses and higher consciousness.

The highest chakra of the body, the Crown chakra, is placed directly above the crown of the head and is where our spiritual essence appears to reside. A

Bingen
ROOT

Bad Kreuznach
HARA (SACRAL)

Disibodenberg
SOLAR PLEXUS

Johanniskreuz
HEART

Dahn
THROAT

Col du Litschhof
BROW - CROWN

Chakra-landscapes

Crown chakra can be difficult to place in nature. For one thing, it can be difficult to distinguish from a Brow chakra. For another, it may not even be a particular physical characteristic but may float above the ground. In such places one can experience the dividing line between heaven and earth as unbelievably narrow. As if one is very close to the divine. I feel that closeness here at the airfield. I cannot say where Brow ends and Crown begins.

I continue from the airfield up through Notweiler and into the forest, and at Col du Litschhof I cross the unmarked border into France. I choose a forest track which after a while turns out to have old milestones posted along it. Again I have struck an ancient highway and it takes me straight to Lembach. My first French town. I consider staying the night but Mary wants me to reach a new landscape system today, so I carry on.

The energy changes. I am clearly on my way into a different landscape temple. The French atmosphere contributes to this. The road leads through small groves and over farmland, past a pilgrim Chapel to Mary in Hoffsoffen, taking me westwards to Niederbronn-les-Bains at the foot of the Vosges. Just before I get there, I come to a hilltop where I am met with a breathtaking view over the town and the neighboring mountains. It is as if the next stage – the next temple of landscapes – is being presented to me, set in the south along the edge of the Vosges. I have walked 30-odd kilometers today, a lot of it up and down hills. I am tired, find myself a hotel and want more than anything to throw myself onto a bed and sleep. It takes a huge effort to postpone this and get on with my washing. I have got into the routine of washing my socks, underwear and shirt every day. Today I do my trousers as well, so everything is clean and ready for tomorrow's new stage. This seems to give me fresh energy and I wander up through the town, observing the goings-on, and then dine at a little restaurant. I walk awkwardly due to my aching muscles.

Bent slightly forward and with stiff legs. I must resemble an old man who has lost his walking stick. But this old man is staying at a posh hotel, and knows how to appreciate a good mattress and a soft eiderdown. He sinks down into a deep, rejuvenating sleep!

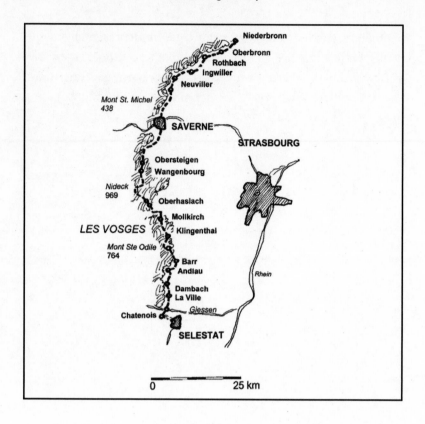

2

Soul and Polarity

Alsace

I slept well. The stiffness has worn off. It is as if my legs are actually raring to go, and thus rejuvenated, I head for the foot of Les Vosges. In Oberbron I find a large convent. The convent of 'Maison Mère des Soeurs du Très Saint Sauveur'. Men are allowed to enter the church. Here I manage to tune in – to find the frequency that connects me with Mary. A new stage has begun. A new landscape-temple. From now on, I will try to take note of the qualities of the landscape as I pass through it and notice when I go from one chakra to another.

I follow a track a little way up a slope. On my right are tree-covered mountains, on my left a wide valley. The numerous villages I walk through bear witness to the fact that this fertile strip of land between the river valley and the mountains was inhabited for thousands of years. This is an ideal sort of place in which to walk. To one side the beautiful view over the lowlands below, while to the other the freshness of the woods and mountains.

I meet a couple of Dutch hikers carrying only small backpacks, the rest of their luggage being transported for them from one hotel to the next. We walk together for a bit. They choose to take a slightly different route from me and I am glad of it, for I have discovered that it is difficult for me to focus on Mary when other people's energy interferes.

My intuition is not sufficiently evolved to be able to ignore the influence of other people. In the hotel that evening I happen to meet the two Dutchmen again and here there is no problem. We chat till quite late.

Walking southwards, I clearly sense that the quality of this landscape temple is quite different from that of the previous one. I ponder on the differences between the landscapes. That different energies are connected to different areas and that they link up into systems. That these can be interpreted as chakra systems.

I hesitate to talk to Mary about this as chakra systems are hardly a recognized idea in Christianity. Still, after several faltering attempts, I manage to summon up the courage to ask her. Warily, hesitantly I ask whether I can speak of chakra systems in her context. *'Certainly,'* she answers, surprisingly. Mary gives a rather long talk on the energy system of the body. The understanding of energies in the human body has never been the reserve of Eastern philosophy, though modern Western translation of chakra terminology has unfortunately not been very good. But now the terms are internationally accepted, and it is practical to use them. She points out that in the Western world in earlier times there were parallel interpretations of these energy systems.

Wandering along an idyllic path at the edge of the forest, Mary helps me to understand the chakra system in a simple way: Man has three essential body parts: the lower body, the upper body, and the head. Each part has a main chakra. Between the body parts there are two connecting chakras. Above the head and below the lower body there are two further, connecting chakras. Mary comments specially on three of the chakras: Root, Crown and Heart. Man is an earthly being. The lowest connecting chakra is the ROOT.

From here, metaphorically speaking, the body is plugged into the energy of the earth. What an electrician would call an 'earth'.

Man is also a spiritual being. The highest connecting chakra, the CROWN, is basically similar to the Root, but here one plugs into the energy of 'heaven', the spiritual energy. That is to say a 'live' wire – to stick with the electrician!

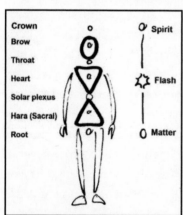

Chakras and polarity

The chakra in the upper body, the HEART, can be thought of as the engine or pump that keeps everything going. Like other pumps it takes a current to keep the engine running. The current arises in the field of potential between the earthly and the spiritual 'terminals'. Therefore it is important to be connected to both earth and heaven – matter and spirit. Metaphorically speaking, the field of potential creates a spark in the heart. The life center of the body.

In my mind's eye I see the human body, between the two terminals, surrounded by a field of energy, with a spark flying from one to the other. This reminds me of something I once read. That according to an old Jewish way of thinking, we are all sparks from the divine ocean of fire.

Mary comments on the other chakras too, but understanding the basic polarity is the most important part. She stresses that she has simplified her explanation. Each chakra has several specific functions, and there are many more chakras in the body.

Up until now I have waited till evening to note the events of each day in my diary, but Mary has just given me a good deal of material and I dare not wait till tonight to write it down. I find a small pavilion beside the path. Here I can sit and write undisturbed. Mary follows this up and asks me to make notes several times in the course of each day. She has so far been teasing me a bit over my cappuccino breaks, but now she says that they are actually good opportunities for writing things down. 'And that will slow down the tempo too,' she adds.

On the way to Neuwiller les Saverne, Mary and I talk about church architecture. I gather she is fond of the Romanesque style. She especially stresses the wonderful way a sunbeam can enter through a small window and give life to a dark room. Almost fertilize it. In Gothic architecture all space is very brightly lit, and femininity, the maternal, disappears. Masculinity takes over.

As I arrive at the old, significant town of Neuwiller les Saverne, I understand what she means. In earlier days, the town had several convents and monasteries. The church, St. Peter and St. Paul, is basically Romanesque, and Mary leads me to her chapel where her statue – as if by order – is illuminated by a ray of sunlight. Here I see for myself the sunbeam fertilize the large dark room. I see her point. Mary talks of Peter and Paul. The use of male power was essential for the spreading of Christianity. In this, Peter and Paul made outstanding contributions. But certain qualities in Jesus' work were lost through this male approach.

'*We had not imagined that it would become so one-sided.*'

Mary and John formed congregations themselves – here in the French area too. Their understanding of the Christian idea had a stronger female inspiration. '*But look around – that impulse is as good as gone now,*' Mary ends.

On the map I have noticed a small mountain called Mont St. Michel. I want to see it. In the middle of the town of Ernolsheim I find a signpost and a path to take me there.

Soon I am in the woods, and after a few meters I feel the presence of a special energy. I will call it 'angel-power'. Whenever this happens I usually perform a small ritual asking permission to enter and to speak to the angel. Halfway through, I am interrupted by a familiar teasing energy. It is obviously St. Michael, laughing because I have not noticed him until now.

Now begins a memorable climb. Mary almost bubbles. I have so far sensed only her face somewhere near my head, but I now sense that she has both body and feet. She is dancing about in happy expectation. Something big is about to happen. I tease her, saying that she must be going to meet her lover. '*That is right,*' she says. '*We are lovers – in the way that all God's angels are lovers.*'

A misty figure of a young man who resembles Michael comes towards us. He welcomes us and invites us to follow him up to St. Michael.

We start chatting. He very courteously calls me 'Sir', but I ask him to just use my Christian name. He also welcomes Mary and asks when she was last here. Mary answers that it must have been about 1,200 years ago, in the company of a monk. She casts me a sidelong glance and winks at the disciple. '*Was it this gentleman?*' he asks. '*That I am not allowed to say,*' Mary answers.

The climb feels endless although it probably takes less than an hour. '*Unless you are absolutely prepared to meet St. Michael, you will be frightened away,*' the disciple warns. I am put through several small tests and am then told that I only have one more to go.

We emerge into a glade, and straightaway I can feel the

presence of elves, even of a queen among them. Respectfully I address the queen and the others and thank them for their welcome. Being able to sense the elves and the queen was the last test. In one long procession we all go on together. The path now climbs in hairpin bends up the side of the mountain. Exhausting! Halfway up the path we come across a fantastic sight. A colossal, long rock is hanging out from the cliff over a small valley. The cliff is called Wasserfelsen. Water Cliff! But there is no water. This place is obviously an ancient site for water worship. Small, round pools have been hewn out in the surrounding rock and you can tell that a waterfall once flowed down the cliff.

Mary puts the words of a blessing into my mouth:

'In the name of God I bless this place as being part of the pilgrimage route of the Virgin Mary. May this be revealed to everyone who travels here. This place was once blessed with water that flowed down over the cliff face. It was a place of rejuvenation. This is no longer the case. I ask men and all beings of nature to help bring water out of the rock again, so that the place can recover its old function. I also ask all you elves to help me with this. Amen.'

As we climb a bit further up, I can see that a well has been constructed, presumably to draw off the water for the use of the town down below. I have since read that the water was in fact stopped and piped back in 1892 in order to supply Saint-Jean-Saverne with water. It must be possible to do something about it!

We carry on up. I have the Michael disciple and Mary on each side of me. Behind us follows a great company of elves.

We are getting near the summit. We glimpse the sky between the trees more and more frequently. I am led past a chapel out towards a ledge of rock. Out on the ledge I am met by an amazing view over the Rhine valley. I am led right out to the

The ledge of rock on Mont St. Michel

edge, towering 373 meters above the valley. There is a circular pool here, about 30 centimeters deep, hewn out of the rock. A very powerful location.

Now Mary and I go forward alone. I have long sensed St. Michael's presence, but now he appears in an inner vision. Like a giant figure he floats in power and beauty over the pool. He asks me to come out into the pool, and there he takes on the size of a man. We lay our hands on each other's shoulders and greet each other warmly. 'Mon frère! (My brother!)' I exclaim. A very deep recognition moves me to tears.

Michael asks Mary and me to sit down on each side of him at the edge of the pool. A short time passes, during which Mary and Michael also exchange energy.

Then Michael tells me that the pool was formed by man several thousand years ago. It was used for ceremonial meetings between angels and consecrated people. Everybody would sit on the edge of the pool with their feet in the water, while the light of the power of Michael came down from above and fused with the water of the power of Mary from below.

This fusion was the holy matrimony between heaven and earth. Between fire and water. Between spirit and matter.

Michael asks me to go out to the middle of the pool and turn towards him and Mary. I close my eyes. Feel the water and the power of Mary round my feet. At the same time I feel fire descending from above with the power of Michael. Like a long-drawn-out explosion, the water and the fire meet in me, shaking me through and through. I am asked to stretch my arms out sideways, and water and fire rush and roar throughout me. I feel a whorl forming in each of the four sections my cruciform position creates.

The energy flow

Michael and Mary move from a vertical axis to a horizontal one and now stand on each side of me. They move towards each other, and at the same moment that they come together inside me a mighty flash of light is discharged, which I understand to be pure power of God. They glide apart and return to their place on each side of me. After a while they repeat their union in me, again shaking my body. Again they glide apart. The ceremony is finished. They bless me and ask me to sit down.

Michael explains: *'When the power of God divides in a polarity, the field of potential between the poles is pure love. Mary and I continually yearn to unite, and as you see, we then become pure power of God. It is, however, our task to work in polarity. It is due to you that we can now unite. We thank and bless you. Our love is in you.'*

Michael goes on to explain that the feeling of happiness I am now experiencing is the highest feeling of love I will ever know.

In the meantime a woman has come out onto the rock. She is standing a little aside and seems to be rehearsing a story. I get talking to her, and she tells me that she often practices story-telling here. It is the most inspiring place. After rehearsing she usually goes out to the pool and presents what she has prepared. She has been coming here since she was a child. I tell her about my pilgrimage and my experiences. She understands, as she and her husband have themselves made pilgrimages.

I leave her on her own and go back to the little chapel which is – of course – dedicated to St. Michael. At one point, while standing in the chapel, I feel that Michael points out that there is no difference between the Michael out there on the rock and the Michael in here in the church. He is one and the same. I understand that I must stop seeing the Michael of the churches and the Michael of nature as two different beings.

In the chapel I notice a stone built into the south wall. Two hearts tied together round a center. I feel it is a beautiful picture of the two heart polarities I have just experienced.

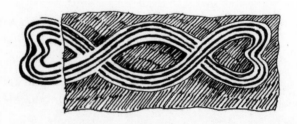

Stone with heart polarities

MICHAEL'S MOUNT AND CHAPEL

'Mountain with rock ledge at first called Hertenberg [12th century] then Bruderberg [16th century] and finally Michaelsberg. Before the Christian era sun worship was performed here ... In the Middle Ages it became a chapel and a hermitage. In 1593 the chapel was rebuilt and a St. Michael fraternity was founded. In the chapel (earlier a well-known center for pilgrimage) mass was said on Sep. 29th (Feast of the archangel Michael). Also, on the evening of June 23rd, there was a midsummer bonfire (*Johannesfeuer*).

In the rock ledge there is a hollow: "Witch school or dancing place for witches". In a cave below, a grave and a "witch's hole" have been hewn.'

Board in the Chapel

I have since read up on Michael's Mount and its surroundings. The area has been inhabited for thousands of years. In the cave under the rock ledge, objects have been found both from hunters and gatherers from the 6th millennium BC, the Iron Age and the Romans, as well as from more recent times.

It was here that the Gallic-Celtic area bordered on the Germanic. A main Roman thoroughfare ran through Saverne up to Neuwiller and from there on to Wissenbourg. More or less the same route I have walked.

It is late afternoon. I begin a quick descent. Mary says she will guide me down through the forest. Full speed down. On the way, we emerge into a glade, and here all the elves are waiting in a ring. I stop in the middle of the circle and greet the queen and her whole ring of elves. I thank her from the bottom of my heart and take my leave. She speaks, saying I am to receive a gift to take with me. A small sword is handed to me.

'This sword is from the elves of St. Michael. It is a present for you on your journey. Other elves will know what it is. Farewell!' I thank her and we start off again at a jog. We run beside a deeply sunken road, which bears witness to hectic traffic in times gone by. Just as we reach the backwaters of Saint-Jean-Saverne, the church bells strike six. We made it out of the forest in daylight.

My experience with the cross in the rock pool is on my mind, and I wonder what exactly it was that I saw as the horizontal polarity.

Mary says I saw *my soul.* She explains that the vertical axis is to be understood as a primary axis, a basic axis. The axis of Life. Every living being has a basic axis.

Mary continues: *'The horizontal axis is the axis of your soul. The soul is a spark – a polarity from God's ocean of fire – with its own quality, determined by level and experience. At your present stage of development you see your soul as a polarity between the angels St. Michael and the Virgin Mary.'*

Mary also draws my attention to dance. Spinning round like a whirling dervish or spinning round with another person like in folk dance, is life-giving because your arms are held outstretched and so mark the soul axis. Such spinning is an acceptance and an animation of the soul. I wonder whether dervish dancers are in fact dancing in praise of the soul.

I also ask about the whorls I saw in the four fields between the axes. I should very much like to know more about them. Mary starts explaining, but breaks off and says that I lack a frame of understanding, so she cannot make it clear to me.

Through Grethe, Mary later talked in greater detail about what happened on the mountain:

'The actual meeting of the polarities is also important. Your soul would not be able to develop further unless this dynamic process between contrasts took place and continues taking place. For your soul to grow, it must be able to unite ever greater contrasts –

without becoming these contrasts – and still burn.

'If you can pass on your own experience it will echo in other hearts. This experience lies in the depth of all souls. If not with Mary and Michael as polarities, then with other constellations.'

After Saverne the road climbs again. For three hours I struggle along woodland paths to Obersteigen. Here lies a chapel, dedicated to Mary's Ascension, of which she is very fond. She hints that we are now in the Crown of the landscape chakra system which began in Niederbronn-les-Bains, and of which Mont St. Michael is probably the Heart chakra. The atmosphere in Obersteigen and the next town, Wangenbourg, does in fact have the scent of a crown. A sense that the atmosphere here is very thin, and that a divine presence just behind it is on the point of breaking through. There may even be a great Crown-angel over the area, but I cannot make contact with it. The air is clear. The sun is shining, and here in the late afternoon I allow myself to enjoy a beer at the pavement café in front of the old hotel where I will spend the night.

* * *

The next day's stage goes through a large forest, up to the Nideck waterfall which cascades down in several beautiful, long free falls. I come upon the waterfall at the very top and as I descend I follow the many free falls for quite a while. It is a beautiful experience. I deem the waterfall to lie between Crown and Brow.

A voice inside me asks if I want to stay up in the Crown but I refuse the offer. Prefer to walk the whole way down through the system. I am delighted to find a little café at the bottom! Even out here in the wilderness I can satisfy my cappuccino addiction. On down to Niederhaslach where there is an enormous church with roots back in the 8th or 9th century. The church is dedicated to Florent whose bones are still preserved here in a casket as relics.

I read that Florent originally dedicated the church to Mary but that the name had later been changed.

Today's stage has been exhausting and I look for a place to spend the night. In Molkirch the only hotel is in the wrong direction, so I pull myself together and head on to Klingenthal where I expect to find somewhere to stay. On the outskirts of the town I suddenly see a signpost to Mont St. Odile, 9 km. Can I make it all the way to the convent hotel in St. Odile? I have walked a very long way and am exhausted. I also know that the path is very steep. I take a deep breath, defy all objections and start up the mountain.

Mary has been very quiet all day, but when I decide to go all the way to St. Odile she livens up. I can sense that she wants to go there.

A thunderstorm over Mont St. Odile has been brewing for the last hour. It has kept in front of me and has so far let me walk on its calm edge. Halfway up, however, the thunder catches me from behind. Lightning and thunder intensify and a violent wind picks up. The trees sway dangerously and I have to hold on to my hat and glasses. The storm is advancing and the rain can catch me at any moment. And now it is getting dark. I still have to make the last climb. I am desperately tired. Have walked more than 40 hilly kilometers. Up to the Nideck waterfall at an altitude of 560 meters, down to a level of 300 meters in Klingenthal and now 9 kilometers up to St. Odile at 800 meters altitude. Even so, mustering my very last resources, I manage to put on speed and I enter the convent at the same moment the clouds burst.

I am happy, but frantically tired and long only for a bed. I nearly black out when the receptionist says the hotel is full. I explain that I am a pilgrim and have walked 40 kilometers today. After a few nerve-racking minutes, during which I imagine having to sleep out in the forest, he manages to find a room after all. I hobble down to the restaurant and just manage to get a meal before they close. The other guests cast sidelong glances at my sweaty clothes. The smell of my feet may also be starting to tickle their noses because, hidden under the table, I have sneaked out of my shoes. I allow myself to take no notice and relax in the enjoyment of sitting still and sensing the smell of food steal into my nostrils.

The bed is good, but my feet, legs and hips are so sore that my sleep is constantly interrupted.

* * *

Mont St. Odile

The place is impressive. The convent buildings rise up on a steep rock overlooking the Rhine valley, just like Michael's Mount. One can walk about on the edge of the precipice and enjoy the impressive view both north and east. In favorable weather, one can see as far as Strasbourg 30 kilometers away.

MONT ST. ODILE

The history of man on Mont St. Odile goes back thousands of years. Archaeological digs under the convent buildings have revealed potsherds that prove the existence of a Michael Cult here in 4200 BC. (Archaeologists use Michael's name for this cult, despite the fact that Michael – as a biblical figure – is from a much later period.)

A colossal wall of worked blocks of stone runs around an area of 118 hectares. This 15-km-long wall, which the Germans call Heidenmauer, is reckoned by archaeologists to date back to the La Tène period (170–60 BC). The arrival of Julius Caesar in the area heralded 'Pax Romana', 400 years of peace under Roman rule.

In the 7th century the first missionaries seem to have arrived. In this period Odile was born, the daughter of a brutal local duke. Odile was blind, and her father wanted her disposed of. Her mother, however, gave her into the care of a convent. According to legend, she gained her eyesight while being baptized at the convent. After many years she returned home and after even more battles she succeeded in founding a convent up at the earlier stronghold.

The convent existed right up until the Thirty Years' War in the 1600s, when it burnt down. After being rebuilt several times, it is now a small place with its own hotel. Today the convent consists of about a dozen nuns and their priests.

In Mary's time the Romans must have been ruling the area for less than a hundred years, and presumably Celtic and Roman culture lived on side by side. Mary has told me about Mount St. Odile. '*I had a dream. God came down just here and kissed the earth and said that from then on, this place would be hallowed.'*

On the rock overhang is a small chapel, the Chapel of Tears. In here a piece of rock juts out of the floor, the Stone of Tears. This must be the place God kissed in Mary's dream.

Before breakfast I go down to the Chapel of Tears and meditate. Suddenly I realize why the chapel has been given its name. Many, many people have sat here, out in the open, on this dizzyingly high cliff which God has kissed.

They have sat in the light of God, in a strong force-field and have beheld the valley, as from a cloud in the sky. To be in God and see this world from on high is redeeming. Anybody experiencing this would easily be moved to tears. Tears of joy, of course.

I have a feeling that there is an angel above Mount St. Odile. It is standing with outspread wings and has a circle of stars dancing round its chest. The Statue of Liberty in New York has a circle of stars over its head. Here, the circle of stars has been moved down round the heart. I wonder if the influence of this angel stretches as far as the European Parliament in nearby Strasbourg.

Michael has said of my journey from Mount St. Michael to Mount St. Odile that it is: 'From heart to heart'. I think this means that Mount St. Michael is the Heart chakra on the way up, and Mount St. Odile is the Heart chakra on the way down, in one great landscape system.

* * *

The next day I spend a lot of time in both the church and the Chapel of Tears. My body is still very tired and I find it difficult to concentrate. It being Sunday, the place is swarming with tourists, and I cannot sense whether there is more for me to do here. Later that morning I decide to go on.

I have read about a druids' cave, which I have planned to see on the way down. I misread the signposts and end up on a broad road to a car park. Continue down this road, but suddenly discover that Mary is not with me. I have simply trudged along without asking her properly which way to go. From bitter experience I know this will end badly. There is nothing for it but to go back a kilometer and start again. Now I ask her to lead me along the route they originally took. She leads me east of the castle/convent. Further on, right round to the north side. I am sure that this is quite wrong, as we are supposed to be heading south. But I stay with Mary down a tarmac road which does in fact eventually turn south, and turns out to be a good road with no cars and an even slope. Pass the Well of St. Odile where I fill my water bottles. Continue along this back road. Old milestones appear, indicating that this is an old main road.

At one point I tell St. Michael about my detour on the way to the druids' cave, and that I never actually got there. *'Just as well,'* he says dryly. *'There was much good in the wisdom of the druids, but it no longer exists. It is not alive today, and that is critical. Other energies can take over and use such a tradition for other ends. Therefore one must be careful at these ancient places of cult worship. Take care. The stone which God kissed on the mountain is today surrounded by living spirituality and may therefore be used safely.'*

The mountains grow smaller, and along narrow roads I am drawn into the bottom of a valley where I am surprised by an enormous church in the little town of Andlau.

THE HUGE CHURCH IN ANDLAU

The crypt is the oldest in Alsace and is dedicated to La Vierge, the Virgin. The church was founded in 880 by the disowned wife of Charles the Fat. The place is much visited by pilgrims.

On again, I travel along an old wine route through luscious vineyards with no traffic. Further and further down into the low country, away from the mountains.

I have to cross the Rhine valley. The only question is: how and where? One evening I sit and study maps. I know that in her time Mary crossed over to Kaiserstuhl. Did she go across the flat, marshy floodplain down to the Rhine? Nowadays there is actually a cycle path further south straight across the valley. Perhaps that is the way I am to go. She may also have sailed down a tributary and over to the other side of the Rhine. On the map I find several watercourses which at that time must have joined the Rhine. The River Gjessen, for example.

* * *

Next day I get down to the flat country on my way to Chatenois.

At one point Mary asks me to sit down and meditate beside the next watercourse. We come to a brook and, rather skeptical, I contemplate the water quietly seeping among the stones at the bottom.

I doubt that it would have been possible to sail from here. Mary assures me, however, that in her time there was more water in the brook. I sit down and she presents me with two choices. She could have taken a boat from here. Or she could have crossed the valley further south. I am free to choose either way. I hope she sailed across, for then I shall not have to walk the 15 kilometers across the valley. I realize that I am not unbiased, that I am hoping for the easier way. I try very hard to find an unprejudiced answer. A sincere impulse grows inside me. 'Of course I will follow wherever you have walked.' '*Good*,' says Mary. '*Come on, then.*' For a moment I feel tired just thinking about the 15-km-long walk across the plain. I pull myself together. My soul seems to have answered, and whatever the effort demanded, it is a great joy to know that I have made the right choice. A long trek across the valley awaits me.

After a few hundred meters I come to a new, bigger bridge and a watercourse considerably larger than the first one. The minute I reach the bridge I see Mary boarding a small barge in the river. She waves and calls that she is going to sail to Sasbach. Completely flabbergasted, I sit down. I had just prepared myself for the long walk. Was that not what Mary had just said? I realize now that by the last watercourse all she had said was that we should get a move on. I see a signpost stating that the river is the Gjessen. So she was going to sail down this river after all. In other words Mary has just been testing me. I cannot help laughing.

So Mary did in fact sail across the Rhine valley. Nowadays it is difficult to make the same journey by boat, as the rivers have been regulated. Mary lets me take a bus or train, but she stresses that I must symbolically follow her – as if wearing seven-league boots while sitting in a bus or on a train.

For the first time on my journey I let go of Mary. I am in Chatenois, in the Root chakra of this stage. Strangely enough, I feel free and without responsibilities.

I arrive in Selestat by bus, and take another one towards Marckolsheim. I am the only passenger. The driver asks me where I am from and where I am going. I tell him. *'Ok, then I'll take you to the border,'* he says. I am surprised and ask him, 'Does this bus go to the border then?' *'No, not normally. But we can make it,'* he answers laughing. And believe it or not, he drives right to the border – without stopping once. He sets me down at a big roundabout. I thank him sincerely.

Walk the last stretches up past an enormous lock system and further on, across to the other side of the Rhine itself. Now the Kaiserstuhl Mountains are before me and I am looking forward to finding Mary again. Although for a while I felt free, I am quickly beginning to miss her company. It is she who gives meaning to the whole enterprise.

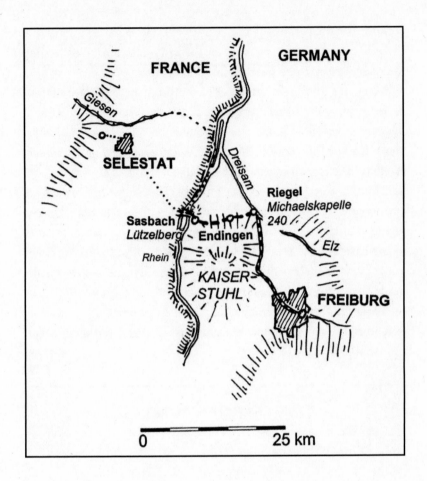

3

Well-nourished and Powerless

Kaiserstuhl

Back to Germany. After crossing the Rhine I immediately turn right, down a road along the river. In earlier times Sasbach may have had some sort of harbor here, and I choose the first ramp that runs down to the water. I picture Mary arriving by boat and coming ashore. I welcome her at once and, after gathering up the threads of the route, we walk in towards Sasbach. I sense that Mary is pleased to be near mountains again.

Mary has told me of her love of mountains. '*I love them. In the flatlands where the earth is cultivated, people are very industrious – and the force of nature is less visible. The mountains are not so marked by man. Here one feels the breath of nature, and the love that flows through all things is clearer. The mountains breathe love.*'

There are certainly mountains here. Kaiserstuhl is in fact an extinct volcano and, as at other volcanoes, the earth here is very fertile. Nature is bountiful. The rivers are bursting with fish both to the east and the west, the volcanic slopes offer exquisite vines and, towards the north, at the foot of the mountains lie fertile lands abounding in fruit trees. Kaiserstuhl is blessed with the warmest climate in Germany, and as it is strategically speaking exceedingly well situated, the area has attracted settlements for thousands of years.

AN ANCIENT JUNCTION

Celts lived here at Sasbach, and even erected a bridge over the Rhine. The Romans conquered the area and restored the bridge. A Roman highway ran from Sasbach via Endingen to Riegel. (Mary probably used this highway.) A find of a Roman silver spoon with a monogram of Christ shows that Christianity was here from very early on. The Romans were driven out by the Alemanni in the year 260.

I have not gone far before I come across a small signpost to the chapel on Lützelberg. The road winds up the mountain through bounteous vineyards and, once up, I find a beautiful, large chapel – as big as a church. The chapel has been a place of pilgrimage, though it is not known why. It all has a mild and very friendly feeling to it.

Outside, a small sign says that, as in Endingen and Riegel, sun worship may have taken place here before Christianity was introduced. In those very towns I think I have earlier felt Root, Heart and Crown in what now becomes my third landscape temple or chakra system.

I walk through plantations of ripe cherries, morellos and large plums. Very tempting. I tell myself I must not go scrumping in the plantations but that it is alright to taste anything within reach of the public footpath. It is a good rule for I have only to stretch out my hand and help myself. After a few kilometers I am full, and for the remainder of the walk I must, with great regret, be content merely to observe the abundance. I wonder if all this magnificence has brought the people closer to or further from the 'love which runs through all things'.

Endingen is a biggish town with a remarkable church. One May day, the statue of Mary on the church altar started to weep. Tears fell from her eyes. At first the townspeople wiped them away, but then tears also began to flow from the eyes of the Christ child. A natural explanation was sought, but in vain. The news spread fast through the town and many people came to watch the miracle. Since then the church has been a place of pilgrimage.

At the base of the church tower there is a small room set aside for meditation. The outside of the tower is decorated with a relief of St. George fighting a dragon. St. George is, in a way, a human version of St. Michael. I therefore feel that Michael is present in this meditation room. He tells me that the walk to Riegel is in itself a pilgrimage and that I must think of it as such. The goal in Riegel is a chapel of St. Michael which stands on a small mountain.

Two years earlier St. Michael had accompanied me on this same walk. The crowning event of the tour was a ceremony where I accepted serving St. Michael just as I have accepted the call to serve the Virgin Mary. At that time Michael finished the ceremony by saying that I might call on him for help at any time, and that he would stand by me. The experience has been lucid in my mind ever since, and I have not hesitated to ask his assistance.

Now I am back here again and I am looking forward to a new journey in his company.

On the way out of Endingen I have to choose between two possible roads – and I choose the wrong one. I continue eastwards, but imperceptibly the road gradually turns south, and I do not realize my mistake until I see Bahlingen, 3 kilometers south of Riegel. This is very upsetting and I get quite agitated. Try to get back on course by going straight through several vineyards, down into a valley and up through a wood. But I am forced to change direction again and end up back on the same road I came by. Jog back a good bit until I find a road up to the right ridge.

I have failed on an important point and have missed a fantastic trip with St. Michael.

This is not good! It is a great let-down and I am devastated. Soon I sense Michael. He is very large. I greet him bashfully and walk on. Then he takes on my size and says seriously, *'Now I will show the way!'* He ascertains that I have missed the lower two chakras on his short pilgrimage.

'It can't be helped. But later we must pick up what we have missed. You may have to stay in Riegel for an extra day, or take the two chakras on the way up the mountain after Freiburg.'

I am very unhappy, but say that of course I must answer for what I have done and do whatever is necessary to make up for my mistakes.

It is now late afternoon and I hurry forward, trying to make up for my error. Down from the mountains, into Riegel and up onto Mount Michael with its small chapel. The last part of the way is very steep, but I make a final great effort and stride up the hill. Panting for breath I arrive in the garden south of the chapel, and sense the presence of both Mary and Michael. I ask them to excuse me while I get my breath back. Sit down for a bit, let my pulse slow down and then step in front of them, ready for a ceremony.

I take the floor straight away. Contrite and very serious I greet them and review the route I have walked. I say that I have made mistakes here at the end, but that I nonetheless intend to continue across Schwarzwald, the Alps, Italy, Greece, across the Greek Islands and all the way to Ephesus. While listing all the places, I visualize the long journey in front of me. I realize that it is a very long way. A very, very long way and that so far I have only done a minute part of the whole route. Suddenly the whole thing appears quite insurmountable and I cannot help crying as I hopelessly contemplate the remainder of my journey. I feel really sorry for myself. It feels hard at the moment, and it will probably get much harder. I am devastated. I have no energy to embellish anything. I cannot go on. I am at my absolute physical and psychological limit. The harsh reality of a further 2,000-km-long walk is glaringly clear to me

After much heaving and sighing, the spark of life inside me seems to kindle and burn once more. I pull myself together and a short while later I can declare that I am now ready for whatever must come.

Michael says: '*You have failed with the first two chakras ...*' He pauses and then continues: '*... but you are forgiven.*' He strikes me first on my right then on my left shoulder and says that this burden has been lifted from me. I am greatly relieved.

Michael and Mary move to stand on either side of me, creating a field of tension around me. They glide into the center of me and out on the other side. Back again, causing me to tremble violently each time.

'*You are free now! You can choose to stay in Riegel or you can go into Freiburg to your room there,*' Michael says.

I look about me. This is a heavenly place, at the tip of a small ridge jutting out from the Kaiserstuhl Mountains. There is an open view all round. The River Dreisam runs along the foot of the mound.

The chapel, however, is unfortunately locked.

Michael's Mount and the River Dreisam

MITHRAS WORSHIP AND THE CHAPEL OF MICHAEL

A shrine devoted to Mithras, the god of light, has been excavated. Traders probably brought the cult from the Middle East in the 1st century AD. Mithras was already known under the Persians in the 14th century BC, but later on Mithras became a god of light also worshipped by the Romans. His followers were expected to lead a chaste life with spiritual discipline. In the years 41–54 AD a Roman fortress was built in Riegel. With a god of light already connected to the place it was only natural to devote the town's promontory to St. Michael, the biblical angel of light.

The original Chapel of Michael in Riegel presumably dates from as far back as the arrival of Christianity in this area. It is first mentioned in 971. The present chapel dates from the 14th century. For centuries it has been a much visited shrine. Today it is falling further and further into disrepair.

I have now finished this stage of the pilgrimage and I go back down into town. Again I am free to choose my own form of transport, in a place where Mary sailed. The train is due to leave three quarters of an hour later and I go to a café to enjoy a glass of Weissherbst from Kaiserstuhl. I have walked on the edge of an extinct volcano, and the whole stage has certainly provoked strong emotions. I do not feel up to the task. Sit feeling sorry for myself. Tell Mary that they expect too much from me. 'I am just a country bumpkin dropped out of the heavens!' Mary laughs and asks if I realize what I am saying. *'That is precisely what you are and that is why you were chosen.'* I cannot help laughing either.

As I climb on board the train, I see Mary boarding a boat in Riegel harbor near the present-day bridge. *'See you later!'* she calls.

In Freiburg I go straight up to the cathedral and into the Rappen Hotel where they let me have my old, modest room, no. 41. Pay for two days, for I will now take my first day of rest. Have walked 364 kilometers – about one-sixth of the tour, I suppose.

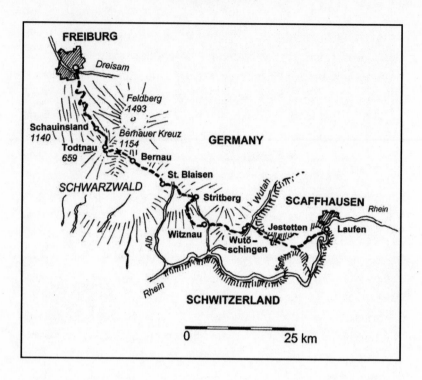

4

In Heaven

Schwarzwald

Freiburg is reputedly the town that most Germans would prefer to live in. I can see why. The huge forests of Schwarzwald lie practically in its backyard, offering the townspeople a wealth of outdoor activity. And Freiburg is quite unique, famous for the little, open runnels that run along the streets carrying the mountain water through the town. The water cleanses and refreshes the air, cools the summer heat and provides great entertainment for the children. Running water clearly vitalizes the entire town.

· After a day of rest I am ready for the next stage – for a new landscape temple. I tune in at the cathedral, which is dedicated to the Virgin Mary. It is exquisitely uplifting to wander through the cathedral's apse. It is like walking among tall trees on the outskirts of a forest. I find the Gothic idiom delightful, especially when the sun casts its rays in through the tall windows. Maybe because the human dimensions of this narrow passage are in such contrast to the rest of the building that towers up, disappearing into the light of heavenly heights.

THE FREIBURG MINSTER

The impressive 116-meter Gothic tower of the cathedral is praised in Freiburg as 'the most beautiful tower in Christendom'. The cathedral was built between 1200 and 1513.

I leave through the town gate, Martinstor, crossing the River Dreisam at the point where I sense Mary must have arrived at the town. Had planned to follow the pathways from the train station but Mary has other plans. She just wants us to take the major road from the Martinstor. Once outside the town I am led into the forest and follow small tracks and paths up the mountain. At some point I join the main hiking path, Dreiländerweg, which runs straight through Schwarzwald. The ascent is severe. I have to climb to an altitude of 1,100 meters. One stretch is so unbelievably steep that I have to take it bit by bit, but finally I am rewarded with an old café from where there is a wonderful view over Freiburg and the surrounding countryside. I can see all the way to Riegel in the north. Schwarzwald has a beauty all its own. It varies from great forests to wide, open meadows full of grazing cattle. The name 'Black Forest' might suggest a dark and dim place but that is not my experience at all. Walking in the splendor of the trees feels purifying. I think trees affect you. As if they are asking your body to remember a natural ancient state of being, where all things are in balance within themselves and with each other. As if the beating heart of nature is calming you. Maybe the great pounding heart of Mother Earth.

Feeling good, I continue up across the open meadows. Mary stops me by two big trees.

'*Sit down on the bench by the trees!*' she says. I sit down expecting to have to meditate, but soon I am asked to get up and place myself between the two trees. Almost of themselves, my arms shoot out into the shape of a cross. I tune in and wait for something to happen. But nothing does. I sit down again and ponder the situation. After a while Mary asks me to take up the crucifix position once again. Now I can feel that something is weighing on me and so I start to unburden my heart.

I ask everything that is not pure and transparent to let go of me. My arms want to move backwards and upwards, but my shoulders are so stiff they move more forwards than backwards. I look around. Ex-gymnast that I am, I am a little embarrassed about my stiffness and would rather not expose it. Using small gymnastic exercises I press my arms backwards. 'I am light at heart,' I say repeatedly, and each time, my chest is able to open up a little more. 'Joy is within me,' I claim optimistically and a little cry of joy escapes me. The ceremony is over and Mary is getting ready to move on. She concludes by saying: '*Be blessed and have a good journey!*'

Apparently, at this stage Mary's teachings are about the heart.

Continue up across the open countryside and along forest footpaths to Todtnauberg, which lies in the midst of a huge forest area. I check into the youth hostel at the upper end of the town. That night the air is heavy and needs clearing. A violent thunderstorm sweeps over us and lightning flashes round the horizon. In spite of this, morning brings the most beautiful sunlight and the air is thoroughly cleansed. Beneath Todtnauberg runs a stream which bursts out into a cascade of waterfalls. It is balm to my soul to experience this symphony of water, chatting, babbling and roaring. An enchanted world of dancing water nymphs.

Mary seems quite at home in this kingdom of water. She says she is not directly involved with the work of the angels of nature. Her field is the soul, which is why she works with human beings.

After Todtnau, I find my way onto an old forest footpath leading up to the pass at Bernauer-Kreuz. Again it is a tough climb of about 600 meters on a long and at times very steep path. Utterly exhausted I reach the peak. Mary asks me to stop. I take a rest where several roads meet.

I want to concentrate and get the feel of the place but the crossroads is pretty busy with other hikers. So I stand aside at the edge of the wood and tune in.

An angel takes me by surprise and asks: *'Has your heart been purified?'* I nod affirmatively, explaining how I feel cleansed and light at heart. *'Anything else?'* the angel asks. I dive into an ocean of self-pity and talk about aches at the back of my right calf and a stinging in the front of my knee. The angel asks me to sit down and move my right leg up and down as if I was having a medical examination. The angel concludes that it is nothing serious and that my blood will now become thinner and rinse out the waste products that are bothering me.

After this 'medical examination' the angel asks me a highly surprising question: *'Do you want access to Heaven?'* Thinking of Heaven on Earth, I answer yes. Shortly after, however, I begin to wonder whether perhaps we are talking of a quite different Heaven.

As I flounder in doubt, the angel interrupts me, saying: *'Heaven is in the heart. Be in it, and walk down the mountain with it.'*

That is all. I bid farewell and begin my descent.

On the way down, I sense that Mary is not quite satisfied with my answer. She says bluntly that my idea of Heaven on Earth is a little thin.

As we walk we talk about Heaven and with Mary's assistance

I come to the following understanding about Heaven:

- The Heaven of the world is in the heart.
- The Heaven of the spirit is in the heart.
- The Heaven of the soul is in the heart.

The forest now opens out onto meadowlands and a view of the beautiful Bernauer valley. Fortunately for me, there is a café in the first little group of houses where I can satisfy my thirst for a cup of coffee.

A little further down the valley I take a shortcut across a meadow, down to a bridge over a mountain stream. Here I stop up. I am sorry I did not answer the angel up at the pass properly.

Sorry that the question is unresolved. As I stand there, losing myself in the lively babbling of the water, I get an idea. I ask the angel of the stream to take my threefold answer up to the Heart-angel on the mountain. I make contact surprisingly quickly and the angel replies that I can now be admitted into Heaven.

I see a vision of a gate opening into a golden world. I approach the gate, but just as I reach it, it is slammed shut by two male guards. For a moment I think I have been denied access, but I realize that the gate now closed is an illusory curtain – a veil. I sweep the veil and the male figures aside and walk through the gate. As I cross the threshold I realize that I am not just one, but three forms: soul, spirit and body. A voice tells me that in this Heaven I can exist as all three, separate and yet united. It is pointed out to me that all three are equal.

I am pleased to have a proper ending to the ceremony initiated on the mountain. Mary is pleased as well.

'*You now have access to the third level of the heart,*' Mary says. I understand that these levels are like windings in a spiral. 'How many levels – or windings – are there in the heart?' I ask. And Mary replies briefly, '*Seven.*'

I do not know what these windings mean. Wonder whether

they represent initiations because I have been told that the pilgrimage is a journey of initiation. There are probably very specific traditions for initiation journeys but I do not know them and I do not really want to know them either. As an ex-athlete I might be tempted to strive for initiations; instead I will just let come what may.

Through Grethe, Mary later spoke of the third level of the heart:

'Every state of being has its Heaven, and the gate to the Heaven of earthly life is in the heart.

'Paradoxically, when you walk through that gate you come into contact with the eternal part of the spiritual world that is independent of physical existence. This is where the concept of Heaven comes in. This is where you are admitted into the world of the angels and to the flowing of the spiritual world into all life.

'It is in here, in the Garden of Eden – I call it the Garden of Eden because in many ways that was Heaven on Earth – it is in here that your grail is. It is in here that your higher being can linger while you walk on earth. It is also in here that we can talk freely and be equals. Here, I am not a high Virgin Mary residing in the world of Spirit and you are not an earthly being that needs to bow humbly in order to talk to me. Here, in your own Heaven, we walk side by side.'

Mary stresses that what opens the gate to eternity is being present in all three states – soul, body and spirit – and then she continues:

'This three-way division is present in all living organisms. Duality is important to life on Earth, but it is only through trinity that life manifests itself. Just as it takes a man and a woman to create a child, but it is not until the coming together of the two that the third part comes into being. The child is created. It is not enough that the man

and the woman are joined; something other must arise. This is the basis for incarnation. The number three equals incarnation.

'It is hard to write about because it is a magical three-part harmony which appears as one sound, but which you must see in its three parts in order to understand.'

I find my way back onto the path, the Dreiländerweg, and it takes me right up to St. Blasien. From afar, the town's enormous domed church appears unexpectedly like a mirage deep in the Schwarzwald forests.

The Domed Church in St. Blasien

THE DOMED CHURCH IN ST. BLASIEN

Europe's third largest domed church, modeled on St. Peter's Basilica in Rome. Built 1772–1783 as church for a large Benedictine monastery. In the dome Mary's ascension is shown and next to the main entrance is a small intimate chapel dedicated to Mary.

The following morning I find I am tired inside and out. After yesterday's experiences I was expecting to wake up encouraged and clear. But instead doubt has crept in. Not just a minor doubt, to be washed off in my morning shower. No, I am in doubt about the meaning of the whole thing. I go across to the Chapel of Mary and ask her what is going on. She tells me that my old way of living, full of certainty and abundance, is now over. A new way of living, where nothing is known, lies ahead. My ego of course wants to protest and that is what is causing my uncertainty.

This answer eases my mind. My body may be tired but not my legs. They do not have any doubts. They want to walk! And so I let them. Upwards and further upwards – to Höchenschwand. In the church there I find a statue of Mary pierced by several swords. This Mary is carrying almost too much suffering. Maybe I should take it as a sign and throw off the heavy burden of self-pity. Ease my heart.

After the church I get onto a road with a wonderful panorama. Here, at an altitude of 1,000 meters, the view is very wide. It gives my heart a breath of relief. I arrive at a small village, Strittberg, where there is a newer church. Even though it does not look very impressive it is quite significant to the pilgrimage. It is dedicated to St. Joseph. In front of the altar there is a statue of Joseph and on the wall behind the altar a statue of Mary and the baby Jesus framed by a radiant halo. It is obvious that the church has a special place in Mary's heart. She lets me know that she feels sorry that posterity has relegated Joseph to the background. He has as big a part in Jesus as she has.

From Strittberg the road descends. I follow a forest path along a stream. Soon I engage in conversation with Mary. I have been here before and it is on this stretch that the big questions can be asked. Cars are few and far between and the soft trickle of the stream is conducive to spiritual conversation.

The morning's doubts about the entire pilgrimage are still at the back of my mind and I ask Mary what it is all about.

Mary replies:

'Revelations are important nowadays: Divine revelations are not reserved – with intervals of hundreds of years – for the few.

'These days it is possible for everyone to have revelations. Depending on the individual's attitude towards "something higher", they can be called revelations from the divine, from love or from the source of life. One can receive revelations on many levels and all of them are of equal worth.

'A revelation is an obvious opening to the spiritual sphere and there is a message in every revelation.'

I ask how to deal with revelations:

'Revelations must be understood. The message has to be interpreted. As a rule a revelation suggests an action. The action is performed and is acknowledged with a thank-you. Thus a channel for communication with the spiritual world is opened and a dialogue can begin.'

I ask whether one needs help to deal with revelations:

'These days most people do not need an intermediary to interpret and explain a revelation. But because some of the revelations concern more than the individual himself it can be useful to gather

in groups to help each other to understand revelations. In this work it is important to remind yourselves that all revelations – regardless of nature or level – are of equal worth.'

Then I ask: 'If there is no need for intermediaries then how do you view the various religions with priests who assume that role?'
Mary replies hesitantly:

'The question is controversial because in the Christian world I am considered a holy figure. And yet I must say: all religions are culturally determined and all have their time! In Christianity it is time for renewal. Some of the original ideas have faded and a good deal have been added. Some ideas are directly rooted in the conditions of society at a certain time, conditions which no longer exist. The guardians of the religions are having a very hard time adapting thousands of years of culturally determined religious framework to modern life. The core of Christianity, and other religions too, is basically a set of important truths that provide a fundament to build on. A new day is dawning!'

Mary gets back to our pilgrimage and says,

'Pilgrimage is an excellent tool for working with revelations and connecting to the spiritual realm. Walking anchors you physically, and in the right landscapes there are numerous opportunities for opening your personal spiritual layers as well as those in the surrounding nature. Man is capable of – and strongly encouraged to – communicate with the angels of nature and other similar beings. This – among other things – is a prerequisite for the survival of the Earth. My pilgrimage route, which you now follow, is designed to be filled with challenges.

'By walking this route you fulfill two purposes. One is to experience the route on a spiritual level. It is all about your soul. The other is for you to be an inspiration and an example to others.

'That is why it is necessary to publish your experiences of this trip, based on your notes. And you are thinking about publishing something – are you not?'

A little hesitantly I answer yes.

The lecture draws to its close, and yet again I am left in awe of how spiritually revealing this part of the journey seems to be.

The road leads to Witznau, which is nothing more than a crossroads and a few houses, but fortunately one of the houses is an inn where I spend the night – as once before.

A couple of hours earlier, I had gone astray.

I had seen on a map that there used to be a monastery in the neighboring village of Berau. This was at the back of my mind. So even as I walked the preceding stretch, I had been getting ready to take the path up to Berau. I was distracted from the perfect ambience for conversation along the stream. My talk with Mary stopped. Mary even told me that we were *not* going to Berau. Said she had gone via Witznau. When we reached a path leading to Berau I felt drawn up there. After only a few meters I realized that Mary had stayed down on the road. I asked her if it was wrong to take this path. She said it was not wrong but that she would stay down on the road. Warning bells were actually ringing, but then she had earlier allowed me to walk on footpaths parallel to her route. It should be OK, I thought, and carried on. It was a delight to walk on this path. For a long time I could sense Mary down on the road, but as I walked up the path, which became narrower and narrower, Mary changed character. The Mary now present was not the usual mild, middle-aged woman but an older and more severe Mary. When I asked her about it she replied shortly that this was necessary here.

Nevertheless I continued upwards. In spite of all I had learnt, my self – or my ego – forced its own project through. To begin with, the path was fine but it soon became so narrow that one wrong step could mean a fall of 30–50 meters. In places the path was cut by rockslides with only a vague track across the loose stones. And, unstable as they were, it wouldn't take much to start a landslide. On the map I'd seen that there should be a waterfall. This lured me on, but when I reached it the attraction was a great disappointment. It had almost dried up and was filled with rotten branches. As I turned the next corner I suddenly saw a big mountain goat walking towards me. It took a few steps before it saw me and then stopped. We gazed into each other's eyes for what seemed to be an eternity. This was not a tame goat but a wild mountain one. I gasped but then calmed myself and raised my hand in a friendly gesture. Instantly it fled over the rockslide. I was able to continue. After the next corner I seemed to sense a dark being of some sort. A confrontation ensued. I got through it unharmed, perhaps due to the little sword given to me by the elves on Michael's Mount.

I finally reached Berau and now hoped to meet Mary in town, but she was far from clear here. Not in the church either. Lit a candle at a statue of Mary holding the baby Jesus. There was no response. Then it struck me that this was the surliest statue of Mary that I had ever seen. Now I clearly heard Mary's voice. She announced dryly that her route did not go to Berau but rather to Witznau. How stupid I felt! So stupid that it almost made me laugh. Here I had gone 4 kilometers up this outrageously impossible path and now I had 3 kilometers down. Had I listened to Mary and continued on the road straight to Witznau, I would have saved myself 5 kilometers as well as a lot of unnecessary effort. It taught me a lesson though. I had to pay for my folly with a lot of extra effort. I was glad to finally find Mary and the inn at Witznau.

* * *

The next morning the landlady in Witznau promises nice weather which holds almost until noon.

As we walk I ask Mary: 'What is grace?'

'God set up the world according to an ingenious set of rules. One of the basic rules is that as you give, so you will receive. There is a very delicate balance in all types of energy exchange. This applies to man too. In all circumstances and at all levels. In this way your world can function and fulfill itself without interference. Yet God allows himself and the highest divine forces to interfere when certain circumstances require it.

'Grace originates in compassion and can overrule the basic laws of justice. To achieve grace requires understanding of both the deep regulation of the energy of justice and the innermost being of the power of love. Grace can be given if asked for by the human being himself, by other humans or by other divine forces such as angels.'

In the rain I walk through Detzeln and Wutöschingen and up to Ofteringen where there is a small convent called Marienburg. It is a former castle but was converted into a convent in 1862. Nuns from Au by Einsiedeln moved in.

Am in the convent church for almost an hour. No clear meditation and several times almost fall asleep. Cannot seem to be able to pick up Mary very clearly. I am pretty sure that this place is on the route, but it has not been easy to tune in here so I must have been careless opening it up.

I continue directly eastwards on the road from the convent. On this road is a megalithic grave marked by an ancient stone with a hole in it. The grave is from approximately 2000 BC. It is said that the hole in the stone is a 'soul hole' through which the soul could move freely in and out of the grave. I guess we are back in the age of the Goddess and I have assumed that this place is on our route.

Before I reach the grave, Mary asks me to stop. She advises me not to get too close to the stone. She says there is something dark there that could cling to us. After passing the stone at a fair distance I start to say to Mary that it is nice to have got by it, but I am interrupted as I suddenly sense a dark being behind her back. Immediately I invoke St. Michael and ask him to cut the dark being away from us. He does this quickly and after a couple of kilometers Mary is once again clear and distinct. I think about Michael's explanation of how the dark beings can cling to ancient places of worship. This was obviously the case here.

Look for a hotel in Enzingen but the only hotel in town is closed. I am not sure what to do, but decide to tackle another stage of the road. To Willsweil, along the main road. Coffee at the local inn and onwards east up into a forest. The path crosses over a tongue of Switzerland, but crossing the borders by day is permitted. In the forest I make contact with the angel of the place, whom I take to be male. He seems a little fierce, but he offers me a present: '*A feather for your cap*,' he says. I realize he is teasing me and reply, '*Go blow your own trumpet*.' He laughs out loud and says, '*You're alright*,' and concludes by saying, '*Take the feather as a token of my friendship*.'

Continue to Baltersweil where I come upon a pilgrimage chapel.

PILGRIMAGE CHAPEL

A sign says: 'The holy chapel in Baltersweil to Appolonia was for centuries a resting place for pilgrims who passed by on their way to either Maria Einsiedeln or to Santiago de Compostella in Spain, with the grave of the apostle James who was executed by Herodias Agrippa in the year 44 AD.'

Appolonia lived in Alexandria in the 2nd to 3rd century. She was a Christian and was tortured, in the course of which she had her teeth knocked out. For that reason she became the patron saint of dentists but presumably also because the pilgrims of old greatly feared toothache.

For the first time, I meet an official pilgrim route – in fact two routes that cross each other here: the James Way and Mary's Way.

The hotels in the next town, Jestetten, are also full and again I have to keep going. My left foot is starting to give me trouble. If I step on it hard a pain shoots up from my ankle. I limp along. A shower has drifted over me and emptied itself – or so I think. It clears up and I shed my waterproofs. Shortly afterwards the shower hits the mountains, and how it happens I do not know but it comes rolling back, sending down a huge amount of water. It is raining cats and dogs. Soaking wet, I trudge through the border town of Nohl into Switzerland. On down to the bridge over the Rhine. This side of the Rhine Falls is normally extremely beautiful but due to the rain and the pain in my foot I do not take much in. The pain is now unbearable and I am afraid that the injury is so severe that I might have to give up my journey. At long last I reach the old castle town of Schloss-Laufen, on the south side of the Rhine Falls. I hobble into the youth hostel. Can barely walk after 40 kilometers of exhausting hiking. The downhill parts were the worst. Must have strained a muscle between my calf and ankle. Decide to stay at the hostel for at least two nights in order to allow my foot to recover.

Luckily there is a vacancy and I am put in a room with four other people, a German couple and an Irish woman and her son. As is often the case in hostels, the forced intimacy between strangers leads to interesting conversations. The doughty Irish mother understands what I am doing and sincerely encourages me to publish a description of the route.

A stage is over, and in the church in Laufen Mary asks me to sum up that which I have not done fully. I go through the entire course of the trip, listing the incidences where I did not act according to Mary's instructions, endangered us, and was not focused and prepared. I hope I now have learned to listen properly and that I will now be able to follow Mary's directions. In order to avoid

The Rheinfall

endangering us again – through dark forces clinging to us – Mary encourages me to perform purification in all the churches along her route. *'That is why you have to visit so many churches,'* she says with a smile. By so saying she responds to my unspoken surprise at having to visit such a tremendous number of churches. Mary says, *'Think of them as depots for purifying and recharging.'*

She also asks me to understand the landscape temples that we have walked through. Some things I had already understood while others only make sense to me now: All pilgrimages are like a chakra journey from Root to Crown and back again. Except that on a journey like this you do not come back to the place from where you started. You make the whole journey from Root to Crown and then back to a different Root. That is what is significant about a true pilgrimage.

Bungling things up is apparently a theme on this journey. I am tired of it. Tired of not being advanced enough to submit myself and my intellect to intuitive instructions. Often I do not feel at all worthy of doing this walk.

Through Grethe, Mary later explained to me:

'At this stage of development it is a very important challenge to humanity to be able to accept one's own dark sides – that you are not as pure your spirit longs to be.

'It is very important to have the ability to forgive oneself – when you feel you have been too much in another consciousness.

'Wastebaskets need emptying. There will always be things to cleanse. The more you work spiritually, the more you need to purge old insults, and hurt feelings – the part of you that belongs to Earth. As long as you are incarnate your body has an affiliation with Earth. It needs to demand its right to territory and to express needs and longings.

'Your body has its own path of development which can lead in the opposite direction of where you want to go on spiritually. Everybody on a path of development will have to struggle with this contradiction. You are on your path. It is important to carry this awareness with you. Be ready to encounter your lesser nature and afterwards to forgive yourself.'

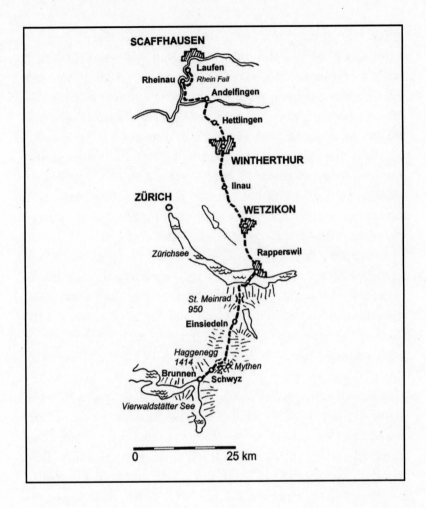

5

Angels – The Soul of Europe – Spirit

Switzerland as far as the Alps

The Rhine Falls have fascinated me since the first time I saw them. Every second, huge volumes of water are hurled down over the rocks, a cloud of steam shooting up from the point of impact. On the southern side, the Laufen side, there are steps down along the waterfall from where you can look up into the furious, threatening masses of water and even stick your hand out into them. It can inspire both wonder and fear to have this force of nature thundering over you. From the western side, the Neuhausen side, you can go on a tour boat out to a rock in the middle of the falls and climb up onto the top of it. For me it was a tremendous experience to stand there – a fragile, tiny human being in the midst of the crushing masses of water – and experience, together with the water, an inner upward-moving transformation – from an element of water to one of air.

I spend my day of rest at the waterfall. I relish it. Regain my strength and my foot slowly recovers. An occasional cappuccino helps too. Having sat writing in a café on the Neuhausen side, enjoying the wide view of the falls and Schloss Kaufen, I walk slowly back to my hotel. Suddenly it dawns on me that there has to be an angel here. I turn my attention to the area above the waterfall and an angel answers, *'Have you only just noticed me?'* This is embarrassing but true and I immediately find a suitable secluded place. I ask permission to enter the energy realm of the landscape. It is quickly opened to me. To my great surprise the angel asks: *'Do you not recognize me?'* and starts to laugh. *'You helped me, you know, when I first started here.'* I have just read that the Rhine found its present course 15,000–17,000 years ago when it broke through here and cut a new bed. A lot of laughing and giggling ensues and I am very confused. 'But I am only a human being and you are an angel. How can this be?' I ask.

'You were also an angel. You chose later to become human, and so you had to go through the "fall" into the material world. I am very glad to be able to talk to you again.'

In my understanding of the world, one may perhaps become an angel at some time if one behaves oneself. But I am surprised that the opposite can happen.

I try to imagine myself as an angel here. But it is more than I can grasp. I do love it here, but I can at most see myself messing about in a small branch of the waterfall.

What is a nature-angel anyway? If I have been a nature-angel then that 'I' must be my soul, which can apparently occupy the body both of a human being and of an angel. Obviously an angelic body is not material but is it then only spirit and soul? Hardly. I have a feeling that it is physical – an accumulation of energy can be said to be physical. At any rate angels seem to have tasks to perform in the physical world. To create places, regulate them and bring life to them. They do not seem to have been awarded the same free will as human beings though. It is rather as if God's creative power works consciously and directly through them. Mind you, I do not see them as puppets on a string. They are very individual and have their own character. Nature-angels, that is. I cannot conceive other angels, such as archangels, in this way.

Early one morning, before breakfast, I sit and meditate at the foot of the waterfall. A splendid time of day, tourist free! In the depths of the water I seem to see an imaginary figure breaking his walking staff in two. I am surprised because I do not carry a walking staff. My only support is my maps. Am I supposed to give these up then? *'Try to follow your inner guidance without looking at your maps at all. Only inner guidance,'* says Mary. *'Then at night you can look and see where you have walked.'*

This will be difficult, I think to myself. But I accept.

We start in Laufen and walk southwards. Follow the Rhine downstream. I manage perfectly well without maps. After 9 kilometers the island of Rheinau appears. Years ago, the widely influential Rheinau Monastery stood here. Today it has been turned into a public institution, but the impressive church still stands.

I carry on southwards through the town. Imperceptibly the road turns west and I end up by the Rhine again. I am surprised that we have to go west. At Ellikon I am directed to turn away from the river. Along a small road running eastwards. Enter a wood. The road now turns slowly north. I get the feeling I will end up at the waterfall again and am convinced that this must be the wrong direction. Keen to compensate, I turn onto a path along a little brook and come to another path which I follow for the next couple of hours. There is not a single signpost, and the area becomes more and more desolate. I do not meet a single soul and fear I will end up in a complete wilderness. At one point I walk along a river through flat, open countryside. In the far distance I see somebody running towards me.

Closer in, I can see it is a man – and that he is stark naked. An energetic man, it seems. In one hand he holds a purse or a sack. Nothing else. We greet each other politely in passing. It seems quite surrealistic in this desolate place, and I am so disconcerted that I do not think to ask the way. I turn back to the path and carry on along the river. After a long walk I come at last to a bridge, and I can escape from what feels like a wilderness. A couple of kilometers further on is a town. I have no idea where I am and very much doubt Mary's instructions. When I finally collapse in a chair in a café, I immediately pull out my map. I need to know where I am.

I have reached Andelfingen and it actually looks quite sensible. The map also shows that if I had stayed on the first path, instead of turning down and following the stream, I should have found a straighter – and more 'civilized' – road. 'We got there in the end,' says Mary.

I am tired and not entirely happy about doing without my map, but after two cups of coffee I cheer up and agree to try again. At first all goes well, but just outside a small town, I choose to skirt it and go through a beautiful little coppice. This is a mistake. I realize that Mary has gone straight into the town. At the far side of the town I try to go back and find the right way. No luck. So I carry on southwards. I end up on a busy road and I know that I am well and truly lost. With great difficulty I find my way to Wintherthur.

That evening we review what happened. Mary tells me that when I make a mistake she has to expend a great deal of energy on correcting the route through the next choices we make.

We agree on a compromise where I in each case first listen to Mary and then check it on the map.

* * *

Am woken in Wintherthur at 6am by thundering church bells. Another quick snooze and it is suddenly nine o'clock! Well, well, a decent sleep at last! At least my clothes got a chance to dry out after a wash in the bath last night.

Tune in at the church and then walk down to the train station. The marked path, Wanderweg, starts here and is well signposted.

In the woods I sense an angel willing to talk. Happy to collaborate on future pilgrims. We somehow get round to talking about me perhaps having been an angel at the Rhine Falls. He has too. We are almost old friends. Before long the angel asks me a pressing question: *'What was it like falling down into the physical world?'*

As I have absolutely no recollection of it I cannot really help him. We compare our respective functions. One big difference is that human beings can move about from place to place while the nature-angel is tied to one place. I suggest that it too could become human and it says it will think about it.

In another wood a little further on, I twice stumble over some roots and then find my way completely blocked by a fallen tree. Think at first that there is something bad going on, but decide to take it as a good thing.

Ask the fallen tree what it wants with me – and at the same time tune in to the local angel.

'At last,' it says. *'Welcome, Hans. How are you?'* I answer, 'So

you have heard news of me from the angel at the Rhine Falls too?' *'Yes, I was there at the same time as you,'* it says. *'I remember you very well. What have you been up to since then?'* Again we have a friendly chat. This angel likes being a Root chakra angel and will not consider becoming human. It says goodbye to me with a beautiful expression: *'May the soles of your shoes kiss my soil.'*

Later I ask Mary if there is anything we ought to talk about. She wants me to ask about the relations between the different countries in Europe.

During the next hour we have a very interesting conversation.

Mary starts: *'The European countries are uniting. Serious disagreements between the nations are being resolved. Many forms of international connections are evolving. Borders between the nations are being erased. Each nation's characteristics seem able to develop on a basis of equality. Europe is finding its soul. Consider how Europe got its name.'*

Mary refers to the myth of the princess Europa and Zeus which I remember like this:

Zeus, the god-king, espied a divinely beautiful princess in Phoenicia. He transformed himself into a great powerful white bull, and in that shape he went ashore. As soon as Europa saw the bull she was enchanted. Whether the bull then abducted her or whether she herself mounted it we do not know. Both versions exist. In any case, the result was that they returned to Crete, where Europa and Zeus were married.

'Please note where Europe came from,' says Mary and continues: *'From the same area as Christianity. Just as the continent adopted the name of Europa so it also adopted Christianity. I also have a part to play in this,'* says Mary. *'As a figure in Christianity it is my aim to inspire the peoples of Europe to adopt the old myth. Recognize Europa as a feminine being and let mercy be a common basic value.'*

She continues: *'To make this pilgrimage is to give Europe a soul. Among other things by recognizing Europe as a holy landscape consisting of much more than human beings.'*

Mary stresses that her field is not politics, but the opening of hearts. That more and more people will seek the way of the heart.

Mary and the infant Jesus on the altar in Liebfrauenkapelle

Leaving the highlands, I come down to Rapperswil, set at a crossing between two lakes. By the town hall square there is a small chapel dating from 1485, the Liebfrauenkapelle.

The chapel has a lovely atmosphere and is very pleasant to be in. An unheeded but important Mary site. She tells me that on her journey she was received here by very hospitable people, and that she stayed here for some time.

I have walked 24 kilometers and can stop for the night here without feeling guilty, but it is only two o'clock so I rashly let myself in for the last 17 kilometers up to Einsiedeln. Mary's pilgrimage route now joins a route of St. James going to Santiago de Compostella. The signposted James Way includes an ascent of 600 meters on paths that involve actual climbing. At one point I give up on the path and follow the road instead. I guess the path must have been made by a mountaineer.

But like other pilgrims, I prefer gradual ascents and not too many 'flights of steps' which strain other muscles. At 1,000 meters above sea level I cross the St. Meinrad Pass. Continue by narrow lanes to the town of Einsiedeln, with its famous abbey.

Two church towers stand out over an impressive abbey complex with several four- and five-storey buildings. For hundreds of years this has been a place of pilgrimage for millions of people.

Einsiedeln with the Mythen Mountains in the background

THE CONVENT OF MARY EINSIEDELN

The abbey is said to have been founded by the monk Meinrad in the 800s. He came from a monastery on Reichenau and settled here as a hermit – in what was then a wilderness. He lived here for 24 years till he was brutally murdered. A couple of robbers believed that he had a hidden treasure and killed him. The robbers were hunted down and sentenced to death but during the next 80 years the place was never without one or more hermits. In the 900s a hermitage was built. As the result of a vision the church was dedicated to the Virgin Mary.

In the 1200s this Mary's Hermitage was extended with a Lady Chapel. There are also reports of a spring welling up just beneath the chapel. Sometime in the 1400s we hear the first reports of a statue of the Black Madonna in the chapel. The same statue that is there today.

The place became famous not only for the hermitage chapel but also for the healing waters in 'Our Lady's Spring'. Countless pilgrims streamed to the site. Thus in 1466, for example, there were reports of 130,000 pilgrims.

Today the pilgrim chapel with its Black Madonna now stands within the great abbey church.

I go into the great church, sit down in a pew in front of the chapel and contemplate the Black Madonna. She is dressed up in a big flared dress, and from the postcards on sale I can see that she has a dress for each church festival. Mary does not come through to me immediately and I become absorbed in the scene before me. There are many dark-skinned people here. I notice a black woman walking past, who suddenly catches sight of the Black Madonna. She gasps, stares at the Madonna and claps her hand to her mouth. She then runs over to her husband and pulls him in front of the chapel to see the Madonna. She is beaming with joy. I understand. It must be wonderful that a central religious figure has one's own skin color.

The Black Madonna in Einsiedeln

Although I several times try to tempt Mary to comment on the Black Madonnas, I get no answer. I only sense a vague unwillingness to take so much interest in skin color. As if it is quite unimportant.

Though it is only a few days since I last had a break, I feel in need of another one. So I stay in Einsiedeln for two days. Am in the church for several services. One afternoon I go and see a large iron cross on a mound south of the church square. Jesus is on the cross, flanked by Mary on one side and John the Disciple on the other. The inscription repeats the sayings of Jesus to John, that Mary is now his mother; and to Mary, that John is now her son. As I am in spirit traveling with both Mary and John, the cross has a special meaning for me. In a way this place is more intense for me than the church.

On my way up to the cross Mary asks me what I have learnt so far.

Some things I can describe, others not. Mary asks me to find a place to sit down. I go out into a field, find a good place to sit, and turn my thoughts inwards.

With Mary's help I piece it all together:

I see the pilgrimage as a giant chakra system, where each stage is not only a small system of chakras, but also a single chakra in a much greater system. The first stage in Germany was Root, and here I was given the introductory test on Disibodenberg. The French stage was Hara, and here I was introduced to my soul. I became conscious of myself as soul, body and spirit. Solar Plexus was clearly Kaiserstuhl, and here an ego structure died in me.

In the Heart, in Schwarzwald, I was asked if I wanted access to Heaven, and I learnt that Heaven's gate is open when you are conscious of yourself as soul, spirit and matter, and see all three of them as equal.

In the Throat, around the Rhine Falls, my understanding of my soul was broadened. I learned it has a history through many levels, from angel to man. The organization of society is apparently also of interest to my soul.

Mary explains that now, in the Brow chakra, we are working on spirit.

Mary asks me to go up to the statues. I do. Sit at an angle where I see Mary in front of Jesus.

I open the discussion by describing what I see and feel, and I happen to say, '… when Jesus gave up the spirit and it ascended …'

'*Exactly!*' Mary interrupts. '*That is what happens when you die. When the axis of vertical polarity between spirit and matter is broken – e.g. by the organs of the body ceasing to function – the energy of matter sinks down, and the energy of the spirit rises up. But the soul is still there as a polarity and may stay there for a certain length of time before it also turns towards home.'*

I ask Mary to explain what really happened by the grave after the Crucifixion. Mary says that the body of Jesus was laid in the grave, and that the three Marys kept watch outside. The stone had not yet been placed in front of the entrance to the grave. This was done according to their tradition of leaving the grave open for a time, usually a few days, expressly so that the spirit might leave the body and the grave more easily. Mary also tells me that Mary Magdalene was the first to see the soul of Jesus. *'She was consecrated and very open.'*

I get back to the tripartite division: spirit, body and soul. Argue a bit against them being equal. That the body presumably is given us as a tool, and that it is the soul that is our real self. Mary explains that this is not right, and that it undervalues the body.

'But if they are all equal there must be a fourth authority to collate experiences for the other three?' I ask. 'Yes,' says Mary. *'That is God! You are body and soul as well as spirit. Experiences from all three are gathered. You are a spark in the divine ocean of fire and you help to nourish that fire.'*

I go round to the other side of the cross to see John in front of Jesus. I ask John how he experienced the death of Jesus.

'Terribly. To have lived every day with this clear and radiant light and then suddenly be left alone in what felt like darkness. And knowing that our task now really began in earnest. It may have been harder for the other disciples. After all, I was given my task very clearly and simply. I was to look after Mary and at the same time receive instruction from her. I was given some of that light that she had also given to Jesus..'

'So what will happen now then?' I ask. *'My apprenticeship is nearing its completion,'* John answers. *'Now I shall pass from one level to another. I will become spirit and will be given tasks in connection with the field of tension between spirit and matter that holds the human body. I will keep the recollection of my soul's experiences – let us call it* one insight among several. But I can no longer be compared to a human soul. Mary stays on the level of souls in the role of universal mother.'

Finally I go round and look directly up at Jesus. This involves looking almost straight into the sun.

'What is happening to you now, Jesus?' I ask. 'I am going to sit at the right hand of God the Father Almighty. I shall be so near the source that you will not be able to experience me. Just as you cannot look into the sun as you are now trying to do. You are in me and I in you,' Jesus finishes.

Finally I go round the cross again and ask if there is anything else. John says, 'My time is coming, and it is important that men are prepared to understand my impulse. You have an important part to play. Pass on your insight. Fertilize the ground.'

Mary says, 'Now go and write it all down.'

I lay a malachite stone on the ground and bless the site. Walk down full of joy.

That evening I embroider a small white dove on my hat. As a sign of Mary and the Holy Spirit. A symbol of Mary's pilgrimage.

The Dove

Through Grethe, Mary later expounded on our talk of death.

'Dying can be compared to moving away from somewhere you have lived for a long time. You leave an imprint, and perhaps something you have created there too. The spirit drives you on towards new goals. In your soul you still have your identity which you take with *you. Even if you must let go of something physical, everything will still be divinely connected. Both in the reality that existed in the life you have lived and in the one to come.*

'*The spirit that goes on when we die will still carry its spiritual experiences with it, but it will also go to God. It is surely a basic dogma in every religion that when you die in the physical world you go to God. That is to say that the spirit, with its spiritual experience, goes to God. There it will also have access to everything that has been experienced in your life if necessary.*

'*The whole ethereal web around the Earth is made up of everything that has been thought, done and acted out. Everything that has happened on Earth. The moment somebody leaves Earth they will also leave their imprint on Earth. That way nobody lives in vain. There will always be a greater meaning in the great fellowship – for everybody. Acknowledging that you are an individual in a greater brotherhood inspires greater responsibility for the fellowship.*'

* * *

Now I am definitely getting into the Alps. This last week of my walk I have clearly been able to see two distinctive mountaintops right next to each other on the horizon. They seem like a great gate into the Alps. They are the Mythen Mountains. In Mary's day they must have been just as important points of orientation as they are for me today. I must get up to the 'gate'. A James Way leads from Einsiedeln all the way there. From Alpthal the path rises steeply up towards the 'gate'. In many places it is beautifully cobbled, proving itself to be an ancient thoroughfare. It does not in fact run between the two mountaintops, but across the Haggenegg Pass, just beside them. I am 1,414 meters above sea level. In the pass itself is a farm with a simple drinks stall in front of the barn. I take a coffee, with milk straight from the cow. Just on the other side of the pass there is a beautiful wooden church which Mary is very fond of. 'Liebe Frau Kapelle, Haggenegg' it is called. It boasts a very expressive coal-black Madonna figure.

Follow the tarmac road through Schwyz down to Brunnen. Very steep. Falling 1,000 meters. I cannot help thinking that for every meter I go down, I shall soon have to climb another up again to get up to the St.Gotthard Pass.

Mary wants me to stay the night here in Brunnen. Tomorrow a new landscape system begins.

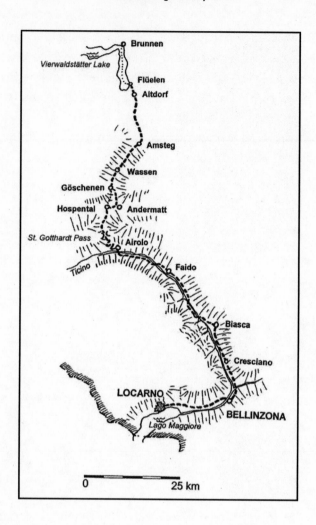

6

About God

St. Gotthard

Here, in mid-Switzerland, lies the vast and beautiful
Vierwaldstätter Lake. Precipitous mountainsides dive down into

the depths of the water, and at the river mouths thousands of years of sediment have formed bases for the building of towns. Brunnen is one such town. A port and also the gateway into the Mythen valleys. Today a busy main road runs south, blasted out of the mountainsides along the east bank of the lake.

I am anxious to find out whether in her day Mary would have been able to forge a way through the mountains along the lakeside, and whether in that case I shall have to take this busy road. I quickly realize that I need not have worried. Mary gives me to understand that she went by boat to the southern end of the lake.

Eagerly I board the ferry and give myself up to a beautiful sail across the Vierwaldstätter Lake. How blessed and wonderful it is to be borne over the water! We put in at Rüstli, where the William Tell Festival happens to be in progress. Sail on to the southern end of the lake. Disembark in Flüelen and carry on to Altdorf, which seems to be the starting point for the Crown chakra stage across the St. Gotthard Pass. Next to the church is a Chapel to Anna. I feel Mary's presence very strongly, especially in the crypt. Perhaps Altdorf was the first town by the lake in Mary's day.

Was given this saying for my walk: 'Go with mildness, lightness and openness.'

Slowly I near the St. Gotthard massif. In my hotel I find a beautiful edition of a book on the area and read that the pass was first brought into use in the year 1000. According to the author, the greatest obstacle was the deep Schöllenen Gorge which was not bridged until about the year 1200. Does that mean that Mary did not come this way at all? Curious, I pass the question on to Mary. She answers that in her day they made a short detour, and she promises to show me where they turned off.

After Goschenen I begin the first major ascent, going from 700 to1,500 meters altitude. Walk along the side of the motorway several times and see cars caught in long queues. It is fun to overtake them. At one point the cars disappear into a long motorway tunnel. Peace!

Just before the Schöllenen Gorge

I am eager to see if Mary can show me an alternative to the route through the dramatic Schöllenen Gorge. Just before we get there, she draws my attention to a small road snaking up the mountain on my right. That was where they crossed the ridge, Mary says. I do not know where that road ends today so I continue over the bridge through the gorge to Teufelsbrugge. Walking through the gorge is very awe-inspiring. Three bridges from three different ages span the narrowest point. The scenery is very dramatic with masses of water thundering through the gorge deep down under the bridges.

I am not surprised that very little traffic came through here until they managed to build a bridge.

After the gorge I reach a flat plain just outside Andermatt. Mary says that she has not been in Andermatt, and when I look back I can see that she must have crossed the mountains further to the west, which would actually have been a shortcut to the old Roman town of Hospental that I am heading for. That route must be shorter, but then you would have to climb up to an altitude of 1,800 meters. Mary tells me that in her day the plain was almost a bog with rushes and open water, so you could not walk across like you can today. A bit further on we meet an old road coming from exactly where Mary must have got through. Here I sense Mary joining me again.

I have since read more well-founded tales of the Gotthard crossing. It is even supposed that an indigenous Roman population lived in the valley north of the gorge. Archaeological finds from the church in Goschenen show that there has been an unbroken Christian tradition there dating right back to the Romans. So they must also have known the St. Gotthard crossing and how to use it. As did Mary.

The church in Hospental is dedicated to Mary's ascension and is an important point on the route. The word 'Hospental' has the same root as the word 'hostel', and the town was originally a Roman outpost.

I stay in the youth hostel which is small, primitive and cheap. But then 30 men do have to share one shower. A real pilgrims' hostel.

Mary tells me that they had heard of the refuge in Hospental, and that this was the reason they came here.

The next morning Mary leads me through a prayer in the church in which I ask the angels in the next area to open their energy to me. This turns out to be very effective.

From Hospental I follow the road further uphill. It is rather busy, and in the first valley I choose to turn onto a narrow footpath. A very few steps take me into a totally different world.

The surrounding mountains close in around me. The hum of traffic disappears. A gentle quiet descends. There is only me – and a flock of grazing sheep. This valley is something quite special. Pure and majestic. Walking on this path is like a blessing, and a few minutes later I am in contact with the angel of the area who welcomes me warmly. Tells me to just enjoy myself. I am quite sure that it is the St. Gotthard angel and that it is a Crown chakra angel. There is something glorious over the valley, so I name it 'The Holy Valley'.

It occurs to me that the Crown-angel of St. Gotthard is at the same time a Heart-angel in an east–west chakra system consisting purely of Crown-angels. 'Of course I am crossing the heart of the crowns,' I think. After all, I am walking the heart-road.

The old main path up to St. Gotthard

I climb along the Holy Valley and am still several kilometers from the pass. Am led onto small paths, sometimes beautifully cobbled. It is obvious that people have walked here since time immemorial. Very steep now. The vegetation is becoming sparse. The air is sharper to breathe. It is quite cool in the shade. I have to rest several times.

At last, exhausted, I reach the pass at 2,100 meters. Finally I am standing at the top of the St. Gotthard Pass and can survey the mountains on both sides.

The sun is shining and there is hardly any wind. I am lucky as there might just as easily have been a biting cold wind blowing.

I have been looking forward to this moment as the highlight of my journey. Not only is it the highest point of the route, but now I have proved to myself that I can stand the physical effort.

I sit down on a bare rock and enjoy the moment. *'Seated on a high, bare pinnacle, beholding the expanses stretching before me, I can say to myself: Here you rest directly on ground that reaches right down to the deepest parts of the Earth. No more recent layer, no piles of old ruins are laid between you and the firm ground of the original world.'* These words could be mine, but they are in fact Goethe's.

I feel a deep, deep connection to the center of the Earth and at the same time feel in very close contact with Heaven. A mighty pole seems to connect the two.

The Gotthard massif is central to Europe. Here the Rhine rises and flows north, the Rhone west, and the Ticino south.

I am thrilled to read a sign saying that the St. Gotthard Pass was used in antiquity, and especially that many coins from the period 15 BC to 400 AD have been found here. That is the period of Pax Romana, and the Romans had colonized areas right up to Bingen.

Now the place is crawling with tourists and it all becomes a bit too hectic for me. Have to queue in several places. The hubbub of tourists distracts me so much that I cannot tune in to find out if there is anything I should be doing. I feel I might be overlooking something. Impatiently I take one last look, inhaling the enchanting landscapes. Then I set off down the path towards Airolo. In some places the path is slippery with water or very sandy. I slip three times but just manage to avoid falling. It is all I can do to find a foothold. So I turn onto the cobbled road zigzagging down the mountain. Over 9 kilometers I descend from 2,100 meters at the top to 1,100 meters in the first town, Airolo.

In the church in Airolo, Mary advises me to stay the night. Right opposite the church there is a hotel, and I check in. Suddenly people are speaking Italian.

I am strangely tired, lacking energy and confused. Mary says I have expended a lot of energy on the mountain.

* * *

The next morning I am reasonably clear-headed. Start well in the church. First a climb over a small mountain, but otherwise there is a good path down through Chiuto, Fiesso and on to Faido.

On the way I ask Mary if there is anything we should talk about. She says simply that we can talk about God.

'*What is God?*' Mary asks, and continues, '*God never came from anything or nothing. God never becomes anything or nothing. God is continually being created.*'

Mary has disclosed this prayer to me before and I have used it many mornings.

Mary then raises the question: what lies behind the words 'God is'?

She explains that as human beings we cannot normally grasp the basic idea that 'God is'. But we will be able to grasp the idea that God is continually being created. We are all part of the power of creation, and the side we see of God is the creator. We have that side in ourselves, each and every one of us.

On the subject of being continually being created Mary says, '*Time is a condition which you are subject to. However far you enter into one of the three forms of energy, spirit, body or soul, time will pull you back. You can experience glimpses of divine existence on all three levels. A few, a very few, can experience these glimpses as longer lasting states of existence.*'

The way I understand it, the glimpses can be in a spiritual direction, as I have experienced on this pilgrimage. But they can also be in a bodily direction like a top athlete who feels that everything comes together in a perfect jump. Or a musician, transported by wonderful music etc.

'Everybody who experiences these glimpses will want to relive them. Some people can do that; others cannot.'

I follow the River Ticino for several days. It is wide and powerful. It carries the rain- and melt-water from the Gotthard massif right down to the River Po and on into the Adriatic. It feels as if the masses of water carry the spirituality of the mountains down with them. I reflect on the thought that *God is continually being created*, and that we create constantly. Why must there be this unending stream of possibilities for choice and creation? Mary explains that God needs angels who can independently find God's being through any veil or resistance.

This reminds me of a myth I heard some years ago.

Once upon a time God was sitting in heaven planning to create a new sort of high-ranking angel. Lucifer, who could read God's mind, said straight away that he wanted to be that sort of angel. Lucifer was given the post, but he had not imagined that it would involve a fall down into the material world. From there, like humanity, he must now work his way up, to be able to become this new, higher-ranking angel.

According to this myth we – like Lucifer – are placed in circumstances which continuously train us to be able to find God.

We are given freedom of choice for exactly this reason – to find God. To be able to make the right choice we must also be able to make a wrong one. Therefore we have several choices. In the extreme, the density of matter limits the damage our human choices can cause to the universe.

The factors of time and cycle mean that we can perpetually

make new choices. Day by day, week by week, month by month, year by year, season by season, age by age. Each choice helps to make the soul more experienced. This is in fact how the soul is formed.

'How can we optimize the process?' I ask. Mary answers that this is done by continually following your soul when making choices. Taking responsibility for your decisions and being conscious of the consequences.

Also it is important to always keep spirit, body and soul side by side. We do not only leave imprints on our soul, but also on our matter and spirit.

If for instance you have no contact with your spiritual aspect, you should seek it.

There can be many different spiritual approaches, and each individual must examine what touches him deeply and what moves him. The way in may be through religion, nature or something quite different.

If you have no contact with your soul, you can practice by asking yourself whether your current reality is what you in your heart of hearts really want, or how you deep down really see yourself.

If you have no contact with matter, you may choose to lovingly occupy yourself with, for example, the body.

'Understand your choices and their consequences, but never become trapped in them! You constantly decide whether something old is finished and something new can begin,' says Mary, and goes on to say, 'In every single choice there is a small spark of God. By concentrating your thoughts inwards you can feel this and know whether the choice is expedient.'

For long stretches I follow the Strada Romanica, an old Roman highway that in some places is just a path. It leads me up to a charming little town on a mountain plateau, Chironico. Spend the night above the bar in the only hotel in the town.

Tune in the next morning in the Chironico church and

continue along the path through a wood. I find several chapels of Mary and finally come to a deserted monastery. According to a signpost it is called San Pellegrino. The brickwork is dilapidated and the windows are boarded up. I sense monks around me. They seem to be asking me to ring the bells three times. What bells? I wonder. Are there still bells in the ruins? After some searching I find a bell tower, and, believe it or not, there is a rope. I start to pull it. The rope moves and after some pulling a bell rings once, and then twice more. It sounds good. As if something new is being created or something old is re-awakened. The imaginary monks seem to rejoice. Perhaps new pilgrims bring new life to the place.

Carry on downhill. I make the mistake of taking a farm track west of the motorway.

It surprises me that there is nobody else on the track at all. As if it is never used. Suddenly a black snake one and a half meters long shoots out a few meters in front of me. I do not like snakes, but this one is obviously more afraid than I am and disappears like lightning on the other side of the track. Tell myself that I must be careful about sleeping out in the open. The black snake may have been a warning though, because a few kilometers later the track ends at a big wrought-iron gate. It does, however, continue on the other side, and I think naively that the gate must have been closed by mistake. I manage to get through the fence and carry on – till I find myself in an area full of large buildings. I clamber down a concrete slope, down into a broad depression covered in giant concrete slabs. I look about me a bit and at length realize that I am in a power plant, and that I am standing in the middle of the bed where the mountain water usually pours down. Luckily there is no sound of water coming, but all the same I hurry to climb up the opposite concrete bank. Here I come up against another fence so I climb through that too. Now I am luckily in an area where other people are about. After some time I find the main entrance and on going through it I politely greet the astounded gatekeeper.

It is a relief to get back onto a public road.

In Biasca there are two churches. I visit the newer one, which is octagonal, first. Then the old one, which is dedicated to St. Peter and St. Paul. A very unusual church that is no longer in use. Mary seems a bit sullen. She tells me that just behind the altar there is a powerful ray where the fire of Heaven and the water of the Earth meet. I can feel it when I try standing there. '*It was I who consecrated that place!*' says Mary. It is one of the places that had later been taken over by Peter's and Paul's energy.

Towards the end of the afternoon it begins to rain heavily. The hotels along the road are closed, but luckily I manage to find a private room in a basement.

* * *

The next morning it is still pouring. My kind hostess brings a jug of boiled water for me to drink, as I like to do every morning. I take it easy. Wait for better weather. By mid-morning the rain seems to be stopping and I risk going out. It soon gets worse again, however, and carries on for the next two hours. In Bellinzona it eases up, but I am soaked through and my shoes are so full of water that they squelch with every step I take. Like this I sail all the way to Locarno.

I have asked Mary several things, but her answers have not been forthcoming. She says finally that what I'm asking about comes later. Right now we are working on fervor. What about '*pure heartedness*' and '*pure heart*'? she asks.

At Locarno I know that I have to get up to the monastery of Madonna del Sasso. It is situated high above the town itself. I hope that Mary will let me take the mountain railway, the Funicolare. But no, we have to walk all the way up. Had I not been so tired I would have enjoyed this walk, which winds up a flight of steps into and through a heavenly valley with picture chapels and beautiful panoramas. At length I reach the monastery and, soaked in sweat, I sit down in the church to get my breath back. The church is dedicated to Mary and her statue behind the altar is beautiful. Mary advises me to stay an extra day in the energy up here. We are in a Heart chakra, and as we are to talk of the pure heart it is important to be in heart energy.

Look everywhere for accommodation but it is impossible to find a single room. Even at the 'Muller Garni'. But as they sounded friendly, I later decide to go back and ask again. By pure coincidence another guest has just cancelled so I get his room for the two nights I want.

It has been rather hard walking on 'webbed feet' in wet shoes all day. But at half past seven I can sit down on my private balcony and enjoy the view over Locarno and the Lago Maggiore.

The Sanctuary Madonna del Sasso

* * *

Day of rest. Washing day. My muscles are so sore that I can hardly climb the stairs – even without my backpack. Am in the monastery church morning and evening.

Here I ask Mary whether I have left anything undone on the way, and she answers that at times I have been so occupied with my physical exertions that it has hindered her messages from coming through. That was for instance the case at the top of St. Gotthard. Generally it is very important to gather energy for a Crown chakra, as I have done. It is important for the soul of Europe that more people do this.

'When you come to a Crown, review the experiences and insight you have achieved and let them rise up into the Crown. Then – if you are open to it – an energy will come down to you. Perhaps in the form of a word or a sentence.' I sit and meditate on this and feel that the sentence I have been given is: 'Go with an open heart and show love!'

* * *

The next day I again start in the monastery church. Hope to go by boat from here. I am quickly told, however, that I am not sailing but walking. Soon get onto a path, Sentiero Romano, which takes me down to the Italian border. Here I spend my last francs and cross the border. The pavement disappears and I have to walk on the busy road.

Carry on till I see a sign to San Bartolomeo. Argue a bit with Mary as to whether it really is necessary to make the 300 meters climb up, when Cannobio is less than 4 kilometers away. But it is necessary, so up, up, up to San Bartolomeo, Formine and Cinzago.

The path goes through a wood where I pass one chapel after another. The church in San Bartolomeo is a woodland church and is not in use. The place is obviously used for picnics, understandably, as there is a quite wonderful special atmosphere here. Go on through Cinzago to Socragno and find the town's huge church, St. Agatha. It towers majestically on the edge of the mountain, and from beside it there is a fantastic view over the Lago Maggiore. Then comes the descent, again by a small path where there used to be a road, but where there is now only bare rock and gravel. Although the climb down is arduous it is obviously important. 'The forgotten holy road,' I call it. Mary has walked here and she wants to show me what it was like in her day.

I ask if future pilgrims will have to go this way too, and she says that it is desirable. But if quite special circumstances call for it, they may be allowed to stay down among the cars.

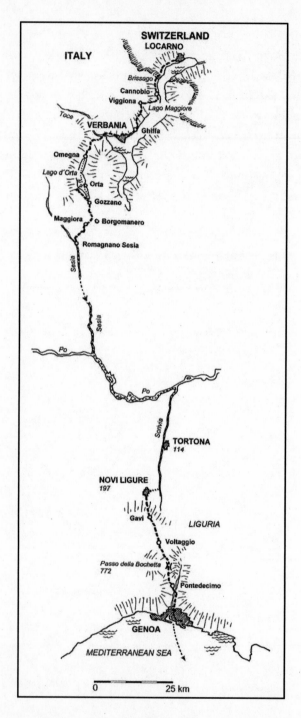

7

Polarity of Models

Down to the plain of the River Po and the Mediterranean
Pass through Cannobio. Out in the middle of a forest, I suddenly
find myself walking on an ancient but rather fine pavestone path.
It has been carefully built up with supporting walls and is just
wide enough for a cart. You normally see paths like this in parks
and at tourist attractions, but out in the middle of a relatively
deserted forest it is quite unusual. This must once have been an
important thoroughfare, perhaps an ancient main road. It is
getting a bit run down. Some of the stones are missing and the
edge has disappeared in places. It takes all my attention to avoid
missing my step.

At one point I remark that the physical exertion and the need
to concentrate so hard on finding a foothold are spoiling our
conversation. Mary says, with a wry smile: *'You might take the odd
break, you know.'*

She asks me why I am here. She knows
very well, but I summarize the whole
story from the winter solstice three and
a half years ago, my ensuing research
and my earlier walks. She then asks
what I intend to do with it all when I get
home. I must admit that I have contem-
plated writing up descriptions of the
route with detailed maps. I then tell her
that I am not sure whether I should just
write about her teachings or whether I
should include my personal adventures

The old highway

as well. *'You can combine the two so that your personal experience becomes an opportunity for teaching,'* she says.

From Viggiona I carry on up to Trarego, at an altitude of 770 meters. Here I find another Black Madonna in a side chapel in the church.

Now I come to a deep valley and need to find a way across. On the map I have found a path, but I cannot quite seem to locate it. Finally ask somebody, who says that the path I am looking for has been closed and that I will have to take another one. She shows me where to find it. I must, however, have got onto the first path after all, as after having walked downhill several kilometers I come to a bridge over a deep gorge and find it barred by a fence. Being an architect, I reckon I know enough to see that the bridge will carry me. Heedlessly I remove the fence and cross. Further along the path, I discover that the real problem is not the bridge but the path itself. It has simply disappeared. Torn down by a great landslide. There is a 30–40 meter gap with a drop of about 50 meters down to the bottom of the gorge. At first I try to clamber over the loose ground, but I begin to slide and just manage to jump back. It is far too wet and unstable. There is nothing for it; I'll have to retrace the many kilometers. Or will I? I begin to weigh the possibilities. Climbing down to the bottom of the gorge is too steep, but I may just be able to climb up over the landslide. I can see a few tracks, but they are too indistinct to tell whether they are left by deer or people. I tighten the straps of my rucksack and begin to climb up the 45-degree slope. Slowly – with three-point holds – I kick my feet into little holes and grasp roots and stones with my hands. My heart is pounding. I pause every so often to get my pulse down. I am very conscious that one careless movement might have catastrophic consequences.

I am especially aware of the fact that my rucksack causes my point of gravity to shift treacherously. After a long climb I eventually get to the top of the landslide. I try not to look down. It is dizzyingly far. I slowly climb down on the other side and at length slither down onto the path again. I am immensely relieved to have made it. My body is trembling with the tension and I am exhausted.

And then, after only 100 meters, the path has again been torn away by yet another landslide. The whole slope is nothing but pebbles. I can vaguely see a faint track and inch my way across, with stones rolling away from under my feet at every step. I manage to get across in one piece. On my way out of the forest I find the fence barring the path from the other side. At long last I am finally out of danger.

I go into the church at Oggiogno and give thanks for having got safely across. I should have asked for more information in Trarego and taken another path.

It was not Mary but my own stubbornness that had led me the way I went.

'What is willpower?' I ask Mary.

'Willpower is contained in the vertical polarity between spirit and body. It comes from conditions determined by your upbringing,' Mary answers.

She goes on to say that my clambering across the landslide was an expression of willpower. I ignored signposts, fences and common sense, letting my willpower actually overrule my judgment. Was it courage or foolhardiness? Mary thinks it was foolhardiness. She agrees that I had a good estimate of my physical ability, but I crossed limits others had set, and I knew that it had rained a lot so that the earth might be loose and might slide again. That was foolhardy. I got away with it, but Mary let on that I had been helped considerably underway.

Pass very interesting churches in Cadessino and Rondo, but by now all I need is a bed and I think of little else.

There are no hotels and I blunder on towards the lake where I hope to find somewhere to stay. At long last I reach the old respectable Hotel Paradise. It is expensive, but I dare not pass up this chance and I check in. The price includes an evening meal, and I do not remember ever having had such a delicious dinner.

The next day I go back to Rondo and tune in at the church of the nuns. I have seen a signpost to a 'Sacro Monte di Ghiffa', and I ask Mary if I am to go up there. She says she would like that.

I start the climb and notice that Mary is wearing a beautiful long dress. I sense that something is about to happen and cannot help feeling that Michael must be somewhere nearby.

On the 'Sacred Mountain' is a large building complex built in the 1700s. A church and elegant cloisters decorated with paintings depicting the story of the crucifixion. We are very high up and have a fantastic view of the Lago Maggiore. A lovely place.

I realize there is going to be a ceremony and I get ready. Climb onto a rock and immediately sense St. Michael standing in front of me. We talk a bit. Among other things, he asks how many times we have met on this trip so far. I make it three but he says four. *'You didn't notice me up in the mountains.'* At once I think of St. Gotthard and the sense that something was lacking. So I missed a meeting with St. Michael up there!

'Are you ready to enter a higher level?' Michael asks. I answer yes, and I feel as if he is putting his hands on my shoulders. A moment later, quite unexpectedly, he passes his shining sword right through me from the front. Mary moves behind me, and we stand like that for some time. The sword becomes a ray of light connecting Mary and Michael. At one point Mary and Michael change places.

Standing behind me, Michael says that, when necessary, I can always re-create him there. Then they change places again, and Mary says that she will always be there when I need her. *'And remember I have a big heart!'* she concludes.

The ceremony is over. Michael explains that we are now more or less done with the mountains and that I am going down to the lowlands. He gives me to understand that I may cross the River Po and go to Tortona. *'Mary will explain more about what happened here.'*

On the way down the mountain Mary explains that they used a front–back polarity to show me how a person becomes one with his spiritual ideals or role models. In other words, a model axis.

I think this ceremony was an initiation.

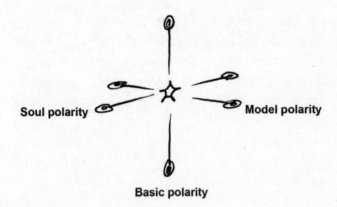

Basic polarity

Model polarity shown with polarity of the soul and basic/base polarity

I ask Mary, 'Why did this happen and why now?'

Mary answers, *'We carefully contacted you at your soul's request. You knew who we were, but not that you had a special connection to us. You sensed our presence and you spoke out loud. You worked in our fields. You declared that you would serve us. You have served us.'*

'But why just now?' I ask.

'You were ready!' Mary answers simply.

Mary goes on to explain that what has just happened is something enormous, and that I should rejoice.

Later I will be shown how it will influence me and my environment. Mary also explains that on the model axis she takes the role of Mary, the mother of Jesus, and Michael that of the archangel. That is to say, the Bible figures, with the qualities I ascribe to them. I create my own pictures for myself, but they are not far wrong, Mary says. On the other axes Mary and Michael are archetypical figures more comprehensive than the figures in the Bible.

'I can imagine that some people may have just one role model; what happens then?' I ask. Mary answers that it is an advantage to have a pair of polarities, but if you wish you can place a single ideal in the middle of the polarity axis, and dissolve it into two.

'Can a football star be a role model?' I ask cheekily. Mary's answer is yes, in principle, but that it would be right down in the Root or Hara chakra, and it would lack a female polarity.

'What about Nelson Mandela, then?'

'Mandela has much heart in his doings and will work as a role model close to the heart. His polarity will undoubtedly be his present wife.'

'What about Jesus?'

'Jesus, my son?' asks Mary. *'Many people will see him as being close to the central divine light. And there he will be. Jesus possessed a very outgoing power and will therefore also have a receptive female polarity. Mary Magdalene would be a natural choice for that role. She was a worthy polarity in their lives and can continue to be so today. Polarities are not bound to time and place.'*

I understand that the model axis is also about how I meet the outside world, about which ideals I use to measure the world, and how I step out into it. In other words about creating my ego.

I realize now that one's father and mother are the first role models in one's life and that they will prevail on the models axis until one replaces them with somebody else.

It is a good idea to replace one's earliest models with new ones that correspond to one's level of development. Even though they have been replaced, the old models will be able to return in situations that remind one closely of childhood experiences. One will once again react in the same way as when one's parents governed, and as the governing models determine the polarity, and subsequently the nature of the tension one's organs are subject to, old physical reactions may therefore recur, e.g. stomach ache and tensions.

* * *

I have now been walking downwards from St. Gotthard for six days. The surrounding energy has changed.

In Verbania I sense a strong Root chakra energy. A couple of youngsters are out for trouble but I ignore them. Get lost a few times. Have to make a few detours before I find the right road again – a very busy one. I walk on the edge of the road, the rush of the passing cars making my trouser legs flap. Dreadful! The Italian ministry of traffic and all their traffic politicians must all be car drivers. They certainly do not spare a thought for pedestrians – or cyclists. Mary explains that she was punted across the river delta in the next valley. We agree that it would be a good idea for other pilgrims to do this lethal stretch of road by bus.

We enter a new landscape and I end the day in Omegna by the lake, Lago d'Orta. As so often before, I look for a cheap hotel, and usually a fairly boring room comes with the low price. That is alright, because all I usually want to do is wash my clothes and sleep. After walking around a town like this, doing a little sightseeing and eating a cheap meal, I am normally quite ready to go back to my hotel room where I may have to do a bit of my diary, look at the map for the next day's walk, write a letter or make a phone call home. But this evening I have finished early and it is too early for bed. I actually begin to get a bit bored. Switch on my mobile and play a short game of Patience. That quickly becomes boring so I turn on the TV and get caught up in an action film. A real action film full of brawls, heroism and passionate love scenes. It is late by the time I turn it off.

I wake up next morning to pouring rain. Expect it to stop when the sun gathers strength. But it goes on raining. Tune in at the church. Mary is very faint. I just manage to catch the fact that we are going to Orta, and she finishes by saying that we must be out by nine o'clock. I don't understand why, but I hurry on.

There is a busy main road along the lake. I want to avoid that, so I find a different road up over the mountain. It is pelting down, and as if that is not bad enough, I realize after some time that Mary did not come this way. '*No, I went by boat,*' she says. All the way up over the mountain I try to convince myself that I misheard her, but as I once again land on the unbearably busy main road, I realize that something is definitely wrong. Mary did go by boat. Her words come through only faintly, and when I ask why, she says that it is because I played games on my mobile and watched the TV film the night before.

Mary says that games have their own world – at a low level. The world of games has nothing to do with awareness and intuition but rather cuts one off from the living world. Therefore the world of games also crowds out the impulses from Mary's world – weakens her. The same thing applies to action films. She strongly advises me to abstain from playing games and watching films with sex and violence, as they may exclude her and move the energy level down towards the Root chakra, which is inappropriate on a tour like this.

Arrive in Orta San Guilio and walk straight up onto Sacro Monte di Orta behind it. Another 'sacred mountain' in the same tradition as Sacro Monte di Ghiffa.

'SACRED MOUNTAINS'

The 'sacred mountain' tradition began with a monk who, having returned from the Holy Land, began to construct replicas of some of Palestine's holy places. This happened in Varallo in the late 1400s. In reaction to the Lutheran Reformation in the 1500s, the Catholic Church started a sort of counter-reformation: on prominent pinnacles they built large chapel complexes adorned with paintings and sculptures illustrating the life of Jesus. Through realism and high artistic standards they hoped to move the faithful to humility and submission. These 'sacred mountains' are widespread in south and northeast Europe. They did not always illustrate the life of Jesus. Sometimes they told the life of Mary, Francis of Assisi or of another saint.

At Orta they built onto an existing cult of Mary, the Madonna della Pieta, whose wooden statue is still to be found in the local church. Nowadays, however, Francis of Assisi is the central figure. The life of Francis from birth to canonization is depicted in 20 large chapels. Each scene is staged with life-size wooden figures in dramatic situations. The chapels are scattered among the trees of the park, and a long walk is involved if you want to see them all, interspersed with beautiful glimpses of the lake.

I go into the church dedicated to the Madonna della Pieta.

Immediately I sense Michael's presence, and I take part in a short ceremony with him and Mary.

Michael stands in front of me and tells me that in ancient times the mountain was dedicated to him and that therefore his energy is still here.

'You are now in the crown of the Root chakra,' he says. 'Seven crowns up and seven crowns down!' So I have walked up seven chakras, and soon I shall have walked down seven chakras. I see it in my mind's eye as two sides of a triangle standing on the earth. Each side is divided into seven chakras. As soon as I have this picture clear, the two legs move together and become a vertical axis. This axis is moved into me where it becomes a ray of light shining vertically down through me.

'This pilgrimage is now integrated into your vertical system,' Michael says. 'All experiences and challenges are stored. They give backbone, so to speak.'

The ray of light reaches much higher up and further down than my physical body.

Michael and Mary change places. Mary gives me a hug and a kiss on each cheek. For a second I half expect her to kiss my mouth. I am startled. Mary shakes her head, chuckles and says I am being influenced. It is last night's film with its love story that makes me fabricate this false idea.

Down in the town I feel transported back to the olden days. Historical buildings line three sides of the large square in front of the harbor. Among them the notable town hall from the 1500s with its beautiful arcades. The fourth side of the square consists of an old harbor front facing the lake. At one of the jetties I discover that there is a regular ferry to all the towns along the banks of the Lago d'Orta. The ferry leaves Omegna at 9am. Reading this, I realize that this was what Mary meant when she said that we had to leave before nine o'clock. Instead of the tiresome walk in the rain on a busy road, I could have been sitting on a lovely tourist boat enjoying a beautiful sail. If I had not filled my head with films the previous night, my channel to Mary would have been clearer and I might have caught the hint about taking the ferry.

Anyway, I jump down into one of the little taxi boats, sail out to the island of Isola di San Giulio and visit the remarkable church in the middle of the island. It is delightful to study the old frescos from the 1400s.

Isola di San Giulio

ISOLA DI SAN GIULIO

For thousands of years the island has been central to this area. San Giulio, or Julius, with his brother Julian, was an enterprising church builder. The story goes that they came from the island of Aegina in Greece (also on the Virgin Mary's pilgrimage) and that they had founded 99 churches on their way here. Number 99 was in Gozzano, south of this lake, where Julius fell in love with the sight of this island and so founded church no.100 here. Supposedly in the year 390. In time, the church became a remarkable basilica including a monastery.

Following Mary's instructions I cross the lake, walk southwards and find a roadside hotel.

* * *

The next morning it is pouring again. Continue on the road south along the bank of the lake. This, however, soon becomes a muddy farm track. When I finally reach the southern end of the lake I stand for a moment gazing across the water. I sense Mary landing from a boat. So she sailed directly to here! Together we walk up an old dilapidated road, Via Francisca, to Gozzano. It feels just right.

Unfortunately all the churches in the town are closed. I run around confusedly. I have arrived in a new Root chakra but I cannot find the point of focus. I am literally rooting around! In the end it all becomes too much for me. I sit down and ask God to open a door to let me out of this muddled town.

I know that, on her tour, Mary did not stop here, but made for one of the tributaries of the River Po, from where she could sail south.

Out of my despondency a road opens. We go to Gargallo. Here I find the first open church of the day – and it stops raining too. Wonderful to be able to tune in and purify myself. I feel that powers from above must have intervened.

Today's stage runs through Borgomanero, Maggiore with its enormous church, and down to Romagnano di Sesia, which, as the name indicates, is on the River Sesia.

Mary asks me what I have learnt. I talk at great length, but she shakes her head. I find a number of other answers. But again: no. This goes on for ages, but I cannot hit on what Mary is after. When I give up she says, '*Reverence.*'

I cannot follow her in this, for I have innumerable times acted against her instructions. '*Yes, but you have never blamed me,*' she says. That is actually true. I have known all along that the fault was mine, that I did not have ears to hear with, even though it was tempting to blame others.

We go into the large church in the square, and ceremonially I connect the threads of the stage from Hildegard of Bingen's convent to here. Leave the church and go out onto the jetty. The river is very full and flows evenly. I can easily imagine that in Mary's day you could sail from here. And I do actually see Mary standing on a lower quay waving goodbye before boarding a barge. She has said earlier that she will meet me further up the river from Tortona.

Walk to the station, find a train for Novarra. Sit on the train imagining Mary being punted down the tributary and for a short distance along the Po itself, befor²e turning up into the delta of the River Scrivia that flows from Tortona.

I wonder whether I will be able find her again!

Through Grethe, Mary later told me that at this point, after crossing the mountains, she was very tired. She had pushed herself hard. Had even battled through high, snow-covered areas. So she was near exhaustion when she got here. They sailed in a broad boat, like a canoe or a barge, for several days. When she finally landed and was given food, she became quite euphoric. The journey across the Alps and the plain of the River Po had been quite an ordeal.

* * *

Spend the night in Tortona and try the next morning to find the river. It is a long way off and the whole area is very flat. As I wander about, trying to get my bearings, Mary keeps repeating the name 'Novi Ligure'. Suddenly I spot a bus for Novi Ligure. I jump on and we cross the extremely wide but very shallow river. After a while we arrive in Novi Ligure. I am expecting to have to walk 5 or 6 kilometers down to the river to find Mary, but I am in for a surprise the moment I alight. I see Mary coming towards me, looking very happy. She bids me welcome. She has disembarked further down river and has walked the rest of the way up here. 'We just have to cross town. Are you coming?' she asks, tripping impatiently. I am completely bowled over and need time to get my thoughts together first. Find a map, sit in a café and absorb the town. Perhaps the main thing is that I need to prepare myself for a new stage.

We walk from the station through the very beautiful old district which boasts several large churches. One ought to stay the night in this interesting town!

Mary tells me that even in her day Novi Ligure was a lively town. Covering about the same area as the old district does today. It was a garrison town and a busy trading place. A lot of visitors and a lot of cheap hostels. It was the gateway from the north, and from here the road to Genoa was short, good and well protected.

An old sign

We reach the other side of town where, right enough, there is a road to Genoa. In fact it is actually the ancient main road, Via Antica di Genova. This sounds quite perfect. We walk through a beautiful undulating landscape with woods, vineyards and large estates. After only 12 kilometers I stop in a small town and take a room. I am indescribably relieved both to have found the route on this side of the Po plain and to know that the road to Genoa seems certain. Enjoy having time to explore the town and do some shopping. Buy a new shirt.

I try to determine the quality of this stage. *'The stage of joy,'* says Mary. While tuning in, I was also inspired to say 'The flower-bedecked way'. That is how the landscape appears to me. Fields and woodlands alternating. Everything bursting with fertility. It is a beautiful walk. The mountains are not particularly high. The route is pretty obvious – there is only one road. Lovely just to walk along the road. If anything, I attempt to prolong the pleasure by walking slowly. Practice being present and aware, using all my senses.

Many things come together on this stage. I feel very privileged and happy working with Mary. Just being able to ask about everything is wonderful. It occurs to me that somebody else might want to ask Mary for advice – through me. Can I give answers? I ask Mary. She hesitates a bit and then says, *'We will have to see how the pilgrimage turns out. But I don't think you are established firmly enough yet. At times your own ego may interfere and you will find that difficult to control.'*

I wonder whether I am to give instruction in Mary's teachings. *'Are you going to teach?'* she interrupts teasingly. 'I don't know … perhaps,' I answer, and ask,' Can I contact you if the situation arises?' *'Always. Till the day you die. That goes for all questions concerning my teachings, and all matters concerning the pilgrimage. I will always be there for such questions.'*

This answer gives me a good guideline. This is all about the teachings of Mary – nothing else.

Mary has several times assured me that she is with me always, whatever happens. I have sometimes been afraid that she might give up on me if I was not up to the task. She now sweeps that aside completely.

'You have to know that we never act like that. Why on earth would we do that? We do not give out punishments.

'At times something may appear to be a punishment, for example when you were watching cheap films and playing silly games. The next day you lost your way completely. You took a real beating in the rain. But, as you also understood, it was not a punishment. You allowed something to screen out my impulses so I could not get through. You created that situation yourself. It was not created by us,' Mary explains.

I ask about future pilgrims on this route. Whether they will have the same contact with Mary as I have. *'No. I am with you all the time. Every second. If you only knew how much energy is expended by us in order to carry this journey through. Those who follow you will have a route to follow. I will have fleeting contact with them all, for example in churches and at the natural sacred sites in the wild.'*

Reach the Bocchetta Pass at 772 meters altitude. It is misty, so unfortunately I cannot see the Mediterranean, but I know it is out there.

St. Michael has been accompanying me for a while now. Find a ledge where we can be alone. Having caught my breath, I get up and stand in front of Michael. I am asked to place my right hand over my heart, and my left hand on his left shoulder. He does the same. Mary goes behind me. *'We are working together!'* says Michael. We stand like this for a while, and then just as I think the ceremony is over I see myself standing inside a transparent shell. Michael opens the front as if it were a cupboard door and steps inside to me – inside my front. Mary opens the shell from behind and enters into my back. My immediate reaction is to think that there is going to be a bit of a squeeze in this 'cupboard', but I remind myself that the whole thing is just a vision.

'We are in you. You are in us,' says Michael. Later, Mary explains that I work through them and they work through me.

Downwards now, to Genoa. I have planned to take the road west of the river, but Mary recommends the east side. This turns out to be by far the best. The worst traffic is on the other bank. Now the suburbs become more concentrated and grow into a town. Genova is big. I follow the larger road right down to the Mediterranean and then wander along the harbor to the old town east of Porto Vecchio.

Along narrow streets I find the San Lorenzo church. My goal. I book into a cheap hotel and look forward to a couple of days' rest.

I made it. I have reached the Mediterranean! Inhale the salty sea air. Hear the waves breaking onto the quay – exhilarating!   I have mounted the Alps and walked over a thousand kilometers. I am happy, empty and tired.

A great stage is ended. A fantastic stage. I can see that Mary's teachings on this stage have been all about understanding the creation and the basic elements of man. About what it is TO BE CREATED.

PART II

TO BE MAN

Italy

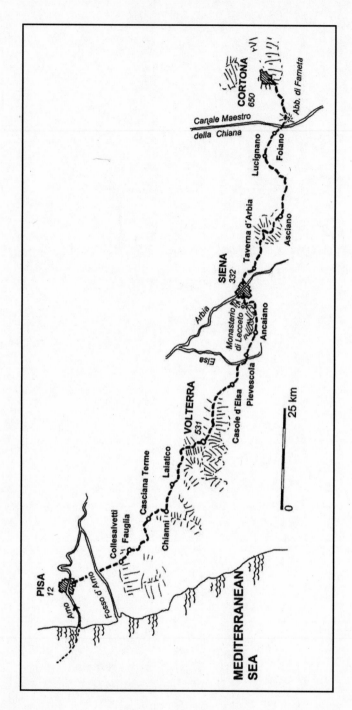

8

Femininity – The Polarity of Laws

Tuscany

From Genoa, Mary sailed to Pisa, but the boat connection is a thing of the past so I have to take the train. The journey is rather symptomatic of my state of mind. The railway runs along the coast, cutting right through numerous mountain ridges. Short glimpses of impressive views alternate with dark tunnels. My pupils are working overtime, constantly opening and dilating. Impossible to concentrate. I am tired.

In Pisa I check into a hotel near the Leaning Tower.

* * *

I have hardly finished the 1,000-km-long stage across the Alps before I throw myself into the next one, from Pisa. I feel time pressing. So far, the tour has taken longer than planned. So I am very keen to get on. In a way I am running ahead of myself, and my soul does not seem to have kept up. Feel as if I am not ready for this town and that it will not let me in. My experiences have not had a chance to sink in and, to be honest, I am not exactly bursting with energy. The first stage formed an entity in itself, and I could easily stop here. The thought does occur to me, but I dismiss it, fully determined to complete the journey. Certainly do not feel like it though. Feel drained. Things are not going right. But I must and will carry on.

It is the middle of August. Italian summer holiday. The cool of the morning is quickly displaced by a burning sun.

Leave the hotel for the cathedral, which is dedicated to Mary.

The Cathedral of Pisa

I am early and the church is not yet open. Wander around the square for a while. Look at the Leaning Tower and the church and end up by the baptistery next to the cathedral. An impressive building – and open. I go inside and tune in. Mary comes through quite clearly, even though I am not really in the right frame of mind and not properly focused. John the Disciple comes through too and he is obviously going to play a larger part from now on.

I am very restless and cannot wait until the cathedral opens. I decide to take to the road straight away, and Mary and John lead the way through the town. We emerge onto road 206 – the direct route south across the Arno plain. The road is straight as an arrow, the whole area completely flat. The temperature rises, the traffic is heavy, and the 13 kilometers across the plain seem unending. It is wearing and I become irritable.

After walking for some time, I ask Mary if there is anything we should talk about. She says that John wants to say something. John comes on and says that I have come to a level where we must think about what it is to *be* human, a discussion he will lead.

He starts by saying, *'Man is constantly being created. From the very moment of coming into existence, one must then concentrate on existing until one chooses to be created anew. This alternation mirrors God's attitude to his work of creation. Be created – exist.'*

John is in full swing, explaining the connections. He has not previously been responsible for teaching me, but it seems that he will be from now on. After a while I decide his teaching is becoming somewhat high-flown and schematic. He seems to arrange things into moralizing diagrams. I suppose this is really because I myself am thinking too categorically, but a sneaking antipathy starts to fill my mind. The sun is scorching in the cloudless sky and the road is intolerably straight, flat and without a single tree to find shade under. Cars are racing past me and there are no cafés open. In the end it just becomes too much for me. I call a halt. It is hard enough keeping in touch with Mary. I cannot cope with more teachers. I have had enough and I refuse to accept anything from John. Ask Mary that all information and conversations may come through her. End of discussion! ... ... Silence.

I slowly realize how categorical my rejection is, but I have had enough and insist.

After some time Mary takes up the thread. Continues in the same groove as John and explains pointedly that it is a question of being completely aware, on all axes: your body, all your senses etc. Being open to the spirit – in nature and in yourself. Not forgetting your soul – being aware of your deepest self.

Really just like when all the axes became a ray of light in my heart. Silence again. The atmosphere is tense.

At long last, the 13-km-long straight road comes to an end. A few bends and it stops at the foot of some broad steps. The road across the plain is almost a processional route leading up to these steps which I now mount. The experience of ascending from the lowlands is amazing. I leave the plain behind me and rise up above the monotony.

. Hope to be able to lift myself out of my critical situation. At the head of the steps is the town of Collesalvetti. I pass straight through, on to the next town, Fauglia.

Here St. Michael is waiting for me in the church of Madonna dei Monte. He is very frank and asks me straight out if I want to stop the pilgrimage here. No sentimentality. Either I am fully committed, or I stop. The situation is critical. But I refuse. In the same breath, however, I ask for a few days off in order to be with my wife, who is coming down to visit me. Michael says that a break will do me good. Go through a short ceremony in which Mary and Michael indicate all axes, which are then gathered into a spark of light in my heart. Very strengthening!

My goal today is Casciana Terme. Just a few kilometers before we get there, I realize Mary wants me to go to Casciana Alta where there is a large church. I take no notice. I have walked 35 kilometers and I am tired. Tell Mary it cannot be that important, now that Casciana Terme is so close. This refusal is not very well received. I sense it at once, but I cannot find the energy to go there. Mary is not very pleased. Even so, I ignore her instructions.

I later discovered that the original main road ran through the Casciana Alta and then on to Casciana Terme by a small mountain road.

Casciana Terme is an interesting and popular spa town. The hot springs were an attraction even in the days of Emperor Augustus, and at the end of the 1800s large spa facilities, cafés and concert halls were erected.

The town is full of hotels and private boarding houses, and I am already looking forward to going to bed. Enquire at the first hotel but it is full. Enquire at the next one, and one by one all the hotels refuse me – are all fully booked. Next I try the boarding houses. They too are all full. In the end I try renting a private room. I find one house where the wife is sympathetic but the husband refuses. It is not possible to find a single room in the whole town. Deeply disappointed and crestfallen, I must settle for sleeping in the open in a park. Under a tree to shade me from the street lights. I see this as punishment for not being willing to listen.

The ground is hard and I wake up repeatedly. At times I have to lie as still as a mouse to avoid being noticed by dogs out for their evening walk. Get up at six thirty and go to a café. I am depressed. I have really put my foot in it.

How could I do it? Refuse John and his valuable teachings. Are they going to cut me off now? I must do my best to reconnect. Go to the local church, but have to wait till it opens at half past eight. At last the doors are thrown open and I tune in. I am told coolly to go out and write everything down. I do this immediately. I am really sorry to have lost contact with Mary and John.

I re-enter the church where there is now a mass in progress. Despite this, both Mary and John come through very quickly and clearly.

Mary asks if I am ready to do the walk as they tell me to, and if I am prepared to accept being taught by John. I have thought about this already and can answer clearly, 'Yes, I am!' Mary replies shortly, *'In that case we can get straight off.'*

I follow them south-eastwards out of the town. *'We are going to Chianni. It is an easy road and we can talk,'* says Mary.

Mary explains that there was no question of punishment. It would not occur to them to punish. What happened yesterday was that *I* chose to cut myself off from them. And because I thus cut my connection with them, they could not come in to help me. There are always helping powers on hand, but when you cut yourself off from them, they cannot assist you. I incorrectly interpreted the absence of help as punishment.

Mary assures me, however, that there were protecting powers around me all night – not even a mosquito got through – only some ants.

Now John comes through and says, '*Dear Hans, I am just as warm and loving as Mary. Mary is in me and I am in Mary. There is no difference in our teachings. The situation yesterday was very instructive. I would not have missed it for the world.*'

John continues:

'*We are explaining about being human. Man is created in the field of tension between the axis of life and that of the soul, axes which each contain polarities between male/female, and giving/receiving. Every human being is both male/giving and female/receiving. To be understood as two sides of the same person. In the new age – the age to come – man will acknowledge his two sides and use them both.*

'*That is not to say that the human being becomes androgynous. You can always choose whether to use your male or female side, whether you are a man or a woman. In your culture, this development has already begun. Your sexual liberation leads to the relaxation of old rules. You are allowed to be both receiving and giving. In a relationship between two people, both parties cannot receive or give at the same time. You must have a mutual agreement.*

'*This development has its dead ends; the sex industry, for example, which is without love, and which is for the most part permeated by old ideals.*'

John tells me about himself:

'*You must understand that the person you imagine me to be stems from the New Testament. But I too am also both female and male. All the values that Mary represents, I represent also. That was made clear by Jesus when he said, "John, this is your mother, and Mother, this is your son." That was the introduction to a long relationship of learning.*'

Walk through the mountain town of Rivalto and on further, along the mountainside to Chianni. Today is market day and the streets are milling with stalls and people. I buy a couple of apples and a coconut bar. Just outside the town is a church, Sanctuario della Madonna del Carmine, which is only used for special festivals.

To my surprise I find St. Michael here. He asks how things have gone since we met yesterday. I tell him what happened and we begin a short ceremony. All axes are made clear. I see myself as a double silhouette around the axes. The two silhouettes glide back and forth from inside to outside each other – as if two layers of aura are changing places. I realize that they are my masculine and my feminine sides. That they are like layers around me and that I am free to choose to use one layer or the other.

I take my leave of Michael and continue down the road. John says, *'In a proper understanding of God he is both male and female. A creative power cannot exist without a receiving one. We do not talk of God who is, but of God who is constantly coming into being. There is a receiving power which continually passes experiences back to God.'*

I try and turn the conversation to the Tree of Life in the Cabbala, but John does not wish to use patterns of understanding that are connected to olden times and therefore, in some spheres, insufficient.

In the course of our discussion I come to realize that God has direct access to each individual through his heart. Therefore there is no 'Up' or 'Down'. Rather a center or a point of balance.

Mary tells me, *'God receives through his female side, except for the divine moments of mankind which go directly to God through the heart.'*

Later on, the heat begins to get to me and there is a break in my lessons. The track crosses a river bed, almost dried out in the summer heat. Mary must have waded through streams like this many a time. Pick up the track again on the other side. Clearly an old highway. I am surrounded by magnificent, undulating hills and valleys, newly harvested and plowed. Here and there, clumps of tall cypresses point skywards, reminding me of the vertical dimension. Tuscany at its most beautiful. I do not meet a soul.

John comes through to me several times:

'We have been through a time of female dominance. Few people have any recollection of that time. We are now in the final phase of a period of male dominance. The transition to a new era is in full swing.

'In the new era every human being will think of him- or herself as being both female and male. Not at the same time, but alternately as he or she chooses.

'The balance between the two is important. From the perspective of society this is a prerequisite for peace. Dominance is lack of balance. Conscious balancing of dominance will be very helpful to all parties.

'Rejoice! A new era has begun. Differences are being reconciled. Friendships built. Polarity is the building block of the world. Understand this on all inner and outer levels.

'The creation of a polarity is the coming into being of an aspect of God. In the center of the polarity, in your heart, you are in direct contact with God, as the person you are. You – and everybody else – are a divine flame.'

The gravel road becomes a busy tarmac highway. The last 9 kilometers up to the mountain town of Volterra are extremely steep. In places the road is so narrow I have to press myself against the guard rail to avoid the traffic. Panting for breath, I stumble into the town and find my way to the cathedral. Tie the threads of the pilgrimage and bless the town. Mary indicates the way to a room for the night. Just as I think she must be wrong, I find a youth hostel. Nice and cheap, and I have a whole room to myself.

Today has been tough, 42 kilometers. All the same, I am in good spirits. I have Mary and John back.

* * *

The next day I began three days' leave from the pilgrimage. Went by bus back to Pisa and met my wife Kirstin. The meeting was warm, and because we had been in regular contact by phone we were not at all awkward with each other. Kirstin had helped me look out the key points on the route and so she could picture the places and landscapes I had been through, which was a great advantage. We went to the seaside and spent a couple of days together.

After that little holiday I returned to my pilgrimage. Once again I stayed in Pisa. My previous start in the town several days earlier had been inadequate so I tried to make up for it now. I waited till the cathedral was open and performed a short ceremony. This time I remembered my soul. Mary told me briefly that the subject for this stage was *what it is to be human – about existing*. She also said that she and John were looking forward to getting going again. Now my way was opened and I could resume my journey. I got back to Volterra in the late evening.

VOLTERRA

Volterra was one of the strongest bastions of the Etruscans, and the town was already a thriving town in the 8th century BC. Its situation on a mountaintop, with its own spring, meant it was the ideal defense post. The cathedral, dating from 1120, and its detached baptistery are important.

There is said to have been a prehistoric temple on the site where the baptistery was built. It may have been a temple dedicated to the Goddess.

The Octagonal Baptistery in Volterra

I sense the feminine strain from the Etruscan culture. As I understand it, the roots of the Etruscans go back to the Minoans on Crete. If one studies their funeral sarcophagi, one finds many similarities. Their attitudes to death and birth have many parallels.

In the baptistery I consider baptism through history. I ask Mary what baptism is really about. Mary answers that from the earliest times it has been a welcome to life on earth. A joyful feast. The water with which the child is baptized is the fluid of Mother Earth, and it possesses the recollection of the qualities of a place.

Water remembers! Therefore it is important that the water is as uncontaminated as possible. A lot of tap water is of poor quality and tainted with other substances, for example, with chlorine.

Baptismal water must be warm in order to be pleasant for the baby. The baptism should preferably take place as soon as the child has decided to take nourishment – has chosen to live. The child may be given its name on the same occasion if a name has already been revealed for it. Otherwise the naming must wait till the name has become apparent.

* * *

Next morning, in the hostel in Volterra, I wake up late. Go to a café for my Italian breakfast, a cappuccino and a croissant. If you are extra hungry you have two croissants.

Mary says that we are going east today, towards Siena. There is a lot of traffic on the main road and I have to balance along the verge with cars speeding past. I find my way onto smaller roads, and walk through one fantastic landscape after another. The road winds its way up and down through farmland and on to wooded hills and green valleys.

A few kilometers before Siena, I lose my way and again find myself on a very busy main road which I have to stick to all the way to Siena. I almost fear for my life. The road is far too narrow for so many cars. The drivers shake their heads at me, amazed at anybody even thinking of walking here.

Mary gives me to understand that we were meant to go a different way. Very annoying! She suggests that I stay in Siena an extra day.

* * *

Rest day in Siena. I have worn a hole in one of my shoes so I shop around for some new ones. Find a pair of super smart, well-ventilated shoes.

Afterwards I sense that there is something from yesterday's walk that Mary wants to clarify. So I think: OK, I'll wear my new shoes in and retrace the last 4 or 5 kilometers. No sooner said than done. Without my backpack I can walk quite a lot faster, and I soon find my way back those 10 kilometers by a different road to the terrifying one I came by. This road is not very busy and it takes me into a large wood where I find a nunnery, Monasterio di Lecceto. In the church a nun is practicing the organ while another sings. It sounds so lovely that I decide to stay for evensong. A priest gives a short sermon, but otherwise it is all singing and music – flute, organ and harp. Beautiful. Angelic. The nuns are Augustinians.

Mary is pleased that I experience this. The convent is beautifully run, and it is on our route. Mary came here. It feels like a landscape heart.

After mass it is time to get my skates on. It is late now. Ten kilometers back to Siena. In twilight I enter through the town gate, Porte Fontebranda. Just inside the gate is a fountain where medieval travelers could wash off the dust. The twilight erases all divides of time and I follow the medieval custom and wash my feet in the fountain.

SIENA

The Virgin Mary is the patron saint of Siena and the cathedral is dedicated to her. The town was founded by the Romans as a military colony about 50 years before she came here. That was under Emperor Octavian Augustus. Before that, there was presumably an Etruscan settlement, but the town was a long way from the main thoroughfares and of no great significance.

It did, however, become very significant in the Middle Ages when it grew to be a flourishing trading center. The cathedral is reckoned to be one of the most beautiful Gothic churches in Italy.

In the cathedral I spend a long time studying the fantastically beautiful pictures in the floor. They are made of black and white marble.

The Cathedral of Siena

* * *

I leave Siena next morning through the Porta de Pispini, out into the Tuscan landscape. Travel along small roads till I reach the little town of Taverne d'Arbia, where I stop at a pavement café and write my diary over a cappuccino. When I get up I see that, in the meantime, two other guests have sat down. I notice their walking boots and a look in their eyes that shows they are hungry for rest and drink. They are clearly trekkers who have walked far. I go straight up to them and speak to them in English. They answer, also in English. They are Dutch, have walked for three months from Holland and are on their way to Rome. Like me, they expect to walk for four months. It is good to finally talk to colleagues. The first on the whole journey. We have a long conversation about our hardships and good experiences. When we part the man says, 'We'll be seeing you!' This is rather odd, as we are going different directions.

I continue along the old highway, Strada Lauretana.

Next morning I have difficulty tuning in because the presence of spirit is weak in both me and in the church. Partly because there is not a single candle burning in the whole church. However insignificant this may seem, lighting a candle is important to me. On top of which, I drank two glasses of wine last night and that was too much. All this means that Mary has difficulty getting through to me. I know that Mary has emphasized the fact that it takes 12 hours to rid your body of a glass of wine. She has not condemned drinking wine. It is just unsuitable if I want to be in contact with her.

It is mid-morning when Mary says, *'Now you are just about clear. Drink a little more water and then we can talk!'* We are going to talk about *values*.

Mary starts with the Ten Commandments. Some commandments are historically out of date, while others still apply. She explains that shared values are important for a community. Shared values keep a community together and give the individual a liberating feeling of security. Mary asks us to revise our values in regard to society as well as between nations.

I consider capitalism and communism. Under capitalism, some people have thrived on being able to develop their opportunities free from constricting morals, while others suffered under the heartlessness and greed of the law of economics. Under communism, some have valued security while others have felt constrained. In both cases a small part of society has seized the wealth of the country and in both cases the focus is on material values.

Mary would like to inspire us to new shared values, but her task now is to point out that laws and shared values reside in the energy system of each individual.

I wish that St. Michael had been here to show just *where* in the system they reside.

Later that afternoon I arrive in Lucignano. A very interesting medieval town built in circles with a surrounding circular town wall, at the top of a mountain.

Among the many churches here, there is an enormous one dedicated to St. Michael: Chiesa Collegiata del Michele Arcangelo. His shining golden statue stands on the main altar and hanging right above him is the Virgin Mary with the Christ Child.

St. Michael Archangel

Full of expectations, I enter the church and seek contact with Michael. I sense his presence and position myself in front of the altar, expecting him to show me exactly where shared values are positioned. Michael can hardly get a word in as my imagination leaps ahead of me. Several times I have to pull myself up and empty my mind. I also get very distracted by four loud-mouthed women who are in the middle of cleaning the church. Michael gives up, saying that I am so full of expectations and ideas that there is no room for him to explain. *'Stay in town and come back here later!'* he says. Somewhat crestfallen, I go out into town and find lodgings. An apartment with a kitchen.

Return to the church at about six. Michael asks me to mark all the axes, and before I know it, he has placed the shared values in a circle over my shoulders. Michael sees shared values as equal to laws.

'*May the laws light up like stars in the sky of your mind!*' he says. I can sense we are not done with values, or laws. There must be more to come.

* * *

The next morning I enjoy shopping for, and making, my own breakfast – rather than just making do with low-energy croissants. Go to St. Michael's Church and tune in. Michael is there again today, but again I have such great expectations of the day's text that it prevents him from speaking freely.

As far as I can understand – or guess – he is talking about the laws of the heart, but I have to leave it and wait for another opportunity.

Go through the town and out by the east gate. Follow the road to Foiano della Chiana where there is another enormous church dedicated to St. Michael: San Michele Arcangelo.

Find my way to an altar to Our Lady and light a candle. At first I cannot see any pictures of Michael anywhere. I look hard and finally find a painting with him in it, in a remote part of the nave. Going back towards the altar, I am accompanied by Michael on my right and Mary on my left. We proceed up to the altar. Here, quite unexpectedly, Jesus appears to me. '*I am Jesus Christ,*' I hear. Hardly have time to wonder how he fits in before he answers my unasked question. '*I am Michael and I am Mary. They are in me and I am in them. We are one!*' And Jesus adds, '*I am the child of man. You are the child of man!*'

Jesus speaks further about laws and values:

'*As far as laws are concerned, you must understand that everything*

is balanced around the heart. If culture or society introduce laws that
are out of balance, they will be made to balance through illegality.
   'There is only one law that is the law of the heart: Love one
another!'

Mary and Michael go up and stand one on each side of Jesus.
They move into Jesus. Unite in him as pure light. Move out again
into polarity. Then they approach me together, placing
themselves on each side of me. Now Jesus passes into me. The
first scenario is repeated. Mary and Michael are united in Jesus –
in me – and I feel a tremendous light inside me. Jesus steps back
again and wishes me a good journey. He grows larger and disappears out to a point which might be the center of the galaxy –
except that it happens inwardly. I feel I am being drawn inwards
and realize instantly that if I follow I shall end in God.

   This lasts a very short moment, like a flash, and then I am
back in the church.

   Michael and Mary are still here. Michael looks me over and
adds energy to my polarity axes. Straightens them out and then
quickly adds laws and values as two circles on each side of my
heart. One over my shoulders and one at the small of my back. The
many laws and values form connecting threads through my heart.

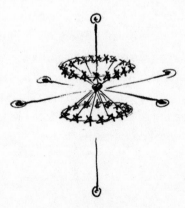

Polarity of laws/values

I am deeply moved by the presence of Jesus and by the whole ceremony. And I cannot help smiling at the way they caught me off guard, letting Jesus walk straight through all my barriers of expectation. Apparently Jesus takes over for lessons on the subject of the heart. I am deeply thankful. Feel that this was probably yet another initiation.

The road now runs through to the other side of a valley, where the town of Cortona towers high up on the mountainside. The ascent is tough going. Just outside the town there is a very large church, Santa Maria della Grazie al Calcinaio. On an earlier visit here, I had found the church shut and had thought it was falling into disrepair. But this time it is quite different! There is going to be a wedding and I am welcome to go in. The church is huge, and not at all run down inside. Large and light with Mary the central figure.

'*This is my church*,' comments Mary, and somehow that makes everything else seem less important. She says that at her time there was a small community here, outside the town wall. She and John founded a small congregation here.

Later, on entering the town, I find that the town gate is called 'Santa Maria'. Ask Mary if she has been here. She has.

I get to the youth hostel, but it is full, and I am told to go to a convent – which is also full. Try several hotels, but without success. There is a big motorbike meet this weekend. Thousands of motorbikes and their riders fill the town and its hotels. I resign myself to sleeping in the open. But on my way across to the last small hotel, I go into a church, light a candle for Mary, drink some water and pray for help. My last chance. The hotel is full, but I think I must have looked so defeated that they take pity on me. The landlord takes me to the upper end of the town and checks me in to a large clerical conference.

* * *

Tune in the next morning at the Cattedrale di Santa Maria. Set off.

First I go down to Santa Maria della Grazie. Join a group of people waiting impatiently for it to open. Among those waiting are a film crew, who manage to open a side door. Several of us go in. Suddenly a burglar alarm shatters the silence. The noise is unbearable and I rush out.

There is something odd going on this morning: First I lost my little pedometer, then I forgot to drink water, I had difficulty hearing Mary properly, the church was closed, and finally that unendurable alarm.

Ask Mary what is happening. *'Lack of synchronization,'* she says. I ask God to put it right, but that is not possible until I understand why it happened. Yesterday in St. Michael's Church I had all my attention focused on Jesus and Michael. Must admit that every time Michael has been present, he has held the floor. Mary has always been in the background. This was thoughtless and unbalanced. I have neglected Mary, the feminine side.

While trying to understand this, I have covered several kilometers. I almost want to go back again to sort out the imbalance. Then something fantastic happens. A new St. Michael's church appears: Santuario di San Michele Arcangelo. A very special church from the 7th to 10th century. And in it there just happens to be statues of Mary, Michael and Jesus. I light a candle and carry it to Mary first, then Michael and finally place it by Jesus, as I focus on the heart. This church is a powerful site.

AN OLD SHRINE

According to a description in the church, this used to be a popular Roman area with a temple to Bacchus – the god of landscape, wine and joy – as its center. The temple was transformed into a Christian temple in the 4th to 5th century. The Lombards later tore down the old church and built a new one in the 7th century. They dedicated it to St. Michael.

I stand near the door of the church. Mary and Michael stand on either side of me and once again we process up the nave. In front of the altar Jesus stands before us. I pray that my lower self may be peeled off and that I may learn to balance the masculine and the feminine in my heart. As in the ceremony two days ago Michael and Mary approach Jesus, passing into him from each side. They melt into each other, come out on the opposite side, and glide back again, while I try to balance the impulses from Mary and Michael equally.

I realize that the external balance between the masculine and the feminine must be supported by an internal one.

A lot of hill-walking today – both up and down. Through sheer tiredness I miss a monastery church. Finally arrive at Castel Rigone high up on a mountain ridge. Castel Rigone has a remarkable church, Santuario di Maria Santissima dei Miracoli. It feels significant. It is said that one day in 1490 a young girl was filling her water sack here. She saw a beautiful lady rising up above the thicket. The lady came up to the girl and asked her to tell the townspeople that she wanted them to build her a small chapel there. Several miracles took place. The town started to collect money for a small chapel, but in the end the Pope granted money for a real church. This money came from offerings that were made to Mary from all over the world.

Have to stay in the only hotel in town, a four-star one. Very expensive. On the other hand I enjoy a cooling swim in the hotel pool.

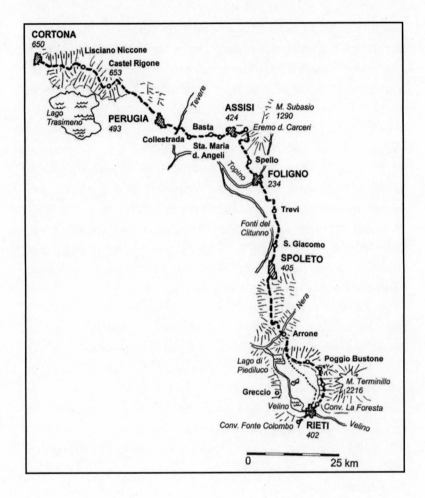

9

Expectations – Francis of Assisi

Umbria

I eat an enormous breakfast at the posh hotel in Castel Rigone. Tune in at the church and pick up the threads of the route. Follow the mountain ridge north-eastwards, and then head down towards Perugia. It is amazing to walk along the ridge of the mountains, 650–700 meters above sea level. Sense Crown ambience. Clouds are so low that at times the view disappears completely. On the other hand the mist lends a fairytale atmosphere to the landscape. This is a gift that lightens my heart.

Mary starts the lesson of the day: *'We are going to talk about the weight of the heart. To be light or heavy at heart.'*

She asks me to remember situations where I have been heavy-hearted. *'How did it feel?'* she asks. 'Almost as if my heart was being squeezed,' I reply. *'That is precisely what happens. Being heavy or sick at heart is a self-inflicted state of polarity, balanced round your heart. It is in principle like a law polarity. A certain incident or situation gives rise to thoughts and thence to expectations. Expectations work in the same way as laws.*

'But laws, or values, are all about relationships between people. They are, so to speak, authorized by society or culture. With expectations it is different. Their source is usually to be found in one's personality or upbringing. They do, however, also appear to work in a state of polarity through the heart.'

It is made clear to me that in the worst case such a polarity can break the basic polarities, causing one to die. Grief is an example. It is well known that one can die of grief. This may be due to the bereaved person's expectation that there can be no life without the departed.

The 'squeezing' may be alleviated in different ways. Weeping may relieve it, having someone to talk to; good friends etc. may also work. Grief is often the result of feeling isolated, in doubt, weighed down by responsibility, or lonely.

When, a few days ago, I had refused to accept being taught by John, I had a clear expectation that I would be punished because I had done something wrong. That was a classic expectation polarity.

Through Grethe, Mary has told me:

'In order to make the stars shine it is necessary to come to terms with and discard old structures that have served their time. During the formation of your ego, it was alright to expect to be punished if you did something wrong. To learn about consequences. At the stage you have reached now, it is time to let go of structures from your ego-forming period. You can achieve an added consciousness from knowing that it was alright earlier, but that it is now a hindrance.

'Reminiscences of your ego will remain. Gradually the voice of intuition will take over and bring you from a level governed by your ego to one governed by your soul. This will not happen from one day to the next.'

Following smaller roads, I arrive in the suburbs of Perugia. The approach road is busy and again does not leave much room for pedestrians. Mary and I agree that one might just as well take a local bus from the San Marco district to the center of Perugia.

PERUGIA

Perugia is situated on a hill which has been inhabited since prehistoric times. To the Etruscans it was an important town with grandiose buildings. The Roman emperor Octavius conquered the town and named it 'Augusta Perusia'. It later became independent but was often divided in violent fights between prominent families.

Perugia is the trading and administrative center for the whole area. Even so, I am surprised how light and lively the atmosphere is at the town center. I especially enjoy strolling down the wide pedestrian precinct, Corsa Vanucci.

* * *

Next morning I leave through the old town gate. Walk down to Ponto San Giovanni where I cross the River Trevere by an unusual bridge: a long wooden house that one drives or walks through.

The next stretch is awful. I am forced onto a slip road to the motorway. Pedestrians and cyclists do not stand a chance. And the sun is burning hot. I seek refuge in an enormous shopping center by the roadside and relish the cool air from the air conditioning. Hardly notice what they sell – apart from a cappuccino. Gradually cool down. More composed now, I go back out into the heat. Find my way under the motorway up to a village – Collestrada. It feels like entering a completely different world. Hardly any cars, just shady, scented trees. After crossing a stream I turn left onto a farm road leading up over a high hill. From the top I can see Assisi on the opposite side of the valley.

Mary appears and asks me to note how Assisi is situated high up above the fertile agricultural valley. Like a heart above the stomach. *'The heart must be kept free of the sphere of production,'* she says.

Having got onto the farm track, I suddenly realize that we are not alone.

Francis of Assisi has joined us. *'I am glad that you have found my path,'* he says. We greet each other, and he quickly lets us know that he has been informed about our journey. He asks about my walk, and in telling him, I happen to mention my shoes. My posh new walking shoes which I bought in Siena and which chafe my feet so badly that I cannot wear them. Jokingly I ask whether he wants them. *'Give them to the first person you meet!'* he says. I start protesting but he cuts me off: *'Try it!'*

FRANCIS OF ASSISI

1182–1226. As a youth, Francis gave up a dissolute wealthy life and founded his own order of monks, the Franciscans. The order was authorized by the Pope in 1209. In contrast to other orders of monks at the time, the Franciscans practiced poverty.

Francis then carries on from where Mary left off the day before. *'In order to be light-hearted, you must free yourself from the constricting duties of ownership.'* He makes clear that the basic rule – that one should take responsibility for one's own life – will often give rise to a discussion of limits of ownership. Ownership brings greater responsibilities in life than one would expect. *'I do not know anybody who has been able to free himself from the thoughts that follow from ownership. Who can abstain from aggrievedly asking "Who is this walking on my land?"'* he explains.

'You must free yourself from pride of ownership – as well as pride of spirit. Taking responsibility for your own life involves the spiritual as well as the productive side of life.'

Find my way through Bastia Umbra to Santa Maria dei Angeli.

And then there are those shoes! I am in fact ready to give them away. A young black man comes past. But because he is black I am worried that giving him my shoes may look condescending. So I don't. To be better prepared, I get the shoes out, clean them and hook them onto my backpack.

The first person to address me – or the first person who seems to need them – may have them. A young man cycles past. I am just about to stop him when I notice that his shoes look even better than mine, so I do not ask him either. When eventually I reach the enormous church in Santa Maria dei Angeli, I see a woman with her child sitting begging in front of the church. I point to the shoes and ask if she wants them. She nods. I put them down in front of her saying: 'Only worn three days!' I do not think she understands my English and she seems to find me strange. In any case she asks for money for food instead. I point to the shoes saying, '*Uomi*' (men's), and give the sign for money. After all, they are worth about 80 Euros, so I try to make her understand that they have potential. Say goodbye and leave. On my way into the church I sneak a look back and see a young man crouching beside her. He is holding the shoes. I presume he is her husband or boss. Later, when I come out, she has gone and I do not see her the next few days. Maybe the shoes were of some use to her.

Later, Francis asks how I feel, having given the shoes away. 'I actually feel lighter and richer,' I admit.

The church, Santa Maria dei Angeli, is colossal, actually the seventh largest church in the world. It was built over the small church, Porziuncola, in which Francis founded his order of monks. The small church – or chapel – is thought to have been built in the 4th century. Legend has it that the name is connected to a stone from the Virgin Mary's grave that was supposedly brought here by pilgrims on their way back from the Holy Land. The larger church was built in the 16th century to accommodate the large numbers of pilgrims. When I first saw the way the humble little church had been walled inside the mammoth building, I was very disapproving. In time I have learnt to be more tolerant. Porziuncola has preserved its strong, radiant atmosphere which I find delightful. I have also now realized that one has to tune in down here before going up to Assisi.

Relieved of my new shoes, I sit down in the nave of the church and find peace. A seat becomes vacant in Porziuncola and Mary asks me to take it. Once again I process with Michael and Mary on either side of me, this time with Francis in front of us. The ceremony is exactly the same as it was with Jesus. Afterwards

Porziuncola in Santa Maria dei Angeli

Francis explains, *'I have striven to become completely absorbed into Jesus. This has given me stigmata, but it has also enabled me to be in Jesus and Jesus in me. Jesus is love. I am love. Jesus is the heart. I am the heart.'*

As I get up from my seat, I am again asked to take part in a short ceremony. I go and stand in the main aisle. First, Mary and Michael stand on either side of me, and then they leave me and go up to the altar where Francis is standing. Francis comes down on his own and enters into me. Francis' flame is overwhelming, and I realize that with this flame of love, it is not necessary to have a pair of polarities.

I am surprised, because I have just got used to the idea that polarity-pairs are a given thing. Having to possess the balance completely in myself is frightening. It was very comforting to have Mary and Michael beside me. I suppose that in my heart of hearts I am afraid to lose my two guides and supports. Being quite alone unnerves me, and at first I will not have it. A corner of a veil has been lifted, but seeing what lies behind it is too much for me.

If one is the flame of love like Francis, one *is* the flame of God. I am miles from this condition, and the slight touch of it that I have felt puts me deeply in awe of Francis and his doings.

Later I have a conversation with Mary about how far I can copy Jesus and Francis. Mary says, *'They serve as models, Hans. You can try and live up to them and identify with them. You can let yourself become inspired by them. Nobody expects you to live like them.'*

Mary tells me that she had sown a light where the church stands today. A long time before anybody had thought of building a church here. Francis sensed that light and made it burn.

'Remember that it is you who sows the light and others who make it burn,' she finishes.

As I am about to leave the Porziuncola, Mary makes me go back down through the nave. I carry light out with me. I am a light – and I must spread light.

On my way up to Assisi, I think about being a light. I like to think it means that we can all be a light if we focus on our task in life and on carrying it out.

Assisi towers up in front of me on the ridge of Mount Subasio. As I draw close, the large basilica erected in honor of Francis steals the picture.

By evening I have checked into the convent of the Franciscan nuns.

ASSISI

Christian preachers came to the town as early as the first century AD and Bishop Rufino was martyred here in 238.

Due to Francis the town flourished. It became a popular place of pilgrimage.

The building of the large basilica was begun immediately after the death of Francis, and it was completed in 1253.

The church is in three storeys. The top storey is the Upper Church with Giotto's fantastic series of paintings in its Gothic nave. Below this is the Lower Church with great arches, darker and heavily decorated. On the lowest storey is the crypt with the tomb of Francis, flanked by four of his loyal followers.

First thing next morning, I to go up to the town square and into the Minerva Temple.

The temple was built in the first century BC. After being restored in the 16th and 17th centuries the inner cell was consecrated as a church and named 'Santa Maria sopra Minerva' (St. Mary over Minerva).

Mary says, *'There was a temple here last time I came. This is my place.'* She had found the temple pleasing and had blessed it.

It is a point of equilibrium between the masculine church of San Francesco and the feminine church of St. Clara. A meeting place for monks and nuns, for Francis and Clara. It is the center of the town.

According to Mary, the holy site where the Minerva Temple stands has been the center of power for the growth of the whole town.

Santa Maria sopra Minerva

MINERVA

The Roman Minerva was goddess of the arts, crafts and war. This strange combination may have come about through two goddesses being merged into one. The Italian goddess for arts and crafts, Menerva; and the Etruscan goddess of war, Minerva. Some people think that the Etruscan Minerva is really Athena – handed down from the Greeks.

I have a very down-to-earth problem to solve. The hole in my shoe has grown larger. I must do something about it. Yesterday I spotted an amusing cobbler down in Santa Maria dei Angeli. I make my way down to him.

At first he says that shoes like mine are not meant to be

repaired. He laughs, takes them all the same and gets going. Fashions two linings and finally sticks on a rubber sole. And Bob's your uncle – both shoes are done. It takes him just under an hour, chattering non-stop, mending shoes for two ladies at the same time. Seven Euros. He asks if the price is alright. I can only acquiesce.

On the way back, I again go and sit down in the little Porziuncola. Somehow it feels as if the walls are full of voices. I seem to hear a fiery sermon by Francis. As if he is preaching to a small congregation about enjoying life and all that has been given to them. *'Everything is divine,'* says Francis. *'Everything that you meet, every occurrence. Rejoice! God is with you! God is in you!'* Francis is full of life; he has drive, radiates warmth and intensity. This must be how he used to sound. Suddenly, he is talking to me: *'Have you any questions?'*

'How did you get into all this?' I ask. *'Superficiality! My earlier life was lively, but it was superficial. Gradually I came to feel the emptiness. My visions caused a transformation in me which lasted two years.*

'During the first year, I learned to turn my back on my old life. The second year I found the wealth of spirit.'

Francis taught me a small exercise: *'As you inhale, you draw God in. Exhaling, you pass God on to others.'*

Between Santa Maria dei Angeli and Assisi is San Damiano. This is where Francis heard a crucifix asking him to restore the House of God. People have since interpreted 'the House of God' as meaning the Catholic Church. In the first instance Francis interpreted it as the house of God right in front of him, San Damiano. He decided to spend his father's money on restoring the church. This led to a break with his family – with Francis, in front of the bishop and the citizens of the town, taking off his clothes and giving them back to his father. In this way Francis chose a life of poverty. He is quoted as saying, 'If we own anything, we shall need weapons to defend ourselves and we shall be forever fighting each other, hampering us in loving God and our neighbor.'

Later, Francis entrusted San Domiano to Clara and her nuns. Clara lived here for over 40 years until she died in 1253. It is a charming spot with a lush little convent garden bursting with flowers. As I stroll about, I hear an inner voice. It is Clara showing me around. She tells me about the ambience of the place: *'Once there was an air of preoccupation here. Over time, it became more usual for people to find deep, intense moments here.'*

At one point as I sit in the Porziuncola, smiling over a debate between Francis and somebody else, Francis asks a bit sharply: *'Are you laughing at me?'* I say I am and explain that it is not meant as an insult. On the contrary, Francis then changes character. He becomes mild, sighs, looks about him in the nave and says warmly, *'I consecrated Clara as abbess here.'*

There is no doubt that there was a warm relationship between Clara and Francis. They constitute a beautiful polarity.

I go up to the Santa Clara church in Assisi and down into the crypt. As I stand in front of Clara's tomb, she and Francis come and stand on either side of me. We walk round the arches a couple of times with me holding first Clara's and then Francis's hand. I struggle with my thoughts. Can I carry out my task? Can I write the book properly? Quote them all correctly and miss nothing out? *'If you believe in God you will know what the right thing to do is,'* Francis says. *'God shines through Mary.'* Finally they take me up into the church and we stop in front of the altar. A voice asks, *'Will you convey the teachings of Mary?'* After some hesitation, I answer yes. *'Then go forth into the world and proclaim them.'*

The ceremony is over. I sit down in the chapel with its original cross from San Damiano. Clara explains that this cross gave them an anchor for their faith.

Finally I am alone. It is closing time. The church empties. I have time to bless it and kneel under the cross before the nuns close up.

I take the local bus and who should get on but the two Dutch people I met just outside Siena a fortnight ago! We have a quick chat, but they need to find lodgings. I expect to meet them again afterwards, and say, 'See you later.' But somehow we miss each other and I do not see them again after all.

Go back to the convent. Do my washing, write some cards and sleep. Am disturbed by some workmen who have knocked a hole in the neighbor's roof. They are making quite a row. Perhaps it is a sign for me to leave. I count up how many days have gone and how far the rest of the pilgrimage must be.

I am surprised to find that I am only halfway to Ephesus. That is to say that at 25 kilometers per day, I still have 52 days left. 1,250–1,300 kilometers! I shall have my work cut out to get there by November 1st.

Walk down to San Francesco's church. Ask Francis if it is alright for me to leave the next day. He agrees. Mary also agrees but wants me to finish up in the Temple of Minerva, from where I will start the next day. Go up to the square and into the temple, but there is a service in progress so I sit down at a café just opposite the temple instead. In a flash I see that the whole pilgrimage is balanced on a knife edge that cuts right through the temple and the spot where I am sitting. A pigeon pecks at my foot as if trying to tell me something. All at once I hear Mary's voice. *'You can stop now and go home, or you can assimilate what you have learned,'* she says, adding: *'The whole pilgrimage is balanced on this knife's edge. This place is therefore also the heart of the journey.'*

However insurmountable it feels – I am only halfway – I am in no doubt. I promise Mary to go on. *'Bless you,'* she finishes.

* * *

The next morning I say goodbye to the warm and quick-witted sisters at the Franciscan convent. Go up to the Temple of Minerva and tune in. Start off up Mount Subasio.

On my way up, I pass several school classes who are making a short pilgrimage. A few pupils are fed up at having to walk so far. But most of them seem to be in high spirits

Reach Francis's wonderful hermitage, Eremo de Carceri. I go in. There is a very warm atmosphere here. I sense it every time I come here. Despite the many school children, I have some time alone in each of the rooms. Outside I sit down and imagine myself in Francis's world. He felt completely at one with nature. He believed every living being to be filled with spirit. A pair of white doves happens to fly out of a window, and I think of Francis's beautiful sermon for the birds.

Francis with the birds

SERMON FOR THE BIRDS

'And the holy Francis saw some trees by the roadside, and in these trees were an innumerable variety of all sorts of birds which had never before been seen in that area. And in the field under the trees were also a great multitude of them. And when the holy Francis saw this great number, the spirit of God came upon him and he told his disciples: "Wait for me here; I am going to preach to our sisters, the birds!" And he stepped into the field to the birds as they sat on the ground. And as soon as he began to preach, all the birds in the trees flew down to him and none shied away, though he came so close that his habit touched several of them.'

Not only is one close to the woods, the animals, the water and the scents here in this valley, but there is also a wonderful view over the lowlands.

Curious now, I ask Francis if he used to sit looking out across the valley while praying and meditating. *'No. I faced the other way. It was the inner depths I sought. But walking on the paths here, looking out on the valley and feeling the life of the animals is indescribably life-giving. One is always filled with life, after being here.'*

By the caves Francis explains, *'Purity and lightness of heart are to be found in nature and you can tune your heart to it.'* Mary elaborates: *'The balanced basis polarity in nature helps man to tune his own polarity.'*

Soon I sense that St. Michael wants to perform a ceremony. I stand in front of an altar stone. Just stand there quietly. I see great gates open before me. *'This is the seventh level. The Gate of Heaven.'* I start to enter. Stop at the threshold and say that, in the sense that Heaven is the clarified balance between spirit and matter, balanced with the flame of the soul, I am ready to enter

Heaven – to enter the heart. Michael changes from being light to being almost clothed. He comes and stands by my left side. *'Then I am ready to come with you,'* he says. I turn to Mary. *'I am ready also,'* she says.

'Good. Then let us start out on the rest of the journey – into Heaven.'

Something significant has happened here. But I must say that it feels more as if Mary and Michael have brought Heaven down to Earth.

Unfortunately the start of the rest of the journey does not live up to the impressive introduction. I get lost and it is some time before I get down onto the right road. I begin to talk with Mary about suffering.

I ask if the path to joy is always through suffering. Mary explains that there are two sorts of suffering: absence of divine help and self-inflicted suffering.

In regard to the absence of divine help, Mary explains as follows: If somebody chooses their path without listening to their soul or the divine, then that person also chooses to be without divine help. *'If you only knew how much help is ceaselessly offered to each of you – constantly!'* Absence of divine help usually leads to blind alleys and suffering. Suffering can be alleviated by the person choosing in accordance with his or her innermost core.

On the subject of self-inflicted suffering, Mary says that this is a polarity of expectation. For example, the idea that a great joy is always followed by a let-down.

Expecting suffering will actually bring about just that – depression and suffering. Self-inflicted suffering can be cured if the polarity of expectation which is causing it is resolved.

In Spello is a church worth seeing, Santa Maria Maggiore, built on top of the ruins of a temple to Roman goddesses. The church has some very distinctive works of art depicting Mary. One picture shows her with John, the disciple, in her lap. Although this is not exactly flattering for a man these days, I like the picture. *'Please notice that he has the stigmata,'* says Mary. John comes in. He is not bothered by the indignity of the painting. On the contrary, he thinks that it shows something central. That he has been schooled by Mary and that he has reached a stage where he is one with Christ.

Mary loves the church. Finds it difficult to tear herself away. She had sown the seed of this church and she and John had founded a congregation here, outside the walls of the Roman garrison. Here were poor people who were given hope through the message that there was a God for them also.

After Foligno I have a job finding my way due to a motorway that cuts across all the old roads. Once again the road builders and politicians have forgotten to consider cyclists and pedestrians.

As if to cheer me up Mary asks, *'What is joy?'* She goes on to explain that joy is a state of mind which temporarily overpowers bad polarities. Relaxes them. This happens when genuine joy streams through the heart to God. A channel is opened and sends energy streaming back the other way, a life-affirming energy. Rejoicing is the best thing you can do for your health.

Via Flaminia

Finally, halfway up the mountainside, I find an ancient gravel road running almost horizontally. I feel as if I am back in the Middle Ages. It takes me to under a town wall where I find steps down to the old main road, Via Flaminia. To my great relief I find a café. Wonder if I have become addicted to my cappuccinos?

Not far from here is the Tempietto sul Clitunno. A small, antique temple set between the Roman road and a narrow river. Further on are several small lakes.

All this running water gives Mary-energy to the place. In antiquity it was a holy place.

I arrive at Spoleto late that evening. Walk up into the old town and check into a hotel.

* * *

Breakfast in the hotel, and who should come down the stairs? The Dutch couple, whom I now meet for the third time. Incredible coincidence. First time we met, he said, 'See you later!' The second time it was me who said it. And now it actually happens. Now we can have a proper talk. They had got as far as Orvieto and are now on a little detour to see Spoleto, after which they are going back to their route to do the last seven days to Rome. They will then have fulfilled their four months' walk from Holland to Rome. We exchange addresses before saying goodbye.

SPOLETO

Spoleto is one of Umbria's major towns. It became a Roman colony in 241 BC. Cicero is quoted as saying, in the 1st century BC, that Spoletium was one of the richest and most beautiful colonies in central Italy. So it was an affluent town when Mary and John came here on their journey.

Tune in at the cathedral, Santa Maria Assunta, which is dedicated to Mary. I dread today's stage because it seems that I shall have to walk on a main road, battling with traffic. I mention this in my prayer to God. His answer comes through: *'Trust me.'*

I start out along the Via Flaminia. After 5 kilometers there is a sign saying 'No entry' and another sign underneath: *'Eccepti residente'*. This is the old main road where it is possible to walk in peace and quiet. I follow it, up over the pass, 650 meters above sea level. Then all the way down again. One peaceful kilometer after another. Suddenly I am faced with a choice. A road going left towards Rieti. This morning I thought that I was supposed to go straight to Terni and the Marble Falls, but that may be wrong. It is a difficult choice. By way of a test, I walk 100 meters along each road to see how it feels. The side road seems best, so I decide to go towards Rieti. Up over the mountain, through Montefranco and down into the valley of the Nera. To find a hotel just outside Arrone.

Walking over mountains, I decide I want to know more about joy.

Mary says that joy is a divine energy that touches one's deeper layers. A great joy will fill and open your heart. So much so, that polarities of law and expectation are neutralized and no longer oppress your heart. This gives a wealth of openings and you feel the energy of life flowing into you. In reality you are being filled with a divine power. *'For divine power is power of life.'*

In Arrone I find a St. Mary's church, Chiesa di Santa Maria, where I tune in. Mary seems glad that I have found it.

I have to cross another mountain to get to Rieti.

After an ascent of 8 kilometers, I cross through a pass and drop down towards Piedeluce.

Mary has not been as forthcoming as usual. I ask why. She assures me that she is there, showing me the way all the time, adding: *'What will it be like for future pilgrims, Hans? They will not be taught. What will they do?'* Whoops, I have almost forgotten what a pilgrimage feels like when you are not receiving instruction underway. I think of the three polarity axes.

THE BASIS AXIS

First there is the basis axis between spirit and matter. I imagine that the connection to the spiritual pole goes through the Crown chakra above the head, and the connection to the material pole through the Root chakra just below the crotch.

'How can I strengthen this basis axis?' I ask Mary.

She replies quickly, '*Note which pole feels strongest. You may feel the Root chakra most clearly, and maybe feel that it is at ground level or even 20 centimeters below that. Then imagine the Crown chakra at a corresponding distance from the heart. Make a note of the two outer poles and try to stretch them a bit further apart. Straighten yourself up correspondingly.*'

I later felt that the Root chakra sometimes seems to have moved up into one's lower body. The Root chakra can then be stretched further down so a balance is restored around one's heart.

THE AXIS OF THE SOUL

The second axis goes horizontally through one's heart. The axis of the soul. The axis that I was shown on Mount St. Michael in Alsace, where I stood with my arms stretched out, and where Mary and Michael stepped in as my soul's polarities.

'How can I strengthen this axis?' I ask.

'*Again note both poles. Let them change places – and back again. Are they both the same distance from your heart? Are they both equally noticeable? Focus on the weaker one. Convey energy to it by concentrating on it,*' says Mary.

THE MODEL AXIS

The third axis, the model axis, was shown to me at Lago Maggiore in northern Italy. The axis which passes from your front, horizontally through your chest and out through your back. Here too it was Mary and Michael who stepped in and formed my model polarity.

'How can I strengthen the model axis?' I ask again.

'*Note who is behind you and who is in front of you. Let them swap places. One is probably nearer your heart than the other. If that is the side you find most useful at the moment, then well and good. If not, you must strengthen the weaker one by paying attention to it and giving it energy,*' Mary answers.

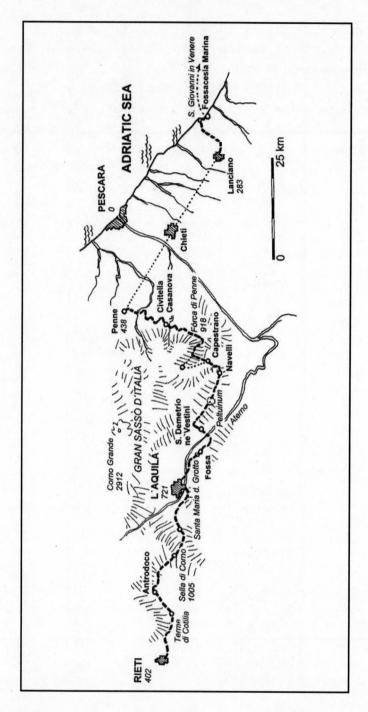

10

Be a Light!

Abruzzo

I am on my way to Rieti. The road is fairly flat and fairly quiet as it is Sunday.

After crossing a low mountain range, I drop down to a very large, round plain completely shut in by mountains. The plain is cultivated and the valley towns sprawl up the mountainsides.

I come to a crossroads and have to decide which way to go. I am very uncertain. Something draws me towards the mountains in the east. There are several small towns that way. Maybe it is the wearying thought of another climb that finally determines my choice. Maybe it is the feeling that time is running out. Whichever, I choose to go straight across the plain to the main town of Rieti.

It is August and in the fields the maize is growing tall. So tall that I cannot see over it. It is like disappearing into a colossal labyrinth. It all feels a bit odd. Odd also that Mary should have walked here, as in her day it must surely have been a lake. She agrees that it may have been, but that she walked closer to the mountains. Somewhat skeptical, I find my way across the plain and arrive at the Cattedrale de Santa Maria in central Rieti.

I later found out that I was right in thinking that the plain was originally a lake; I discovered that a Roman consul had it drained and channeled into the River Velino in 271 BC. This means that the lake had already been dry for 300 years when Mary came through.

RIETI

Rieti is older than Rome itself. The name comes from Rea, the mother of all gods, indicating that the town originally played a central role. The Romans conquered the area and cultivated the land on an almost industrial scale. Since the time of the Romans, Rieti has been called the 'navel of Italy'. It was Christianized as early as the 2nd century AD.

In the early evening I go for a walk round Rieti. On a terrace near the cathedral there is a square overlooking a lower-lying district of the town. I am drawn to the square and here find the most breathtaking view of the southern mountains. I lose myself in the spectacle, alongside a number of amorous couples. Mountain peaks rise up all the way round what used to be the lake. They fence the valley in, protecting it. I sense archangels over several of the mountains. I am intrigued. This valley is magic.

This is where I should have told myself to stay a day or two and explore the valley, but I felt time pressing and decided to move on. I have since realized that I missed something important here. The valley is actually called the Holy Valley. Presumably because of Francis of Assisi. From the year 1209 until his death in 1226, Francis spent quite long periods of time in this valley and in the surrounding mountains. Francis is said to have been especially fond of the area because of its magnificent scenery, the inhabitants' simple way of life and all the miracles he was allowed to perform here.

I was very surprised to learn that Francis spent so much time here. I knew nothing about it before now. His many sojourns in the Holy Valley must also mean that he often did Mary's walk from Assisi to Rieti. Indeed, recently a Pilgrim's Way has been made round the valley, taking in all the places Francis visited. I did miss something important – should probably have walked through the mountains rather than across the plain.

* * *

A year later I went back to the valley and started all over again from the crossroads at the north of the plain where I was unsure of the way. Let me take you a little forward in time and tell you what happened:

First, the path took me to a small town, Piedicolle, with a small idyllic lake. There were bubbles on the surface and a signpost informed me that this was Santa Susanna's Spring. Two swans were preening themselves on the lake, and water trickled gently down small waterfalls. It was a veritable Mary site and I was in no doubt that Mary had been here. I carried on, through Borgo San Pietro, and found an old gravel track to take me further up the valley. The track may have looked exactly the same for centuries. Suddenly Francis was beside me. He used to use this path too. After a hard climb I arrived at Poggio Bustone, a town clinging to the mountainside, with streets that have been turned into flights of steps. Here there was a café, and somewhere to spend the night. Next I continued up through a ravine and arrived at a monastery dedicated to James, the patron saint of pilgrims. Francis followed me discreetly.

FRANCIS AND THE RIETI VALLEY

We are told that Francis came here in 1290 with his followers, 'The Penitents of Assisi', as they were called. They had not felt welcome in Assisi. People simply did not understand that someone, of his own free will, could choose to be poor. They had therefore left Assisi and started out on an expedition to try and learn what they were supposed to do. Francis had many answers to find. Where to go? What to do? In Poggio Bustone they would have been able to live in seclusion and consider these serious matters. A thousand questions plagued Francis and he did not know what to do. He understood that God had shown himself to him and expected something of him, but Francis felt weighed down by his sins and by the fact that he had led his first brethren into great uncertainty. He was troubled and fled to the womb of the earth – a cave where he could sense the divine presence, full of mercy and light.

The unexpected came to pass. He felt his sins being lifted from his shoulders. He let go of them, stood up and welcomed the light. He could now lead his brothers with an inner certainty. If his doubt had won the struggle, we might never have heard of Francis. But his doubt was dispelled, and Francis threw himself into his life's work, which was born here, so to speak, and it was here in Poggio Bustone that he greeted the people with his famous words, 'Good morning, good people!'

Mary gave me to understand that she had visited this monastery too. Francis came closer and asked me what stage of life I had got to, both in regards to my journey and my life at home. I began to give an account of both situations, and Francis made it clear to me that I was facing an important choice in my life. That there was a chance of something new being born. That this choice had to be made, and had to be acted upon.

Poggio Bustone and the Rieti valley

I stood contemplating the mountains and suddenly realized the sort of landscape I was looking at. The monastery is almost enclosed in a very steep valley. Behind it the mountains rise up towards the mighty Mount Terminillo. Below, the valley forms almost a circle. Low mountain ridges curve from either side, leaving only a narrow opening in the direction of the Rieti plain. The heart of Mother Earth seems to beat from the massif, and the small valley can be seen as a mountainous womb, giving birth through the opening towards the plain. Here, I realized, is a divinely devout birthing place, open to those who approach with a pure soul, with reverence and respect.

Francis came this way, accepted his rebirth and went forth, convinced of his task in life. Now, I too felt the same birth-promoting energy. Where had I got to in my life and what was my task? I should be very surprised if other visitors did not feel it too.

Through Grethe I later asked about this place and Mary answered:

'You can use this place as somewhere to get clarification, use it to

create a ritual anchor. It has in fact been used for this purpose before. Not only by Francis. When Francis arrived here, he was greatly troubled and was therefore wide open to the spiritual world. He was actually able to use this place as a sort of womb. In the womb you are in close contact with your purpose in life.

'This place is under my grace and favor, hence the comparison with a womb and something virginal.

'On your first visit here you were not properly prepared. You were a little too eager.'

From Poggio Bustone I carried on southwards. Mary guided me onto the signposted pilgrim's way, Cammino di Francesco, a path connecting all the places Francis frequented in the Holy Valley. I followed this route to the next town. The narrow path winds its way along the mountainside through the sparse vegetation. The view over the valley is impressive, and it is a blessing to walk up there in the quiet, natural beauty. In the next town, Candilice, the houses do not just cling onto the mountain; no, they are practically piled one on top of the other up the steep inclines. It is a challenge to get up to the church at the high end of town. The route continues southwards, across mountain ridges and through forests, sometimes following deeply sunken roads. Francis said that the road looked just like this in his time. About 5 kilometers from Rieti I came upon another one of Francis's haunts, 'Madonna de la Foresta'.

The sun was shining, the birds were singing, and as I came out of the forest a small lush valley opened up in front of me. In Madonna de la Foresta lies an enormous kitchen garden where monks cultivate all sorts of vegetables. The whole valley is a paradise; just the place for contemplation and devotion to the fullness of nature.

Francis was brought here in the summer of 1225, a year before his death. He was in poor health. He was in constant pain and could hardly see. An eye operation was arranged for him in Rieti, and in connection with this he was invited to stay in this friendly place with its hospitable priest. As illness slowly consumed his body, he here recalled all the happy times of his life. There was a lot to thank God for, and what was more natural than expressing the joy of his heart in song? The locals say that it was here he completed his unique hymn to Creation, 'The Song of the Sun'.

THE SONG OF THE SUN
Almighty good Lord in the Highest,
Thine be all honor, laud and praise and all blessing.
To Thee alone, Most High, are they due,
And no man is worthy to mention Thy name.
We praise Thee, oh Lord, with all Thy creations,
Most of all our brother the Sun, who creates the day,
and Thou givest light to us by him,
and he is beautiful and brilliant with great radiance.
Of Thee, oh most High, is he an image.
We praise Thee, oh Lord, for our brother the Wind
And for the air and the clouds and good weather and
    all sorts of weather
Wherewith Thou upholdest all Thy creations.
We praise Thee, oh Lord, for our sister the Water,
Which is exceedingly useful and humble and precious
    and chaste.
We praise Thee, oh Lord, for our brother the Fire,
By whom Thou makest light the night,
And he is beautiful and full of life and powerful and strong.
We praise Thee, oh Lord, for our sister, Mother Earth,
Who keeps us and bears us [carries us]
And calls forth all manner of fruit and colored flowers
    and grass.
We laud and praise the Lord and thank Him
And serve Him with great humility.

As I walked, I heard Francis talking to me. He described how God has manifested himself by creating all things living: birds, animals, plants etc. It is very obvious here – a garden of manifestation. Francis manifested himself, and I could manifest myself too. As he talked, I understood that a feminine way of manifesting yourself is by SOWING. A masculine way is by BUILDING.

They go well together, these two places: birth at Poggio Bustone and manifestation at Madonna de la Foresta.

When we got to Rieti I asked Francis if he had a favorite spot in the town. He led me directly to the southern side of the square to the place where, on my pilgrimage, I had swooned over the breathtaking view. Francis looked towards a certain mountain, and the archangel Michael seemed to appear over it. I was again entranced by the beauty of this mountain and decided to go there.

It is about 5 kilometers from Rieti. All I know about it is that it is called Francis's Mount Sinai, and that the monastery there is called 'Fonte Columba'. The road winds up the mountain. The humble buildings come slowly into view through the thickets. Francis seemed to walk with me, and as we walked, we talked of my task. After visiting the church in the square, we descended a long flight of steps leading down to a small chapel which, I was surprised to find, is dedicated to St. Michael.

Inside, we saw a painting of St. Michael [or perhaps Jesus] giving the rules of conduct to Francis and his 'Little Brothers' here. I sat down and at once felt Michael's presence. He confronted me with my task, and we discussed it. Underneath the chapel is a cave. It is actually a narrow tunnel-like passage, just big enough to squeeze through, where Francis spent a lot of time in quiet meditation.

I read that Francis held St. Michael in great respect and used to prepare himself for the feast of St. Michael on Sep. 29th by fasting for 40 days.

On the way back up from the cave I saw a signpost to the Columba Spring. Beneath towering treetops I followed the path down to the spring, which still flows to this day. Not very strongly, but flows nonetheless. Here I sensed Mary's presence. She too confronted me with my task.

Fonte Colombo

Fonte Columba has a fine polarity between Michael up in the cave and Mary down by the spring. Columba actually means 'dove', and I really felt the uplifting influence of the Holy Ghost. I found it very inspiring. It does not surprise me that Francis kept coming here.

It was as if Francis was showing me in this valley how he was enabled to begin his work. How nature's powerful places helped him, and that today they can help us too.

There is a fourth site in the valley dedicated to Francis, Greccio, on the western side. Greccio is also halfway up a mountain and on the path 'Cammino di Francesco'. I found it very touristy and rather restless, but its situation is beautiful and in Francis's time the energy must have been very good.

Enough about this more recent visit. Now back to the pilgrimage.

* * *

The next morning Mary tells me to take it easy and only walk 15–20 kilometers. I leave about midday, going eastwards through the town gate, Porta d'Arce.

On the road from Rieti, Mary asks, *'Have you done your exercises?'* I have completely forgotten the exercises to strengthen the three polarity axes, so I get down to it at once.

1. My Root is knee high. I pull the height of my Crown up correspondingly.
2. On my Soul axis Michael is very close. I focus on Mary and her energy. Inhale the landscape. Draw Mary a bit closer. Thus the balance is restored.
3. On my Model axis Mary is very close. That is good; because it is her I am following through the landscape.

Mary helps me.

4. *'Visualize the central flame in all three systems. Center them all in your heart.'*
5. *'Visualize the central flame vibrating outwards and creating an oval, spherical field around you, a field containing all the other polarities.'*

'Now you have regenerated your energy field – your aura. It is a good thing to do this every morning,' says Mary.

'Do you have a clear Expectation polarity?' she continues. After a few seconds an old one comes to mind. 'Yes, the expectation that when I do wrong I will be punished.'

I try to envisage where this polarity is located. The word 'punishment' is in front of my mouth, a little to the left. Doing wrong seems to lie behind the small of my back, slightly to the right. The axis between these two positions passes diagonally through my heart.

'Punishment is your interpretation; experience is more correct,' says Mary. *'Try to see it as such.'* I do, and at once it becomes more neutral and something I can use.

'Replace "punishment" with "experience" when this polarity occurs. Use the word "punishment" in connection with crime in the legal sense,' she says.

Having carried out this balancing, I now feel whole. But I would like to know what one does if one cannot feel the central flame in one's heart. Mary teaches me a short prayer: *'Dear God, you who are the light of all things, re-create the light in my heart.'*

I follow the road through the antique spa town, Terme di Cotilla, with its healing sulfur springs. When Mary was here this was a luxurious spa area, and the emperor had his own spa residence here.

On through Antrodoco with its St. Mary's church from the 12th century. On the way up to the next mountain pass, I pass Santa Maria delle Grotte. This cave church was built here, under the vast overlying rock, after a shepherd found a picture of the Madonna in 1601. Was for many years a place of pilgrimage but today seems deserted. The church is now completely hemmed in by a big new main road.

I go through several small villages and eventually reach a mountain pass at an altitude of 1,005 meters. Had hoped to spend the night here, but there is nowhere to stay. Have to go all the way to Scopitto before I manage to find a bed.

* * *

The next day, on the way to L'Aquila, I get onto a very busy main road. Have to fight the traffic for walking room. Arrive in the town a little awkwardly. Go up to the cathedral, which unfortunately is closed.

It is time to send a ton of cards home, so I go to the post office – but have to queue for ages, and in the meantime the tourist office closes. By now all the churches are closed too. As are the two cheap hotels to which I have been given addresses. The timing seems altogether wrong. The town closes itself against me as if it wants to push me away. I seriously think of going on. I then realize that I have not given it a proper chance. Find another hotel near the cathedral and check in. Expensive, despite its low standard. To make matters even worse, there is some very noisy building in progress. Still, I manage to get a short nap, and in the late afternoon I get up and give the town another chance. Go out to see if it will welcome me.

It feels like coming to a completely different town. It has opened up. Literally, for all the churches and shops are now open. Life streams towards me and cheers me up.

Later I discovered that I had entered the town the wrong way. I should have come via a beautiful mountain landscape south of

The Fountain of 99 Spouts in L'Aquila

the town and entered through the town gate, Porta Rivera. Just inside the gate I would have been met by the impressive Fontana Monumentale with its 99 fountains surrounding round the town square. That would have made for quite a different arrival.

Encouraged, now that the town has opened up, I go into the cathedral. Mary seems very dominant, although the church is dedicated to Massimo and St. George.

I sense Michael's and Mary's presence immediately. Walk up the main aisle and find them waiting for me in front of the altar. They have changed sides. Michael asks smilingly if I have missed them and of course I say that I have.

I go right up to them. I see that, between them, they hold a great golden goblet surmounted by a sun. The Holy Grail. I go between them, turn round and stand with the Grail within me and look down the church. The nave is in darkness, but the great west door is open, and through it I see the life of the square in a sharp and blinding light. *'Go out into the world and be the light you have in you,'* says Michael. I stand there for a moment. Sense Mary and Michael coming very close to me. They become the light. The light that I am. They move out again, but I still seem to have them within me and I seem to see through them. It is only for a glimpse, but even so it is very inspiring. I go outside.

Francis is no longer with me. Still, I feel that this was exactly what he wanted to teach me: *'Be a light.'* Just over a week ago, in the small church, Porziuncola, near Assisi, I was shaken to hear that I myself could be a light. That I could unite my polarities in my heart and be a light. Since then, Francis has accompanied me and has several times tried to impress this on me. I have found it difficult to accept, and I definitely do not feel that I am a light. I discuss this with Francis, and he seems to try to spell it out for me. To the best of my recollection this is what he said:

'I was a light and – while trying to avoid being too arrogant – I was

also God on Earth. You must not misunderstand me; being a light is being a spark taken from God's ocean of flame. When you let the flame burn freely – when you are a light – then you are God on Earth.

'*There is no point in being a light alone. You must realize and accept that everyone else is a light too, and that they must burn from their innermost source. You must also accept that all other lights are your sisters and brothers and that you are a fellowship in God.*

'*To see the light only in yourself is to separate yourself from others. To see the light in others is to unite you with them. To see someone shine from his innermost source – being his innermost – means that you see one another. That you are in God. This is true fellowship.*

'*As we have been told, a community must have laws to regulate behavior, laws that must be constantly revised to avoid becoming rigid and outdated, used solely to defend privileges. Every privilege creates a division, preventing you from seeing God in your neighbor.*

'*Even in the religious world there is a tendency to create privileges for oneself. I saw that in my younger brothers. Academic privileges above those of experience. This happens on many levels: men's privileges above women's, the privileges of rulers over their subjects etc. These are all misunderstandings. They may have had their day. But no longer.*'

On my way out of the town I visit the Santa Maria del Collemaggio. A huge church that was the setting for a papal enthronement in 1294. Go south-east and drop down to a flat landscape.

In the town of Fossa I visit the Santa Maria di Grotte church. A neighboring woman lets me in. The church is full of frescos. On walls, loft and vaults. In lively Italian the woman tells me about all the pictures. I do not understand very much, but luckily I recognize the names, and then I understand the pictures. Mary tells me that she slept in what was then a small cave under the present church. Steps still lead down to a small, dark, cave-like room under the choir.

The woman has been my guide and now she kindly, but firmly, asks to be paid.

Continue along narrow roads, through San Demetrio ne' Vestini and up through the valley to San Giovanni Batista, a sleepy medieval village from the 12th century. In the empty, dilapidated streets I feel as if I have traveled back in time. On leaving San Giovanni Batista I get onto a deserted gravel track that leads me up through a gorge into the mountains.

Several times I wonder if this can be right, but after 3 or 4 kilometers and an ascent of about 400 meters, I reach a wide plateau 845 meters above sea level. The whole area is quite deserted but I find a farm road leading east. Several kilometers later the road comes to an end at some impressive ruins. I have reached Peltuinum. In Mary's time it was a tremendous town with about 100,000 inhabitants. She must have been met by a great hustle and bustle. Now, only ruins remain. Totally lacking any respect for the past, farmers have harrowed tiny fields in among the ancient ruins of agora, temple and theater.

Having explored the ruins I find my way to a hostel – an albergo – in Castel-nuovo.

Dream that a good friend shows me a book in which he has underlined everything about ABSENCE. It is written in old Gothic letters.

* * *

Early next morning I go back out to Peltuinum. Mary says that we should not stay there too long. Something unwanted might cling to us. I follow the farm road down from the fortified hill. In ancient times this road was an important thoroughfare called the 'Claudia Nova'. In places it has been plowed up, but I find my way to the town of Navelli on a small promontory. Here I turn north.

On the way, Mary and I have tackled the dream about ABSENCE.

I understand it to mean that it symbolizes my absence from Mary the previous day. Mary agrees and says that it is important to be conscious of absence, as absence has caused problems throughout history. Mary says that absence means *not* being present and aware in the poles on the basis axes. In the root of the basis axis: feeling one's feet, scents and sights – being present. In the spirit: sensing the spiritual side of nature. On the axis of the soul: being conscious of the poles of one's soul and seeking the deep echo – having your soul present with you. I practice carefully. I don't suppose one can be a light without being fully present in one's polarities.

After Navelli I follow the old road through the mountains to Capestrano, which used to be a major town in this area. I think we are supposed to use the pass, Forca di Penne, at 918 meters altitude.

The road up to the pass is like a shelf cut out of the mountainside, kilometer after kilometer. Meet only a couple of cars. At long last, reach the pass. As I leave the valley a whole world disappears; a new one comes into view as I pass between the two mountains that make up the fork. The mountains now slope down towards fertile lowlands disappearing in a mist out towards the sea. The energy changes. Though I cannot see the Adriatic, it still affects the energy here.

I walk slowly downwards, enjoying the beautiful view across the lowlands. In a bar the landlord tells me that there is no hotel within the next 40 kilometers. That sounds bad, but my legs are in good form today and I prepare myself for a long walk.

Pass through several small towns. In Civitella Casanova a young man tells me that there is a hotel, just west of the town, about 2 kilometers from the town center. He even offers to drive me up there. I have walked 32 kilometers but, believe it or not, I refuse his offer. I decide to walk on. Mary nearly swoons! But I am determined, and I continue along the road towards Penne.

On one of the first ascents, I walk alongside a vineyard. The sunlight falls beautifully on the grapes and the foliage. As if the sun's rays are winking at me through the juicy grapes. In order to get a closer look I jump across the ditch. Jumping back again, I fall flat on my face. Lying there headlong, I suddenly realize that this is the first fall of the whole trip. I haven't hurt myself. It must actually have looked rather funny, but it strikes me how little it would take for something to go wrong. Perhaps I ought to pay more attention and concentrate more, instead of just counting up the kilometers. I often get tired and absentminded after walking 30 kilometers and I am no help to Mary like that. I resolve to practice being attentive in spite of any physical tiredness. Am conscious of my surroundings and my body. The singing birds. The wind playing in the leaves of the trees. The cool dampness under the treetops.

Try to catch the supersensory nuances of the landscape. Is the mountain speaking to me? Is there an angel present? Is the sea whispering to me? Is this church telling me that Mary was here?

Try to center myself in my heart. Think about this pilgrimage as having grown out of my innermost self and about taking full responsibility for it. That I am doing the journey of my soul. Mary does not say much apart from showing me the way. Forcing the march is my own project. All the more reason to show her that I can do it in a well-balanced way. Like walking in Heaven.

Downhill, uphill, through several small towns, but not a single hotel. After walking 45 kilometers I at long last find a room in an 'Agriturismo'. It is not very agricultural. Expensive and posh with gourmet dinner and luxurious rooms. Am tired, very tired indeed.

Even so, I still feel that, right through my tiredness, I managed to stay attentive.

* * *

The next morning the kind staff give me a packed lunch to take with me.

I feel, however, that I must have got out of the wrong side of the bed this morning. Am probably not synchronized as a result of my forced march the previous day. Walk the 5 kilometers to Colle Romano, the first hill in Penne. Here, in Colleromano, stands the Chiesa di Santa Maria. A very large church. A service is in progress with modern singing, piano and flute music. A warm and lively atmosphere fills the church.

I expect to go exploring in the old town of Penne, but Mary informs me that I have now been in the one church relevant to our journey. In olden days Penne was a city, as the main thoroughfare through the pass also ran through here. So I have followed the ancient main road.

Between Penne, Chieti and Lanciano the old pilgrim's way has been swallowed up by new motorways and built-up areas. Mary does not want me to walk this stretch. She asks me to take a bus or a train. So I do.

I am to pick up the route in Lanciano, and for the last part of my way there, I take an ancient train. As it slowly winds its way up the mountain, puffing hard, I get the most amazing views of the sea and the valleys. In Denmark, a railway like this would have been closed down years ago. Here they do things differently. Primitive things can exist alongside modern, fast ones. Thank goodness, for the ride is in itself a great experience. Long live this railway!

Reach Lanciano by evening. It is swarming with people. There are market stalls everywhere. In the main street there is even a bicycle race. I discover that the town is celebrating the 171st anniversary of its Madonna statue. I look for a youth hostel. Ask a monk, who shows me the way to an old Franciscan monastery that has been turned into a hostel. At the last minute I catch the manager, and am given a bed in a room for five – all to myself. Have a quick shower and hurry down to the service in the old Franciscan church, Santuario del Miracolo Eucaristico.

EUCHARISTIC MIRACLE

The thanksgiving miracle in Lanciano consists of ancient dried blood which can still be made liquid. It has been preserved in this church since the 8th century and is the first Eucharistic miracle in the Catholic Church. That the blood does not putrefy is a mystery, even to the scientists who have examined it.

The church is jam-packed. Many of us have to stand. As in Penne this morning there is a lot of singing and music. Electric guitars, flute and good singers.

More than a hundred members of the congregation take communion. Mary asks if I want to join them. I feel that I don't quite understand the ritual and do not want to take part. A little later, after nearly everyone has been served, Mary says that she would like me to do it for her sake.

I pull myself together and hurry up the now empty main aisle, reaching the queue before the last person has been served. Mary says, *'This is my son that you now take unto you. May he shine and work in you.'*

I can sense what I am supposed to learn. Jesus is a light. Jesus is Michael and Mary, and thus Jesus also shines in me. I must learn to trust in myself as a light.

* * *

Tune in the next morning at the Cattedrale de Santa Maria del Ponte. Mary says that we are to go down to San Giovanni in

Venere.

Leave town going southeast along the old main road. I reach the coast via a series of small towns. Here I arrive at the San Giovanni in Venere Abbey. The complex towers up above the sea from a fantastic position, on the tip of a mountain ridge that runs right out to the coast. To me, standing looking out over the sea, with the monastery in the foreground, is marvelous. I have finally reached the far side of Italy. The church is open to the public but seems disused.

The Abbey of San Giovanni in Venere by the Adriatic

I sense St. Michael long before I enter the church. Something is going to happen. Michael and Mary are already there waiting in the raised choir. I 'process' alone from the west door to the altar steps. Bless the church as being part of the route.

Walk up the steps and stand before Mary and Michael.

Greet Michael. He welcomes me. '*A stage of your journey is over,*' he says. '*You have reached the sea. Now you must sail down the coast, making a small detour across land on the Gargano Peninsula.*'

After a short pause he asks, '*Are you going on?*'

I have assumed that my Italian stage will end only when I leave the country, so the question takes me by surprise.

Immediately agree, and it is not until a moment later that I begin to realize what Michael has just said to me. For one thing, I do not have to walk down to the Gargano Peninsula. Mary went by sea. For another, this abbey is so important a goal that it would be feasible to end the pilgrimage here. So my journey from Pisa via Assisi finishes here in San Giovanni in Venere. The Gargano Peninsula is a whole new stage.

Michael goes on to say: '*You will sail from Brindisi to Corfu and then on to the mainland, starting again in Parga.*' Short and concise. In other words, the Gargano Peninsula and Corfu are an interlude leading up to the Greek mainland.

Mary takes over. Smiling, she asks, '*Are you glad that you do not have to walk?*' I have to admit that I am, and am almost ashamed to have forced the pace the day before yesterday. It was quite unnecessary, as I have now been awarded a couple of days. '*Yes,*' Mary says. '*Trust your spiritual impulse. Have absolute faith in it.*'

I am asked to go and stand between Michael and Mary. They turn and we all face the altar. Michael talks to God. Tells him that '*the young man*' has completed a stage of the pilgrimage and that he is prepared to continue with the Greek part. God asks Michael if I have learnt anything, and he answers that in some areas I have, while in others there is more work to be done. God speaks to me directly: '*You have done a good deed. Your proclaiming of Mary's teachings has my blessing.*' Then God speaks to all of us. The lessons I am to learn in Greece may be severe, but I will also find them fruitful and enlightening. '*In Michael and Mary you have two good helpers. Bon voyage to all three of you. Blessings on your trip.*'

I am filled with joy. I raise my arms and playfully give Michael and Mary quite a slap on the shoulder.

The ceremony continues. We take a step forward, turn and look down the nave. In my mind's eye I see the whole pilgrimage route, right from the beginning at the convent of Hildegard of Bingen.

I go over it minutely with all its important towns and places. I see a light shine in each place as I pass. And as I finally arrive here, at the Abbey in San Giovanni, I seem to see the whole pilgrimage before me as a string of lights. The ceremony ends.

Later, with Grethe's help, I asked Mary what realization lies in walking Mary's Way. Mary answered:

'Submission is an important ingredient. Trusting that you will be given the help you need. In that sense it differs from the Way of Christ, because his was such a dangerous way. He could not submit himself to others in the same way. It is especially feminine – a privilege – to be allowed to be in submission. That is not to say that the way may not be painful and full of sorrow. But it does not encompass so many dangers.'

On the first stage across the Alps I learnt about what it is TO BE CREATED. About understanding how each individual is formed and how they function. This stage through Italy seems to have been about what it means TO BE MAN. About how the energy of one individual connects with that of others, and about how everyone may enrich their environment by being a light.

Mary asks me to accompany her and Michael down to the harbor to see them off. She also asks me to get out my maps so we can pinpoint where they will land. I look at the map and try to sense where this might be. The nearest I can get seems to be Lesina.

Go right down to the beach. Under the cliff face beneath Giovanni in Venere, Mary and Michael seem to board a smallish sailing boat. They tack out from the cove and veer south. We wave goodbye to each other.

I take a dip in the Adriatic and walk up to the station.

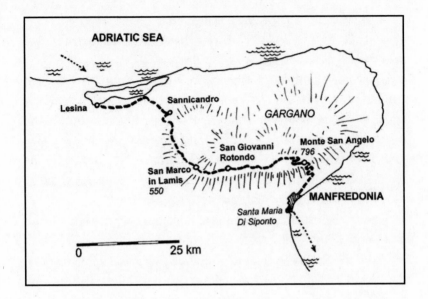

11

Michael's Land and Padre Pio

The Gargano Peninsula

Where did Mary go ashore on the Gargano Peninsula? I am not at all sure. Before I got here, I felt it was probably Lesina, but now, having seen the industrial area round the town from the train, I begin to wonder. I now think that it must have been further out than Lesina. It might be my own imagination but I persuade myself that it must have been as far out as San Nicandro.

Spend the night in San Severo. Go down to the station next morning. The bus leaves in an hour so I have time to reflect on the stage I have completed in Italy.

Mary is always very positive and says that on the whole we have managed to find the correct route. But she does say: *'We*

must go through the route before you go on to Greece. There are seven
or eight places where you have chosen a slightly different stretch of road
from where I went. We should correct that.'

Mary goes on to ask, 'Have you walked in Heaven?' Shamefully
I must admit that I have often forgotten that the three sides –
spirit, body and soul – must be kept together if you want to walk
in Heaven on earth. 'It is very important to remember your spirit. Just
as you practiced doing, the day you walked too far. Being present on all
three levels is important.' As I muse on what she has said, she adds,
'Go to San Nicandro and find your way from there.'

I find this instruction calming. The Italian stage is completed
and I now know where to go on from.

From the flatlands, the mountainous Gargano Peninsula now
rises up like a ship's bow into the Adriatic, reaching an altitude of
over 1,000 meters in several places. Here the climate can be
severe. San Nicandro is situated on the northern slope just a few
kilometers from the coast.

I get off the bus in the middle of the high street. Assume that
I will be able to contact Mary in the parish church. Walk up
towards the old town center. In the first square I come to, there
are two churches. They do not appeal to me, but a church tower
a little further up does. Unfortunately this church is closed, so I
sit down on the steps and rest a while. Suddenly Mary comes
through: 'I am right here,' she says, and I sense her clearly in full
figure. I am greatly relieved. Actually cry with relief. I find it very
trying to be out of contact with Mary and I worry that I will not
be able to find her footsteps again. Mary explains that they
landed further up the coast and walked here.

I have since found out that Mary did in fact land in Lesina as
I first thought. I have been there since and experienced Mary
landing. The town is ancient. In antiquity it was called Alexina.
Not far from the harbor I found the town's large church of St.
Mary, where she is portrayed with nearly all her insignia. An
impressive place and a good starting point for a new stage. Then,

I seemed to sense that Mary walked from there up to San Nicandro.

Back in San Nicandro something induces me to go further up into the town and here I come upon a fourth church – with an open door. It is the San Georgio in Terravecchia. And of course, in this church of St. George, Michael is present. He welcomes me. For once, there is not going to be a ceremony. Michael says only that both he and Mary will accompany me across the peninsula. *'As you know, the peninsula is Michael country,'* he adds with a twinkle in his eye.

Michael takes the lead down through the town and out westwards. On the outskirts of the town I sense that he wants to turn into a side road leading south. On the map I can see that from the end of this road there is a path up to a bigger road. The road leads us into a small valley, becoming narrower and narrower, and I begin to wonder, but Michael insists that we go on.

We cross a railway line and must have gone about one and a half kilometers further when we meet a car. It stops and I understand from the deprecating gestures and words of the driver that this road comes to a dead end and that I must turn back. He drives on, but as I trust the map more than him, I carry on. Shortly afterwards the driver and his car come back. I show him my map and compass and insist that there is a path. He gives me to understand that he lives on the last farm and that there absolutely is no path. He is very firm, though kind enough. He drives me back to the railway and tells me to follow it westwards till I get to the main road, which I do, and then head for San Marco in Lamis. Walking along the official road, I cannot help asking Michael teasingly if there really was a usable path in the other valley. I am sure that Michael is good at navigating, but when it comes to traveling along roads and paths, through woods and over mountains, things seem to go wrong. Mary and I agree that I will stick to her instructions from now on, even though this is Michael country. *'After all, it is my Way we are traveling,'* she says.

Through Grethe, Michael later said to me:

'You got there, didn't you? You could have done it by the road I had shown you, but that man helped you, so you were still looked after.

'You are right, though; I am more concerned with direction and objective. You must expect to have to make corrections on the physical plane. It is Mary's Way you walk, so you must obviously ask her first. I am actually only to be asked when things seem impossible. Then I will lead you through, even though it will take courage – and maybe a few corrections which people will show you, as happened here. You will not be misled.'

Time is getting on. By now it is late afternoon and the next town is 20 kilometers away. I must keep up a good pace. The first 15 kilometers are uphill through a stony and not very fertile landscape.

The few small farms I pass are deserted and run down. Every now and then I pass a small plowed square between the stones. The sun is burning hot, and it must be about 35 degrees C in the shade. If one can find any shade, that is. Very few trees are tall enough to give any. I find it very hard going. I imagine that the landscape in Greece will be just as barren and deserted.

Through Grethe, Mary later told me:

'I too had to accept that nature was not always friendly. I too was accompanied by Michael. I realized that if I was to complete the tour I would need God with me and the help of St. Michael. Not least when I did not get enough to eat, which as you know happened sometimes.'

Five kilometers outside San Marco in Lamis we finally go downhill. I drag myself along. See a large church and plod down to it. Only to find it closed. Continue down through the town. Ask directions for a hotel and am guided even further down, outside the town in fact. Cannot find the hotel and think it foolish to go even further in the wrong direction. Turn back up, taking a different road. At last I find the town center. Here I come upon a sweet little church, Madonna della Grazie, which is of course the church on Mary's route.

After asking several passers-by, I have to face up to the fact that there are no hotels to be found before the next town, 3 kilometers further up. Although I can hardly drag myself along, I somehow find the strength to struggle on up the mountain. Reach Borgo Celano where there are several hotels. The first two are closed, but at the third one I finally get a bed.

* * *

Wake up to a small anniversary. I have now been underway ten weeks. If I could manage the first two long stages I must surely also be able to manage the last one across Greece. Leave Borgo Celano early, and after only 4 or 5 kilometers I find myself in San Giovanni Rotondo, the town of Padre Pio.

PADRE PIO

Padre Pio, 1887–1968, was canonized in 2002, only 34 years after he died.

He received the stigmata when he was only 24 years old, and he lived with them for 50 years. Time and again the doctors examined him but found no natural explanation for his constantly bleeding wounds. He suffered constant great pain but humbly accepted it.

The Catholic Church authorities were very skeptical of him and tried repeatedly to clip his wings. Forbade him to

---

talk about or to show his stigmata. Even attempted to have him transferred, but had to desist due to great popular outcry. Padre Pio was pained by the attitude of the Vatican towards him, but like Hildegard he never opposed the authority of the Church.

He performed several miracles, and was famous for his blunt advice. If those seeking advice were more curious than sincere, Padre Pio would send them away, telling them to come back when they were serious. He placed great faith in guardian angels, and he often recommended people to ask their guardian angel for help.

In a letter, he describes an episode with his own guardian angel: '*At times I feel that I am dying. Last Saturday I thought they were doing away with me. I did not know which saint to pray to, so I asked my guardian angel. After keeping me waiting for a while, he finally came to me. Flew about me, singing hymns to God with his angelic voice. Then it was the old story all over again: I reproached him bitterly for having kept me waiting for so long, as I had done nothing wrong. I had called him as I was in need of help. To punish him I refused to look him in the face. I wanted to run away, to flee from him. But the poor soul came to me – practically crying. He took hold of me, so I raised my eyes. I looked him straight in the eye and saw that he was full of regret.*'

Padre Pio writes further that the guardian angel answered him, '*... I am always near you, beloved youth. I always keep vigil over you with the devotion that has grown out of your thankfulness towards your heart's chosen one. My devotion to you will never die, not even when you die. I know that your noble heart beats for ever for the one we both love. You will cross every desert, every mountain to find Him. To see Him again ... and ask Him to free you quickly from the chains that* *bind you to your body ... You will have to wait a little longer. At the present He can only give you starlight, the scent of flowers, the melancholy of the harp and the caress of the breeze ...'*

Padre Pio Pilgrimage Church

Padre Pio's town has become a colossal tourist attraction. Every year more than 7 million people visit it. Earlier this summer the new church for Padre Pio was sanctified and it is very impressive. Can seat 7,000 visitors. It is designed by the Italian architect Renzo Piano. It is very pleasant, even with hundreds of visitors milling about. I discover many exquisite details, beautiful play of color and exciting spatial effects. Mary thinks that Padre Pio deserves it. *'He was a magnificent example,'* she says, *'and he had great life force.'*

The original church, which is dedicated to Mary and where Padre Pio was priest, is less than a stone's throw away. It radiates energy as if the fiery sermons of Padre Pio are still imprinted in the walls.

I like being here. After a time I sense Padre Pio coming through to me. He observes briefly that I too serve Mary. *'Stay with her,'* he says. *'She is the light of my life.'*

Later, the mass of tourists becomes obtrusive. I cannot take the hubbub, so I decide to move on.

Follow the main road east, straight to Monte Sant'Angelo. Up and down hill for the first 19 kilometers. Then the road climbs the last 5 or 6 kilometers up the mountainside to an altitude of 1,000 meters. It takes tremendous effort, not made any easier by the fact that again today there has not been a single café in more than 20 kilometers. No cool shade either.

At long last, the weather changes. A strong wind comes up and the gathering clouds filter the sunshine. I thank the wind for helping me.

Along the way, I talk with Mary about the phenomenon of hearing voices and disclaiming responsibility. I have heard of violent criminals insisting that they were obeying inner voices and that they could therefore neither be considered of sound mind nor fit for normal punishment. There are certain parallels. If I insist that I am not responsible for this tour because I have been acting under Michael and Mary's orders, then I am in the same position as the criminals.

It is quite clear to me that I and others who hear voices are fully responsible for our own actions. We cannot disclaim the responsibility. We must learn to distinguish between our own voice and inner voices. Regardless of which voice we choose to listen to, the choice is ours, and thus the responsibility too. We must always accept responsibility for our choices and actions.

Do not misunderstand me. I am not talking about distancing oneself from spiritual inspiration, but about integrating it. There is a goldmine of divine inspiration to be had.

Mary explains it to me.

She and Michael are on my model Axis. An intimacy in which she and Michael are part of me and I am also part of them. When I hear a voice, it will be my own voice, but the source of it lies in Mary and Michael. The more I work together with them, the more their voices will run through my intuition.

Monte Sant'Angelo comes into view. The town is built around an ancient shrine, St. Michael's cave. Wearily I take the last steps into the town. Past all the souvenir stalls which are shutting up because of the strong wind that is picking up. Walk straight into the Basilica Sanctuario San Michele Arcangelo. Descend a flight of steps to the grotto. It is teeming with people and a service is in progress.

THE SANCTUARY OF MONTE SANT'ANGELO (SAINT MICHAEL SHRINE)

In the 8th century tales were told of miracles here. The first one is supposed to have taken place in 490. A rich man from Spoleto was seeing to his cattle on the mountain. Suddenly his best bull disappeared. He searched for a long time and finally found the bull in a remote spot, kneeling before the entrance to a cave. Angrily he shot an arrow at the rebellious animal, but instead of hitting the bull, he shot himself in the foot. The occurrence worried him so much that he told the bishop of it. The bishop decreed three days of prayer. Towards evening on the third day the archangel Michael appeared to the bishop and spoke to him:

'I am the archangel Michael, and I am always in the presence of God. The cave is sanctified to me; I have chosen it. I am myself its attentive guardian ... The sins of man can be forgiven at the opening to the cave. Anything asked for here in prayer will be given to you. Go therefore to the mountain and dedicate the cave to the Christian religion.'

There are signs of earlier cult worship in the cave so I assume that this Christian myth has roots in that cult.

This is a very powerful place, and I can see why forgiveness could be found here. During the service, old memories come crowding back to me. Unfinished occurrences where I have behaved rudely. I pray for forgiveness, and it is as if my victims become shrouded in a golden divine glow. I let go of something and I am given something. The merciful gift of forgiveness.

The cave

After the service is over and the zealous verger has run about, telling people off and shushing them, I get a chance to bless the church. Go before the altar and am met by a joyful Michael. He puts his arms about me and says, '*You have done it! I am so glad that you came up here. Have a look around and then come back.*' I wander about. See among other things a figure of Michael and the dragon in a small niche in the rock. Finally I return to the altar. Michael steps back a little and a column of light rises up beside the altar. After a short time the column of light moves over to me and encloses me. Then it shrinks to a long thin spear which I will be able to use like St. Michael does.

Michael tells me that the ceremony is finished, and that I may find a hotel now. '*There is one on the left as you get back up to the street,*' he says. I climb all the steps and am surprised to see a hotel sign 20 meters off. 'Hotel Michael'. Perfect. They give me a room with a view to the coast far below.

Having written up my diary and had a rest, I go down to Mary's Church, Chiesa di Maria Maggiore. Here too there is a service in progress, so I go shopping instead. Come back later and have the place to myself. I bless it properly. Go before the raised altar. Mary receives me warmly and I try hard to restrain my expectations. After a short time a pink column of light rises up with Mary standing inside it. She herself becomes quite pink. She comes down to me with the column of light and enters me. She revolves around my central axis, and the pink column engulfs me. We stand like that for a long moment. Then I take St. Michael's spear of light and place it vertically through my heart. I do not know where that impulse comes from. Time passes and after a while Mary exclaims, *'The miracle has happened! Sit down and understand it.'*

For me, pink means roses, blood and the earth. Michael's light is like the sun's heavenly rays, piercing the rose and making it fertile.

'Yes,' says Mary. *'You are the rose of the sun. The fertilized flower. The flower of life.'*

The ceremony is concluded. Mary appears elevated and very happy. Joy slowly seeps through my body, through sore limbs and great tiredness. *'You may stay a day longer or you may go on.'* I thank her and leave the church. Look up at my hotel window and notice I am staying exactly halfway between the churches of Mary and Michael.

* * *

Choose to stay a day longer. Breakfast with an English couple who live in Portugal. The husband is an architect too, and tells me that I absolutely must see the Santa Maria di Siponto church down in Siponto. The lower storey dates from the 500s and the upper one from the Middle Ages. I am looking forward to getting down to Siponto, the ancient harbor of the Romans and the crusaders, and from where I guess Mary must have sailed.

Am in St. Maria Maggiore again. Go up and symbolically hug Mary and thank her for yesterday's ceremonies and miracle. Mary is happy, and pleased that I stayed. I go to Michael's grotto too. Sit down on a step and ask for forgiveness for several stupid actions. Michael grins and tells me to just go out and get on with it.

Later the same day I go back to St. Mary's. Ask Mary if there is anything I can do for her. I sense immediately that she wants me to look after Michael, but before she can put this into words Padre Pio comes trotting up to me, saying bluntly, 'Have I not told you to do your best?' I am speechless – and yet I am not surprised. This has been my motto for years, and I can only answer yes. 'Then go out into the world and do it!' he says in a peremptory voice.

The room is quite full, even though the church is empty. All those who have been in contact with me on my journey are present. Mary and Michael are among them. We seem to be celebrating the conclusion of a stage. I finally stand up, and as I turn to leave, Padre Pio gives me an encouraging pat on the shoulder.

* * *

My day of rest is over. Next morning I get up early. Yesterday was full of superb experiences, and I am expecting just as much from today.

Mary says that we must reach Siponto before twelve o'clock. Down the mountain I go, very steeply. A descent of 850 meters through countless hairpin bends. Wonderful views appear at each bend. A little rain to start with, but I am soon blessed with dry weather.

Keen to hear the sound of the sea, I make a detour along the coast. This takes time.

At last we reach Manfredonia. Mary advises me to take a bus out to Siponto but I just walk. This takes more time and it is 12.50 before I get there. Only to discover that it closed at 12.30. Very annoying! I should have listened to Mary when she said I had to be there by twelve o'clock.

Mary tells me that the church in Siponto is situated on the site of an old cult, which she has also blessed. She and John founded a small congregation here, which grew big and strong during the first centuries.

I say good bye to Mary, who then disappears down to the harbor.

I catch a bus to Foggia, and then take the Eurostar train to Brindisi. The railway runs along the coast, and on the way I imagine Mary setting out to sea. As far as I can judge, she will have to change boat at least three times. She says five though.

The station in Brindisi is so well situated that one only has to walk down the main street to get to the harbor. Here I buy a ticket for a ferry leaving an hour and a half later.

I now take time to welcome Mary. Go to the great harbor steps. Sense her ship coming in. Hand her down the gangway. Warm reunion. Past the great columns that were also there in Mary's day. Then, Mary had gone up into the town to stock up.

We continue up the street. A wedding couple drives past. Up into the square. Up to the column bearing a statue of Mary. Behind it the crusader building. There are a lot of young people who obviously use this as a meeting point. We visit the large church by the square.

Later on, we again walk together back down the great harbor steps. Mary's boat is now quite clearly visible to me. There are several farm animals aboard and a lot of goods. The boat has one large sail. We wave goodbye with a 'See you in Corfu!' People round about me must think I am mad, standing talking to empty

Column at Brindisi harbor – stood here in Mary's day too

space and waving to nothing. If they only knew...

On board the ferry, I ask Mary if she sometimes sailed by night. She rejects this categorically. One might have risked sailing in bright moonlight, with a starry sky, but it would have been very dangerous. The weather might easily change and then you would no longer be able to see the coast.

I stay on deck for a long time and enjoy the fresh air and the sight of all the lights along the coast.

PART III

TO EMBRACE THE EARTH

Greece

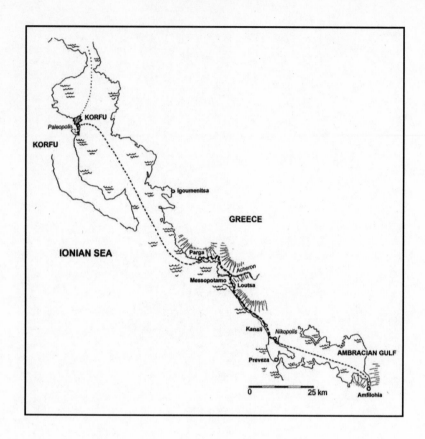

12

The Sea and the Great Sleeping Mother

Along the Ionian Sea

A persistent knocking on the door of my cabin tears me from my sleep. A voice calls that we are nearing the harbor. I have completely forgotten the time difference between Italy and Greece, so the night was an hour shorter than I thought. Hurry on deck and am in time to see the sail into Corfu. The fresh sea air feels good.

Presumably Mary landed on the northern part of the island and walked down to what was then the main town, not far from present-day Corfu. Mary does not expect me to do that. Just the short walk down onto the small peninsula, Kanoni, south of Corfu.

CORFU

Originally Corfu was inhabited by the Illyrians. Around 734 BC a group of political refugees from Corinth settled on the island. They founded a Corinthian colony, Palaeopolis, on the Kanoni Peninsula, which became an important economic trading factor on the Adriatic coast. In 229 BC Corfu became part of the Roman Empire, and in Mary's time, under the Romans, Corfu enjoyed numerous privileges.

Mary tells me that in her day the main town was Palaeopolis. It stood on the Kanoni Peninsula and was, culturally speaking, more Hellenic than Roman. A lively, pleasant culture. Here too Mary and John found followers. She confirms that she landed on the north side of Corfu, and then walked across the island.

When she left, Mary set sail from the old Palaeopolis harbor, and she wants me to bear that in mind tomorrow when I set sail myself. There is no need for me to go right out to the tip of Kanoni. She would rather I wander around the area that was once Palaeopolis.

Having passed several ruins, I find my way along some small lanes to the ruins of a Temple to Artemis, behind a small convent of Theodoric. There is not much left of the temple, which dates back to 590–580 BC, but it still makes a strong impression on me. It is filled with a special energy. Best preserved is an outdoor altar or sacrificial table on the east of the site, with a processional path to the temple.

ARTEMIS

Daughter of Zeus and twin sister of Apollo. Artemis presumably dates back to before the Hellenic Age and may be said to represent one side of the Great Goddess. Is often connected with help for women giving birth.

I make contact with Artemis. She says that she is Mary's parallel and that she possesses the same attributes. In Greek mythology Artemis and Apollo are twins, and Apollo can also be seen as a parallel to Michael. As they are presented as twins, I guess that there was a time when the two energies were of equal value. When the feminine and the masculine were in balance.

Medusa on the Temple of Artemis in Paleopolis

The Temple of Artemis also bears witness to another and more violent feminine power. The terrifying Gorgon (Medusa). In the town's archaeological museum I study the famous Medusa relief which originally adorned the gable end of the Artemis Temple. Medusa is pictured as a muscular woman with two snakes intertwining to form a belt, and two others twisting their way out of each side of her hair.

THE SYMBOLISM OF SNAKES

Snakes seem to have been a symbol of power since the time of the Goddess. A beautiful little statuette of a woman holding two snakes in her outstretched arms has been found on Crete. She is called the Snake Goddess, or the Snake Priestess. The statue is dated to the 14th century BC.

In Minoan culture there was nothing threatening about the figure, but there is no doubt that she was a powerful woman.

Snake Priestess

In several cultures snakes are associated with life after death. A deceased person was able to return from the realm of the dead in order to take nourishment. Or he might actually be reborn as a snake. From a practical point of view, snakes were useful for keeping mice away from sepulchers and palaces of the dead. I assume that snakes symbolized the connection to the realm of the dead, and that goddesses and priestesses were responsible for the connection.

I have also seen Artemis pictured with a cloak woven from snakes. I interpret this as a dignity bestowed upon her. The figure of Medusa testifies to a far more violent and belligerent femininity. Indeed Medusa is said to have turned to stone anyone who looked at her. Zeus could not quite control her and, in the end, according to myth, the hero Perseus cut off her head.

Artemis with her snake coat

Several Greek myths tell of masculine heroes defeating female monsters. There seems some suggestion that Greek culture wanted to settle up with an earlier powerful, female culture. The more innocent traits became integrated in the new culture, e.g. in the form of Artemis, while the more violent and engulfing traits were repressed.

Even though Mary has not asked me to, I still venture out to the tip of the Kanoni Peninsula to see the tiny monastery there. A powerful place, despite being a popular tourist attraction.

On my way back to Corfu, I venture into the park around Mon Repos. A delightful area in what used to be part of Palaeopolis. Follow a long path that leads through the park to a Doric temple. On the path a young German woman approaches me. Apparently, because of my hat, she thinks I am a park attendant.

She is a little afraid to walk alone in the large park. I must have seemed trustworthy because we walk to the temple together. We talk about the myths behind Artemis, Athena and Apollo, and together we walk back to town. I tell her about my journey, which she finds interesting, and we end up talking for several hours till she has to get a bus back to her hotel. I am not at all used to such long conversations. Usually I just exchange a few words with the people I meet. It feels like trying to use an old rusty chisel – slow work until the tool is honed. We could probably have continued the conversation, and this meeting with a nice woman could have developed into something more. But I realize that my guilty conscience would then have weakened the power of my pilgrimage, and I say a polite goodbye.

I am sure that Mary has had a hand in this, but I am not clear about her intentions. In any case, I have met a captivating example of femininity.

Back to my pilgrimage. I have understood that, in her time, Mary sailed from here to the town of Parga on the mainland. Today there are ferries to Igoumenitsa but not to Parga. I happen to hear, however, that some excursion boats sail that way. I find the travel bureau. There is actually a boat the next day. I quickly book a seat.

Early that evening I go for a walk in Corfu. Wonder whether I should go out to Palaeopolis and see Mary go on board. My first instinct is not to, but as I stand at the water's edge looking across to Palaeopolis, Mary says directly, '*Do me a favor and come and see me off.*'

It is getting late so I hurry across. Something feels urgent. It may be that I need to get to the monastery before eight o'clock. But when I want to turn right towards the monastery, Mary shakes her head. She wants me to turn left. I find myself at a Byzantine church, Sts Jason and Sossipatros. It is still open and turns out to be quite remarkable. Built partly with materials taken from the lost town.

Records show that Jason and Sossipatros brought Christianity to Corfu in the year 40 AD, and that they built the first Christian church on the island. They are said to have been pupils of Paul. If this is true, the two of them must have come to the island five or six years after Mary and John.

Mary says, before we even enter the church, that I am to bless it. As I sit there, a charismatic figure clad in black comes to me in a vision. It is John. He says, '*My name is IOANNIS; the disciple they say was loved by Jesus Christ.*' It is quite clear to me that I am to write his name in Greek. '*My appearance is more authoritative now than the last time we spoke, Hans, which is probably better suited to my high-flown manner of speaking,*' he says, laughing self-ironically, referring to our little controversy in Italy.

'*Yes, I also learnt something from that. This is my country. The area where I have lived most of my life and which I love. I quickly learnt to speak Greek, so I have had no problem mixing with and talking to the people here. I have been on the island several times.*'

Of Jason and Sossipatros, John says: '*They were also pupils of mine – perhaps even more than of Paul. But the extrovert drive that he possessed was rather more memorable than my fervor. Mary and I brought the Christian faith to Corfu. But it was Jason and Sossipatros who spread it.*'

'*Hans, I will accompany you and Mary in this guise for the rest of the journey and see to it that you are given the trials you are meant to have. You have passed the first one today. You resisted the temptation from the young woman, who was attracted by the divine power she felt through you.*'

It was lucky I had hurried, for the church is closing now. We go down to the quay and here I say goodbye to Mary. With seven or eight other people she boards a smallish boat full of corn, olive oil and other freight. '*I will meet you tomorrow in Parga,*' she says. '*See you.*'

* * *

At nine o'clock the next morning I leave on the tour boat with a party of tourists. It is a guided tour, so for a while I play at being an ordinary tourist. I sit in the bows and enjoy the fresh sea air. After sailing for three hours we land in Parga. Here I disembark. The rest of the party has a two-hour stop before going on to Paxos.

Though I have been relaxing and enjoying the sail, I am now strangely unfocused. Can only think of finding a cheap bed for the night. Look casually here and there. Enter a side street. Find a boarding house and get a room. It is not what I was hoping for, but it is after all only for the one night. See to a few things.

Then suddenly I realize that I have not met Mary at the harbor as we arranged. And that is of course the reason why my hunt for a hotel was so unfocused and unguided.

I hurry down to the harbor, and suddenly Mary is there in front of me. '*Here I am,*' she says. We stroll over to a jetty and sit down. I ask Mary what I must see here. She points out to sea and answers that there is only the small chapel on the little island in front of the harbor.

Later that afternoon I swim to the island that protects the harbor. As a matter of fact I have not brought swimming trunks with me, but so what – a pair of black underpants should do. I don't believe they look much different from swimming trunks. On the beach a couple of women giggle at me. I ignore them. Later I discover that underpants like mine are on offer up in the town.

In the middle of the island there is a well and a small chapel. Mary's energy is very clear here, and I stand there and bless it all – in my underpants!

In the evening I go to see the newer church up in the town. Mary would like me to start from here tomorrow morning and adds teasingly, '*We cannot have you swimming about in your underpants any more, you know.*'

That night I have a dream:

A team of us have to find a name for Peter Dawkins' new book. We are sitting by a large reservoir. The water level is low, but suddenly, in a split second, the level rises nearly a meter. Exciting, though the thought of the colossal powers behind this – powers which can make the water rise so quickly, and which could so easily drown us – is a bit frightening.

* * *

Wake up the next morning with the remains of a headache. Last night in the restaurant they served us a sturdy dram before our meal, and stupidly I could not resist it. Today I will have to suffer the consequences. When I tune in at the church, Mary says frostily that she hopes this will be the last time that she sees me in such a miserable state this journey.

The instructions for the route are clear: '*Go out to the main road and follow it to the Necromantio.*'

The moment I get onto the road, I am overwhelmed by the beauty of the landscape. The road runs along a mountainside that slopes down into the sea. Crested waves roll majestically onto the sharp rocks where they are mercilessly ripped apart with a hollow roar. All around the horizon, islands jut up out of the water. Looking like teenagers running away from the safe mainland. Inland the mountains rise in great heavy sweeps. One after the other. Higher and higher. Grandiose and massive. There are few trees, and bare rock dominates the picture, like the naked skin of the mountains. Nearby, beautifully scented bushes flower along the roadside. I attempt defining the quality of this landscape, and it strikes me that it is like the body of a gigantic woman – a woman asleep, perhaps a mother.

The road is wide, with very little traffic. Good conditions for a talk with Mary. While we talk, it dawns on me that Greece – or more precisely the ancient Hellas – marks a decisive cultural change away from the Egyptian and Minoan cultures. Earlier, fertility was fundamentally linked with femininity and was a significant factor in the first few thousand years of farming.

Worship of the Goddess of life, germination and harvest was crucial. Contact with the realm of the dead and the world of the spirits also lay deep in the ground and was thus the domain of the Goddess. In the new era, people were less preoccupied with the past and permanence and more interested in the future and expansion. Slowly the Goddess, and therefore women in general, had their powers taken from them. Finally, the societal powers of women also disappeared, i.e. the connection with the world of their ancestors, and the contact with the dead which was kept up in palaces of the dead and other such places where oracles could be contacted. Oracles had until then been the Goddess's domain, and the judgments of the oracles were of decisive importance in public as well as in private life. Now, male priests began to take over the power of these oracles.

Some of the souls from the cult of the Goddess stayed tied to her sites of worship. Much grievance and pent-up anger was entrenched in them, emotions which are still latent in the Greek landscape – the Great Sleeping Mother.

After a while Mary suggests that we talk about my dream. So we do. Some things I understand, others not. Mary helps me see more clearly. I have followed several courses given by the Englishman Peter Dawkins and through him have learnt of landscape chakra systems, angels and temples. So when Peter appears in a dream, I am sure there is a connection to the landscape temple at which I have arrived. The name of the book comes to me easily: *The Great Sleeping Mother*.

This must also be the title of this new stage of my pilgrimage. The second part of the dream, with us sitting by a large pool presumably connected to a great hydro-electric plant, carries a warning. The water, which I connect with femininity, rises violently. Unimagined powers are contained in it, and it is not to be taken lightly. One might easily drown in it. In other words, I am facing the Great Mother – the Goddess – and I must be wary, for she is extremely powerful.

I see the Goddess as the human image of a ground-energy that I call 'Mother Earth'.

Understanding the Virgin Mary – the great mother figure of the Christian faith – is one thing, but understanding and meeting the very Mother of the Earth is something else again. From the very beginning I have had an expectation that this voyage in feminine waters would also take me past some of Mother Earth's sacred sites. Perhaps this is due to happen on this stage.

I arrive in Messopotamo and go up to the Necromantio – the Palace of the Dead. The antique temple ruins stand at the top of a hill, on the banks of the legendary River Acheron. Here lie the remains of the Mycenaean stone walls with their enormous, irregular but finely jointed blocks of stone.

THE PALACE OF THE DEAD

The complex in Messopotamo is a palace of the dead similar to the palace on Knossos – only on a smaller scale. I read that in this area there are buildings dating right back to the 13th century BC, possibly even further. This corresponds to the period of transition from the Minoan culture on Crete to the Mycenaean one on the mainland.

In the palace of the dead, bodies were embalmed or cremated, and the bereaved could contact the dead through priesthood. The entrance is built in the characteristic zigzag, which was supposed to keep out evil spirits and is thought to be a sort of labyrinth.

I have been very interested in classical labyrinths and their history, and I understand the word 'labyrinth' as a name for one of the first palaces of the dead.

The oracle here was revered as highly as the one in Delphi. According to mythology, the oracle stood at the entrance to Hades, the realm of the dead. To get to it, you

---

had to be ferried across the River Acheron. Through the oracle you could ask for advice and guidance from dead ancestors or members of your family.

At the Necromantio, answers from the oracles were delivered in an underground hall. This hall is preserved and, in contrast to other Greek temples, it has curved rib vaults – which disproves the belief that load-bearing vaults were invented by the Romans. The hall is from the 4th century BC. It is the main attraction here and is still very powerful.

The Hall of Oracles

As I stand there trying to sense how the hall was used in the past, a figure of a woman suddenly appears at the other end of the room and looks at me sharply. I find this unnerving and quickly go back up above ground.

I talk with Mary a bit and she asks why I do not question the woman about what she is doing. I pull myself together and go back down into the hall again. I address the figure, who was apparently a priestess, and ask her to tell me what they did in this room when it was functioning. She agrees to answer. Tells me that they were a link between the bereaved and the dead. Many people came here to speak with the dead. Sometimes, after having gone through a process of fasting and purification, they themselves would sense the answers. But more often the answers were given through the priestesses. *'Just as when you talk with a clairvoyant,'* she says, and I realize that I have been thinking of the answers that I have been given at home through Grethe. The woman has been able to read my thoughts. I quickly switch off. I ask her whether their position gave them power. She replies that they had no power and that they had to live off whatever the visitors brought as gifts, which was not much. I thank her and commend her to God. I go back out and leave here, feeling that I have been in contact with something that was not entirely good. Go to a café and write.

As we walk Mary fills me in: the woman in the underground hall had been a priestess there. She herself had said this had been about 500 years BC, but Mary says that must be taken with a pinch of salt. It could be 200 years either side. Mary adds that the woman was in fact the foremost priestess here, and that the renown and heyday of the Necromantio was very much due to her skill. I ask whether Mary is a spiritual mother for the priestess. The answer is yes, but that the priestess does not seem to recognize Mary's energy. She keeps to another energy. One which I, for some reason, understand as ht eenergy of Gaia.

GAIA

In Greek mythology, Gaia is the nearest we get to a 'Mother Earth'. She was born of Chaos and belongs to the world of the gods before Zeus. Her descendants are often enemies of the gods surrounding Zeus. In recent decades 'Gaia' seems to be gradually becoming accepted in Western culture as a name for Mother Earth.

Previously I have always seen Gaia as a positive symbol. Now I am not so sure. I get the feeling that there is something – some unknown force – lurking nearby. Maybe the dark priestess from the Necromantio is following us.

During my research last year, I visited the ancient oracle cave on Mount Parnassus above Delphi and met Gaia. I sensed something threatening there and it frightened me badly. I could not work out what it was, but for some reason I connected it with Gaia. I have often thought of it since, and I must confess that it is not without serious misgivings that I plan to visit the cave again when we get to Delphi. I am quick to picture the dark priestess I just have met at as one of Gaia's priestesses. A moment later, I am imagining myself on a secret mission, on my way to have a showdown with Gaia at Parnassus. A showdown with the dark feminine powers from the time of the Goddess which still linger, blocking the way for new powers.

Even though I repeatedly try to rid myself of this thought, I cannot shake it off. And I am not the first to have been sent on this errand. There are several earlier examples. First and foremost Apollo.

APOLLO

Apollo was the god of music, medicine and prophecies, but he was also the divine archer and bringer of light. Presumably he came to Greece with the great Indo-European migrations. According to myth, he was fully grown by the age of four days and even then filled with invincible might. First he decided to kill Python, the snake who had pursued his mother. With lightning speed he flew to Mount Parnassus where the dreadful animal lived. Until this moment, nobody had dared lift a hand against Python, who was spreading dread and crop failure everywhere. Apollo found the snake on the mountain where it lived beside the shrine of the Earth Mother. The fight began and raged back and forth down the mountain. Finally Python rose up in his frightful might, poised to deal the lethal blow to Apollo. Faster than lightning, Apollo shot one of his golden arrows and hit Python right between the eyes. With a terrifying bellow the snake rose up to his full height and fell down with a crash that shook the mountain. Python was dead.

Python was, however, the son of Gaia, Mother Earth, and the gods did not let this murder pass unheeded. Apollo had to go into exile to cleanse himself before he was allowed to return as the new lord in Delphi.

A masquerade begins. This may sound ridiculous, but I feel as if I am caught in the role of a hero – who once again, in the spirit of Apollo, has to defeat the old dragon of Mount Parnassus.

In fact I am so caught up in it that I start feeling the spying eyes of the dark priestess everywhere I go. I am even afraid to write down events and plans in my diary in case I give away my 'mission'. I decide that from now on I will call the priestess 'K'.

As if this was not bad enough, Mary gives me to understand that my contact with her may become unclear, or even completely cut off, until I have been in the cave on Mount Parnassus. We will not be able to discuss anything until afterwards.

That is almost the worst thing that could happen. I will have to find my way by relying completely on my own intuition.

The road leads up across a mountain and right out to the coast. It is a relief to be by the open, cleansing sea. It is mid-September. The tourist season is over. There is nobody on the beach and the houses are emptying. I enjoy walking alone in the brisk wind on the beach.

John asks me to make up a prayer for those in, on or by the sea. I am surprised by this, but I meditate on it, and at one point it seems to me that I hear sirens or nymphs singing. I realize that the sea is inhabited by angels too, each reigning over his own domain. Ask God to give strength to the angels.

* * *

Find private rooms. Next morning my hosts invite me to breakfast. The wife does all the work and then sits down in the background. Dutifully she hands my payment for the room to her husband, who seems to do nothing. They only speak Greek so we gesticulate a lot. I think they understand that I am on a long pilgrimage, but they completely fail to see why I do not simply take a bus.

So far, Mary is still coming through clearly. I gather that I am to follow the coast as far as possible. John is here too. On the way Mary explains that the sea is vital for the survival of humanity. If the ice on the North Pole melts and the sea loses some of its cold–warmth polarity, thus weakening the currents, it may cause the poles to shift. As a consequence, the Earth's water masses may become rearranged and even the shape of the land may be altered. The consequences for humanity will be unimaginable. *'Look at Mars,'* Mary says.

'The sea is important – vitally important!' she stresses. John adds that this was why he asked me to compose a prayer for all in, on or by the sea. For all living creatures. I am working on that prayer!

As I walk up the hill, a car pulls up in front of me. It is my hosts from last night, wanting to give me a lift to Preveza. I suspect they are making this drive solely for my sake. Once again I try to explain that on a pilgrimage one is supposed to walk. They, however, cannot bear to think of me walking in this heat. It is very kind of them, and I understand their view. Why torment yourself in the sun when you could take a bus? But I thank them politely and reject their offer. It would feel like betraying something in me – and Mary – if I, for no reason, went by car where she walked.

A bit further on is a roadside fruit stall. I want to buy a couple of apples. The man throws in a couple of bananas and will accept no payment at all.

Mary impresses on me: *'Follow the sea.'* And so at Kanali I turn down towards the sea again. On the way there I realize that I need to say my prayer to the sea before we can leave it. I go down to the beach, gather some water in my hands and intone my prayer saying: 'In the name of God I bless the sea ...' I recite the rest of the prayer and walk on. Mary stops me, saying that the prayer was not very well phrased. Among others things, I had blessed the sea in the name of God. She says that I have taken this privilege without having obtained God's permission.

Then something happens. It feels like being switched into an intercom. A voice comes through, and though I cannot tell which plane it is coming from, I am in no doubt that it is a divine voice. *'A prayer is a powerful tool. It is important that it is addressed correctly, for instance to me. The object of the prayer must be clear. What the problem is, and what solution you are asking for. And it must come from your heart.'* A sort of explanatory note is added: *'Not so much beating about the bush. A prayer must be heartfelt and crystal clear.'*

When I next reach the sea, I try to amend my prayer. It is apparently still not sincere enough, for the divine voice tells me that a prayer not spoken from the heart will not be heard. No matter how many times you say it. God hears through your heart.

I am confused about the next leg of the journey. Mary then says that she in fact sailed from Kanali, round the present day Preveza to the old city of Nicopolis.

I cross a neck of land and reach the ruined town of Nicopolis overlooking the Ambracian Gulf. The gulf is connected to the Ionian Sea by a narrow strait running between Preveza and Action. Under the Pax Romana, Nicopolis was an important town of commerce.

NICOPOLIS

The town was founded by the Roman emperor Octavian after his naval victory over Anthony and Cleopatra at Action in 31 BC.

The inhabitants of the surrounding provinces were forced to populate the town, which grew quickly, had its own coinage and held great games every fourth year. From the 3rd century AD onwards the town suffered violent earthquakes and was invaded by, among others, the Goths and Vandals. By the year 1000 AD the town was deserted.

Mary must have arrived in the middle of a period of intensive building. The Odeon and the grand theater were presumably under construction. Mary tells me that she stayed in Nicopolis before sailing on to Amphilohia.

Nowadays you cannot sail from Nicopolis, so I have to go into the nearby town of Preveza to find further transport.

Later that evening I catch a bus to Athens. I can hardly lift my legs after walking more than 40 kilometers, and I enjoy being driven.

The harbor front in Amphilohia

Night falls. We drive along the water's edge on the east bank of the fjord with the moon's reflection sparkling beautifully on the water. Get off the bus in Amphilohia, find a hotel and walk down to the idyllic harbor front and meet Mary.

I am relieved to have got this far and to have found Mary again. Towards midnight I take supper in one of the harbor restaurants. Mary has almost materialized and it is as if she is sitting right next to me. The situation is so realistic that without thinking I automatically ask her what she will eat. We both burst out laughing, and for the whole midnight hour we sit there fooling about, teasing each other and also talking seriously. I forget myself several times and speak aloud to Mary. Notice the other guests gaping so, giggling a bit, I pipe down.

Mary allows me to name a dessert after her: 'The Virgin Mary's Favorite Pudding'. Soured goat's milk in a bowl, topped with dripping honey. Half an oblong nut sliced and strewn over the honey, with the other half placed in the middle of the bowl.

An unforgettable dinner.

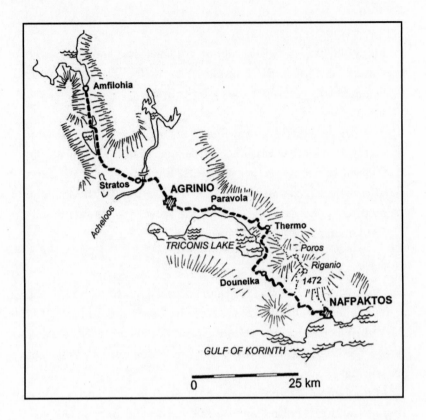

13

The Sea and the Challenge

By Land – Western Greece

The day is getting noticeably warmer. A last wisp of cool wind
blows in from the Ambracian Gulf as I step out into the morning
light. I sense that I need to complete my prayer about the sea
before continuing on my way and losing all contact with it. The
gulf is connected to the sea by a narrow strait. I go down to the
esplanade jutting out into the bay. Slowly the prayer takes form
in my mind:

'Dear God,

I have a prayer to you about the sea. The interconnected waters of the Earth. Mankind's basis for existence. Their balances and their polarities are shifting. Ocean currents seem to be changing.

I beg you with all my heart, through the power of your mercy, to restore the balance between cold and warm water in the sea. To strengthen the polarities that makes the water flow. To strengthen the angels and all other beings of the sea who help to create and give life to the world of the sea and its fundamental energy systems.

Thank you, God. Amen.'

The gulf is really more a lake than an ocean, and I wonder if the same applies to a lake as to the sea. Mary interrupts and says that a lake brings to mind the amniotic fluid of the womb. Lake water is the amniotic fluid of the great landscape-mother, safe and reassuring.

I understand the allusion to amniotic fluid, and I can see that there is an internal influx and overflow from the lake into the sea. The 'amniotic fluid' carries the message of life on land, into the sea. This message is important to the sea. If the 'amniotic fluid' is polluted, there will be no life-giving messages to the organisms of the sea.

According to the map, there should be a lake a few kilometers from here. I look everywhere, but there is no lake. Everything is dried out or drained. In several places farmers have dug holes 2 or 3 meters deep to get water for their irrigation systems. The next largish lake on the map is still there, but the water level has fallen drastically. Tractors with water pumps are working far out in the flatlands to get enough water to irrigate. All this irrigation must cause enormous evaporation, and I am afraid there must be very little chance that the area can expect an equal amount of rainwater in return.

Mary encourages me to say a prayer about the water of the lakes. But it is not very good. Something seems missing. It goes like this:

'Dear God,
I have a prayer to you about our lakes.

Many lakes are shrinking, the water being drawn off for irrigation.

I pray you, help mankind to understand that lakes are wells for life and not for consumption. Help man to guard the water of the lakes for the cool of the morning and the warmth of the evening.

I pray you, help the angels and other beings of the lakes to resist the pressure of man and to restore the beautiful energy systems of the lakes.

Thank you, God. Amen.'

Through Grethe, Mary later said:

'The water of the Earth is closely connected to the great mother and has therefore long been treated negligently, not honorably. We spirits are very conscious of this.

'Our help is continually being sent down to improve the situation of the waters, as human initiatives are being made in ignorance of what water actually is.' Mary's eyes fill with tears, and she says that she knows very well that there are icons in her image that can shed tears, and that of course tears show that the water element in man overflows both in sorrow and in joy. *'Earthly pain is connected to the element of water, the fundamental and life giving element. As it is written: "The spirit of God moved upon the face of the waters." Water existed from the very beginning of creation and so is fundamental to all life. A cleansing of the waters would be an enormous and demanding task. The only answer is for each individual human being to safeguard the waters*

225

with due reverence and honor, and to avoid polluting it when at all possible.

'Great, devastating pollution is taking place ... Running water is being blocked. Dams are being built. Canals are being constructed. Watercourses are being straightened to suit man instead of letting man and water co-exist in the age-old context wherein man fetches, honors and gives thanks for the water. This will take time.

'You will continue your research in this area also. The more you understand and acknowledge the water and the work of the water spirits, the more this will help you to reach an inner humility. A humility and awe towards everything life-giving.'

From Amphilohia I walk south – straight into the sun. I expect to have to find a small road along the left side of the valley. There is one there, but it seems to lead up into the mountains. I find others but they do not appear to lead anywhere, so I stick to the main road.

I am more or less in constant doubt. I reproach myself for not trying to take any of the side roads. At one stage I try going up to a small town, but it looks quite wrong so I go back. Other possibilities do not seem right either. Or maybe I am just too chicken. Furthermore, I have not been able to contact Mary since Amphilohia.

It is unbearably hot. About 40 degrees C. Every 4 or 5 kilometers I have to go indoors and drink half a liter of water and sit in the shade to cool down.

I am afraid that I may have to walk more than 40 kilometers to find somewhere to stay tonight. On top of this, I have to go along the edge of a main road, watching out for the traffic hurtling by.

After 33 kilometers of insufferable heat, I arrive at the ruined town of Stratos. In the 1st century BC Stratos had just suffered a cruel fate. It had been on the losing side in the battle of Action. A new town, Nicopolis, was built, and to populate it, most of the inhabitants of Stratos were forcibly transferred there. Stratos may therefore have been a bit of a ghost town when Mary was here, despite its strategic position at a ford with access to a large lake. The lake has in fact been lost recently, due to the construction of a great dam. A great deal of life seems to have disappeared together with the lake.

I make several enquiries about hotels or rooms, but no luck. So I must tackle another 12 kilometers. I will have to put on speed if I am to reach Agrinio before dark. It is tough going, but I manage it. Probably the hardest day of the whole tour. A long trek in unbearable heat. Moreover not a single church was open today, and Mary was absent. Very odd!

I have problems with my shoes again. I had them mended in Assisi, but one sole is practically worn away and the old hole keeps growing larger. Must do something about it. Decide to stay an extra day in Agrinio for shoe repairs.

* * *

Next morning I wake up a year older. Fifty-five years old. I celebrate with breakfast in the hotel. Many Greek hotels do not serve breakfast, so bread and marmalade have to be dug out and are a somewhat dry feast.

Kirstin phones and sings 'Happy Birthday' to me. Very nice.

The next hour I carry out all my errands. Three shops away, there is a cobbler and he mends my shoes which will be ready tomorrow. Have a haircut and do my washing.

The following morning I collect my shoes. Beautiful new soles. I set out happily, going east. On the outskirts of the town, the road forks. A voice that sounds like Mary says to follow the north fork. I know that our route passes through a town beginning with 'Ka-', and as the northern road does in fact lead to a town starting with 'Ka-', I calmly turn onto it. The voice says that it would be good if I could wait to look at the map until we reach the first town. That is OK by me. A little later there is a signpost saying '110 km to Ka ...' I am still not worried; the sign is dented and a decimal point must have got lost: 11 km seems about right. After a short distance, however, the road turns due north and I begin to sense that something is seriously wrong. So the map comes out after all and I find that the town beginning with 'Ka-' really is 110 kilometers north of here. In other words, completely wrong. Have to turn back. Get back on track.

I have been led astray by a voice sounding like Mary's and I do not doubt that it is the priestess from the Necromantio causing mischief by speaking to me in Mary's voice. I order her to stay away from me and I focus on finding the right way. Not long after this I pass through a small town that starts with 'Ka-'.

Halfway between Agrinio and Thermo is the Trichonis Lake, to the north of which is a small town, Paravola. I have been there before and felt then that it was very much a 'Mary town'. Just outside Paravola, the energy of the landscape changes. As the lake comes into view, a mountaintop just north of the town catches my attention. I sense that there must be a Heart-angel up there. The angel and its fire-force stand in polarity to the water-force of the lake. Right between the lake and the mountain is a hill, a small mountain really, around which the town of Paravola is built. I sense that the energy of the hill represents the union of the two forces, Fire and Water, and may therefore be thought of as their offspring, the golden child. A blessed and glorious place.

The Heart-angel says that we can talk and write openly. The angel's heart-energy seems to form a glass dome over the whole area. I get the impression that it would be good to spend two nights in this energy.

Suddenly I feel Mary taking my arm, saying, '*I am here. It is me, Mary. The mother of Jesus.*' She repeats this quickly three times, and now I dare to trust that the voice is genuine. It sounds heartfelt and warm, which helps to convince me.

We have to climb the hill. I pass a side road with steps and sense that Mary wants to go up them, though I walk past ten paces before I submit. OK, we will try that way, then; I begin to climb the steps. Of course the steps lead straight up the hill. It could not be more direct. I cross to the most easterly part of the hill where there is a churchyard and a small church. I walk round the church and sit down on a brick seat against its south wall. The sun has warmed the wall and it is a warm, cozy place. In front of me are graves with large marble sarcophagi. Small glass frames display photos of the deceased. The place is dotted with vases of freshly picked flowers. An oak tree has dropped a great number of acorns still cradled beautifully in their open husks. One can feel this place is sacred. We are in the middle of Boykatio, an ancient temple area. I prepare myself.

'*How did you get on?*' Mary asks tenderly, and I pour out all my troubles. Then lose myself in the view over the lake and the mountains behind it. It is enchanting. Suddenly sense that John, Michael and Mary are all present. Am told that I am to be purified, but that there is something I must know first.

Mary and Michael are in front of me. Michael enters me and we fuse. Then Mary enters me and envelops both me and Michael's light with her rose-colored aura. Mary, Michael and I are one. John is left standing alone like a polarity missing its opposite. I barely have time to think this strange, before a shining white female figure appears in front of John. I can see no details; she is just shining and pure. I wonder if she is the one that I am to install on Mount Parnassus.

I seem to see unfriendly eyes, watching us. I remark on this but am just told that we are to carry on with the ceremony.

We prepare for the purification.

I pray for cleansing fire from above and water from below. The fire that usually licks gently over me has become a violent sea of fire spreading out far around me. In the same way the water from below has become a rough sea. I am shaken through several times as I stand with my arms outstretched in the shape of a crucifix. The eyes I have felt watching us are swallowed up in the ocean of fire. Suddenly all my muscles relax. The purification is finished and I can lower my arms. All is peaceful and I notice that I am now standing between Mary and Michael. See myself as the tallest. Am ashamed and change the image so that I become the shortest. Am told that it does not matter at all. I thank God. The ceremony is completed. I can move on.

Once out of town, Mary tells me that the priestess actually caught up with us while we were eating and chatting by the lake in Amphilohia. The love in us was very obvious and 'K' caught our scent. She has been following us all the way from the coast, noticing that I repeatedly did not obey Mary's instructions. She quickly found a way to exploit this. Mary says that my little slip-ups were not important. The main thing was that I found my way back to the trail each time.

I promise Mary to stop at the first hotel I find. We come across one a few kilometers later, not far from the lake. In the early evening I go for a walk to see a temple ruin marked on the map. It turns out to be 3 or 4 kilometers away, up in the mountains.

I get a good way up and discover that all my helpers are with me. Cozy. It is as if we are all on an outing. At the ruins I see a female figure. I greet her and introduce us. Ask who she is. She seems to answer, 'Aphrodite'. I cannot understand that. 'Are you not Artemis?' I ask. She is not. I wonder about this. The ruin is in a thorn thicket, and as I have bare legs I cannot force my way through. Instead I sit down and breathe in the cool evening air and enjoy the beautiful view. The sun is low and the clouds mirror themselves in the lake in a multitude of yellow and orange colors. Am about to go down when Mary asks whether I do not have more questions for the angel. I do, and again I try to find out who she is.

'You are Nike, are you not?' *'No, Hans, can you not see that I am Aphrodite?'* and she gives a grin so recognizable that I gasp, 'But you are Mary!'

Mary goes up to her. They stand back to back, and I realize

that they are two sides of the same person. I burst out, 'But you are an angel!' Mary answers, *'Yes, I am the universal mother of the souls of the angels.'* This takes a little time to absorb. Does this mean that Mary is mother of the souls of both angels and human beings? 'But why do you appear as Aphrodite?' I ask. *'Because I feel like it,'* Mary answers with a grin. All my companions laugh. All the way back down, I ask about Mary's double role. Mary answers, *'There is no duality. Human beings are also angels. Did you not think I was with you when you were an angel?'* I had not thought about it. I see now that an angel also becomes incarnate in a form – a body of energy – suited to the assignment in which it is to work. In parallel with the physical body of humans. *'Therefore it is important that man learns to speak with angels. Ultimately we are all one,'* she says.

It is a warm and peaceful evening. I forget all about my tiredness and wander down to an idyllic lake pavilion where I drink a glass of lemonade with a load of lovesick youngsters. The air is full of romance; even two turtles are caught by the mood and mate.

* * *

That night it rains and next morning sees the odd shower. Start off without coffee and food. So far I have always had a chance to put my wet weather gear on before it actually starts to rain. Now my luck runs out. First one drop, then two, and in five minutes it is pouring. I run 20 meters to a tree to put on my rain kit, but I am already soaked. Moreover my shoes and clothes are getting heavily splashed with mud under the tree. I plod dejectedly along the last few kilometers to Thermo. The roadside ditch is full of water and I rinse off the worst of the mud before going into town.

The Heart-angel's 'glass dome' seems to have shrunk, so Thermo is sometimes outside the area where I can count on contact with Mary.

Find a hotel in Thermo. Late that afternoon the rain stops and I go out to see the old town ruins.

ANTIQUE THERMO

A large building complex with stoas 200 meters long, large leveled areas, an excavated pool filled with fresh water and many remains of the buildings. Apollo is a central figure here. He has his own temple, the earliest phase of which dates back to approximately 580 BC. There is also a temple to Artemis.

The Pool in Thermo

Mary says that the area was already falling into ruin when she was here. The Romans did not think it of much importance.

In the Artemis temple there was a priestess whom Mary got on well with. Even the priests in the Apollo temple were quite friendly.

In the archaeological digs next to the Apollo temple an even deeper layer has been uncovered. Prehistoric buildings that have not yet been dated. Some of the remains have lovely oval shapes, bringing to mind Malta and the buildings from the time of the Goddess.

As I leave, the rain sets in again. And thunder. I hurry home.

Back in my hotel room I see a news story on TV about a man who was driving his car and ran into a bear somewhere. I do not understand what they are saying, but I am sure that it is quite near here. Perhaps on the mountain which I have to cross the next day. What shall I do if I meet a bear? I am getting scared.

* * *

Next morning I am up early. I have forebodings about today's walk. I have to cross a mountain and it may turn out to be a long, deserted and dangerous journey. Have a light breakfast, pack and am ready to start just after eight. In the meantime the sky has become darker. Almost as black as night. The clouds are torn by a flash of lightning. The wind picks up. Buckets and sheets of corrugated iron are blowing about the yard. The clouds look threatening. So threatening that I decide to wait half an hour and see what happens. Ten minutes later the skies open and there is a formidable storm. By now a gale is blowing and, had I been out, I myself and everything in my rucksack would have been soaked through. It is all too much and I decide to stay put a day longer. The storm rages for three hours. It would have been ghastly out there.

Fall asleep and dream:

Am walking in an arid landscape with somebody else – and yet alone. There is a flock of sheep. Get close to the flock and a mother ewe prepares to attack. I wave my arms at it and it draws back. Then I see that it is guarding several lambs hiding in the sand behind it. My attention shifts. I wonder if there are any rams among the sheep. See one poking its head up out of the sand. I walk towards it, waving my arms. It backs off and digs itself into the sand. The whole flock actually manages to survive in the arid landscape by staying just below the surface, burrowing their way through. All you see are bulges in the sand until they poke their heads up. A large ram does just that. It gives me a push, and I discover that I am standing in the middle of the flock, and that the other rams are now coming up out of the sand too. They are surrounding me and can now exert their strength. They are stronger than me and I am in trouble.

Wake up. The dream seems to give a realistic picture of the situation.

I am seen as a threat to the mother animals guarding their young. At the end I get shut in by the rams. I am at the mercy of the males.

Early that afternoon I go down to the town square. Have a cappuccino, am restless, and so decide to go out to the temple ruins again. Clouds are scurrying across the sky. Enter the museum, where I meet the guard, who only speaks a few words of English. Still, I think I manage to explain that I am on a walk and where I am going. We have a little laugh. I ask him if I may go into the fenced-off area with the prehistoric digs. He asks me to wait a few minutes till the other visitors have gone. When they are out of sight I am allowed in.

In Artemis's temple, Artemis herself comes to towards me. She tells me to note that her temple is the first one within the north-east town gate. Visitors would first honor the maternal and feminine element which ruled everything in nature. Then they went on to the Apollo temple and prayed for something specific – like good performance in sport. There was a good balance between the two forms of energy. The prehistoric ruins fascinate me with all their organic shapes. In some places, I can see that later temples have been built on top of the remains of the old walls. While I am contemplating these walls, a voice emanates from them and I sense the presence of an energy-being. '*I am Gaia. I ruled here in the days of the Goddess,*' it says. We begin to converse. She asks me to note how her culture has been buried and how everything has turned out. She has had to suffer this for nearly three thousand years. She sounds disheartened. She is keen to hear about the new female power. I am a bit wary and only dare tell her that, as I see her, she is whitish and very intense. This conversation changes my idea of Gaia. Now she says it was good that I gave up the fight and I realize that I have been thinking of her as an adversary – separate from myself. Probably due to the frightening experience I had the last time I visited the cave on Mount Parnassus. This is quite a paradox as I have included Mother Earth in much of what I have been doing.

I honor Mother Earth and I ought to respect the work that Gaia has done.

I cannot stop myself asking her whether, through this whole era of male dominance, she has not wanted to overturn this dominance and regain her honor and dignity. She has, many a time. 'Yes.' I say. 'Old combatants will continue to fight old feuds. It is time for change. Time for new forces to take up the fight.' That ends up sounding like an untimely manifesto, and I can see that it is stilted and badly expressed. I have only just accepted that I must honor and respect Gaia and here I am already in the process of dethroning her. '*I am glad that you gave up the fight. Even so, you will be given a small test when you get to the cave on Mount Parnassus,*' Gaia finishes.

Dark clouds are scudding towards us. They are heavy with rain. I leave the ruins and head for town. Feel the first drops and start running. Kind people give me a lift, saving me from the cloudburst. I hurry into a café and sit with some locals to watch the storm. Lightning flashes right above us, and the rain and the wind grow stronger. Another rainstorm. It is bucketing down. A

Dark clouds over Thermo

repeat of this morning. The streets become rushing rivers and nobody ventures out.

Once more, rain and thunder force me back to my room. Despite my talk with Gaia, I still cannot shake off certain skepticism towards her. Even back on Mount Disiboden Mary told me that everything that happens to me happens on two levels. I feel that there is something I have not understood, and that I am reacting like an old-fashioned male – with confrontation. I must accept that the way forward is through unity, not division. Ultimately, unification in God. This may be why I have to stay here.

Gaia also said something about waters on Earth being compa-rable to the blood of the human body. Life-giving blood. Rain falls, fertilizes the earth, fills the reservoirs, cleanses, is gathered into burns, into streams, into lakes, into rivers, finally to join the sea. Here the water evaporates, and the process starts all over again.

Bored, I turn on the TV and happen on an old English film about elves. About Sir Arthur Conan Doyle and two little girls who see elves. The film is about whether it is possible to see supernatural beings, and whether this can be proved with photography. At the end of the film the magician Houdini comments that he is against all exploitation of magic, but that in the case of the main characters in the film, the two little girls, he only sees joy.

The film makes a deep impression on me. When it finishes, showing a lot of elves, I cannot help crying. Tears pour down my cheeks. My whole ordeal and all the dangers I am facing have made me tense. Hearing the word 'joy' works like a key, opening a cupboard full of tension, fear, loneliness, pointlessness, and mistrust. The long walks in burning heat. The expectation of walks in pouring rain and thunderstorms. The story on the news about the road accident involving the bear. The fear of snakes. The fear of what may happen in the cave on Mount Parnassus.

I see now that I am in the process of convincing myself that I am on a heroic expedition, thinking that I have to introduce a new feminine power in place of Gaia. Even if this should call for me to battle with the powers of old. I am simply demonizing the contents of the tour and forcing out all joy and light-heartedness. Nothing new and good can come of this. Basically I suppose I have dug up some deep layers of dread which I have then built into this mythical story. A story which, to my own ego, can make sense of all the challenges, efforts and privations.

Go for another walk out to the temple ruins. Watch the sunset. Contact Gaia and give her my profound apologies for demonizing her through my fear and old-fashioned ideas. She answers, warmly and youthfully, *'Good! Then we can meet again in joy.'*

All my projections onto Gaia worry me, especially because I cannot let go of them. If I can demonize and mythologize my experiences to such an extent, how can I trust my other experiences? I ask Mary. *'Sort through them and trust those that are built on joy,'* she says and thus repeats the moral of this afternoon's film.

The wind is different now, cold and persistent. I have dug out my thick pullover. I hope the weather will change tomorrow. *'Do not look on the weather as an adversary but as someone who wants to tell you something,'* says Mary.

* * *

The next morning the weather looks good. I had expected to have to cross a high mountain. To my surprise, Mary chooses to lead me along the lake. It seems to me that she makes a deliberate choice due to my special situation. Perhaps Mary chooses the least dramatic road through pure indulgence.

The walk along the lake is beautiful. The sun even shines. Mary and I again talk about water. As I understand it, the Earth is a closed system with water circulating through it. *'What retains the atmosphere?'* Mary asks. *'Why have most of the other planets no atmosphere?'* Mary explains it to me, and I conclude that if the atmosphere were not there, water *'might explode into hydrogen and oxygen'*.

In relation to Mary's statement that water has a memory, I sense that soul is linked with water. Water is the cornerstone of all organic life on this planet. Water is our form of life.

Our road leads through valleys and over low passes. It is a laborious walk and after a hard climb I cross a final mountain ridge and can look down onto the Bay of Corinth. This gives me the strength to tackle the final 10 kilometers down to the port of Nafpaktos. Forty-five kilometers! I feel that I have earned a good hotel. One with a balcony overlooking the bay, even.

Through Grethe, Mary has since told me that she crossed the mountain from the small town of Poros:

'*I was well aware that trials awaited me there,*' she said. '*Crossing by land was part of the road to my consecration. I have always found it easier to travel by water, but I also felt that I missed important chances for personal growth by choosing the easier road. I personally needed to walk the road I took. A road which would present the difficult challenges which life on Earth offers. Challenges such as the fear of not being supported – the fear of being deserted. It awakes one's survival instincts.*

'*I also needed to meet the aspect which we may call the Great Mother. My faith was so strong that I always trusted that I would be helped. That is why I had to go through meeting the negative aspect of the Great Mother – would the Great Mother help me? This experience would not be possible in the water phase, because there I would be carried. So it had to take place in the land phase.*

'*There were times in the Greek world when I was quite exhausted. I had not brought many provisions and I would not have been able to carry them if I had. But I found that I always received whatever help I needed. I even found help from quite unexpected sources. Birds of the sky brought me food. This is difficult to tell anybody about, as there were no witnesses, but I was given olives which birds brought in their beaks and dropped for me. And just as my water carrier ran dry, I found a spring. The Great Mother saw to it that I was kept alive.*

'*Near the springs there were usually a few plants which I could use for food. Occasionally I came upon people who had chosen to live in the mountains. They were very hospitable as they seldom had visitors. I was usually offered mutton, as most of these isolated people kept sheep.*

'*But it was quite a trial, as I could see it was for you too. And of course, as I have walked that road before you, I am the most suitable to accompany you.*

'*It is also true that there are several different routes to choose between. You may perhaps think that I chose too difficult a road. For there was no special reason for me to go to places quite as deserted as I did. So you are right in thinking that I have tried to ease the way for you. I am glad that you did not start out in that terrible weather and that you did not take the road which you quite rightly felt that I followed. I did not cause that weather. It is not in my power to affect the weather.'*

I have been back to this area since my pilgrimage, and have driven the stretch of road over the mountain which Mary spared me for.

It is not actually much longer than the road that I took. But there is a terrible climb, and for over 20 kilometers it runs along a deserted stretch of mountain without a single house. In good weather it is a most beautiful journey, but in bad weather it would be something of a trial. Mary has told me that future pilgrims will be able to choose freely which way they want to go.

If I had chosen this road and had met a violent storm, I might have had to give up and rely completely on the help of the Great Mother – or God.

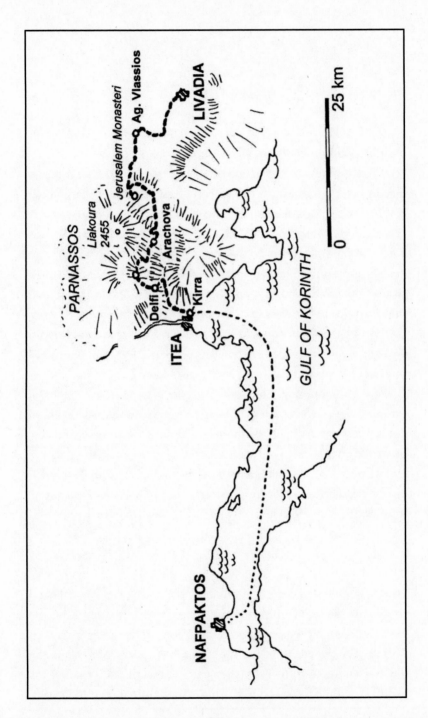

14

Meeting Gaia

Delphi and Mount Parnassus

The first thing I am conscious of this morning is the sound of a motorboat. I go out onto the balcony and see quite a large boat leaving Nafpaktos harbor, sailing east. I may have missed my chance here. Mary has told me that she sailed from here to Itea and that I should try to do the same. Go down to the harbor and ask a couple of fishermen if they will take me to Itea. But they shake their heads and say that their boats are much too small and that I would do better to take the bus. There are no other boats in the harbor that look capable of making such a trip, so I give up and get on a bus instead. As we drive along the Bay of Corinth, I imagine Mary sailing. A couple of hours later I arrive in Itea.

The question now is, how did Mary get up to Delphi? I examine the various paths. 'K' is up to her tricks again so I cannot get any clear messages. In the evening I go for a walk and feel myself drawn out towards the suburb of Kirra. Down at the waterfront it seems that Mary and I can sneak a quick word. I become convinced that Mary disembarked in Kirra and from here found paths up to Delphi.

* * *

The next morning I go straight out to Kirra. I see now what I could not see in the dark the night before – ruins down by the water's edge. There is a sign saying, 'Docklands of Kirra. Port of Delphi'. So my intuition the night before was correct; this is the old harbor of Delphi. From the end of the ruins a road leads north, straight past the church. This is the original road to Delphi.

At first I walk through lush olive groves, then the valley narrows and I continue along the bottom of a ravine. There is something quite special about this road. I sense an atmosphere of gatekeepers. Stop and ask permission to enter into this landscape's world of energy and angels. It takes more explanations than usual. Both about my pilgrimage, about the Virgin Mary and about my own intentions. At length the gatekeeper gives in and opens the gate. Round the next corner, Mount Parnassus rises up in all its might. I sense the presence of a powerful angel above the mountain. It welcomes me and says that it has been looking forward to our coming. I get the impression that the energy of this angel is of the same sort as that of the Heart-angel on St. Gotthard. I carry on through the ravine. A cliff rises up vertically in front of me, and high above I see a hotel in Delphi hanging out over the edge. I actually pass under Delphi and enter into a broader valley. The angel explains that the road acted as an avenue of procession to Delphi, and that this part of the valley was called the 'Valley of Resolutions'. In the olden days, as people came this way, they must all have been thinking of their errands and their resolutions; and of what they would promise the priests up in the temple complex.

I now leave the valley behind and begin to climb a series of hairpin bends that snake their way up the mountain. At the first bend I am confronted by the steep slopes of Mount Parnassus. '*This stretch of the road is called: "Do you dare to look the truth in the face?"*' the angel says. Then the road takes a turn and I get a broad view back across the valley almost all the way to Itea. Here the traveler sees his journey home, and the angel explains that the theme of this stretch is: '*Now, don't promise more than you want to keep on your way home.*' At the next turn, one is again confronted by the threatening, sheer wall of the mountainside. The theme of this stretch is: '*Judgment is nigh!*' The road flattens out, and the theme becomes: '*Let us rest a while.*' There is a small church here, Agios Georgios. It is open, which is unusual but very pleasant. I rest in the church a bit before tackling the last climb.

After a final bend, the road now leads directly towards the Temple of Apollo.

It comes into sight high above you. You feel very small and far down here, and have a sense that the gods reign further up. '*This stretch is about submissiveness*,' says the angel. The rest of the way, my concentration seems to lie in my feet. It is a strenuous climb. I emerge onto the main road just before the round temple of Pronaia.

It has been a great pleasure to walk for 20 kilometers in the peace and quiet of the countryside, without any traffic. I go straight up into Delphi and find the hostel I have stayed at before.

THE ORACLE IN DELPHI

The importance of the Delphi Oracle started to grow in the 8th century BC when Apollo evidently took over the place from the old gods, first and foremost Dionysus and Gaia. Its name was changed from Pythi to Delphi. The temple became very powerful, and its oracular pronouncements became famous. No colony was founded, no lord chosen without consulting the oracle. By the 7th century BC this was the leading oracle in the entire known world, and it was in this period that the first great temples to Apollo and Athena were built. The oracle was allowed to continue under the Romans, although it was plundered by Sulla in 86 BC. It was not given its coup de grace however, until 394 AD, when the Emperor Theodosius banned it, following the introduction of Christianity.

The temple was probably functioning in Mary's time, but without its past glory.

I visit the ruins in the early evening. From the temple square I watch the sun setting behind the mountain ridge. The tourists disappear too and the air becomes blessedly cool. This is the best time of day. I have also good contact with Mary.

Below the Temple of Apollo is the Sibyl Stone. One of the few existing remains from the time of the Goddess. There seems to have been a watercourse tunneling under the temple down to the stone.

Beside it is a small square, considerably reduced by improvements made to the Temple of Apollo in the 2nd century BC. Before that, it was quite large. As far as I can make out, it was called the 'halo square', the 'harvest square', as the most important festival, the harvest festival, was celebrated here. A labyrinthine dance was performed, meant to symbolize Apollo's fight with Python. I have studied the subject of labyrinths closely, and I ask Mary what she saw. She says she saw no labyrinth, but she had heard that people walked one in the square. *'As you are doing now,'* she says, alluding to my pilgrimage. I think about walking in a classical labyrinth, rounding the four cardinal points of the compass. Wonder what my own cardinal points are just now? The answer is swift: *'fear, judgment, faith, and charity'*. Exactly the themes I have worked on here in Greece.

Through the ages there have been several temples to Apollo here. The museum displays friezes from the archaic and the classical temples. On the eastern gable of the archaic temple, Apollo was depicted sitting on the tripod normally reserved for the female oracle pronouncers, the Pythiae. There are three young men and three young women on each side of him. In this early version it was obviously important to stress his abilities as an oracle and to the balance the sexes.

On the newer, classical gable, Apollo is shown driving four-in-hand, entering Delphi where he is to be crowned. Here there is no longer an attempt to balance the sexes. From now on, the male God is victorious.

Other reliefs concentrate on portraying two great fights. The archaic relief centers on the fight against the Titans. The fight against the old gods. Among the very oldest gods was Ge (Gaia). The other great battle is against the Amazons. I am surprised that the fight against the Amazons is so central to Hellenic mythology. Why is it so important to show the defeat of female warriors? Who were those Amazons? And did a period of female power really come to an end? Could Athena with her helm, spear and shield possibly be a mythical Amazon?

As I walk back towards the hostel, Athena seems to call to me from the Pronaia Temple. She tells me that she belonged to the pre-Apollonic tradition, and that people had worshipped her long before him. Some visitors would always visit her temple first with offerings to gain the favor of the mother/the water/the landscape. Then they went on to Apollo.

THE PAST HISTORY OF DELPHI

In describing Delphi's past history, a previous director of the museum wrote: 'The battle for local supremacy seems to have been an important element in Delphinine theology. On the one side there were Python and Delphin – dragons who represented water, cloud, sea, the underworld and chaos (death). On the other were Zeus and Apollo, representing the sun, clarity, sense, order, life and cosmos. The battle was won by the powers of order, but the old gods did not disappear completely.

'It looks as if the origins of the oracle cult are to be found in the Corycian cave on Mount Parnassus, where archaeological findings supporting this theory date right back to the Neolithic age. The cave was home to Python and Delphin, and was the first center for the oracle ... The cave was seen as a gateway to the underworld Hades. It is said that nymphs entered the cave and were driven mad, after which they began prophesying. Contact with the oracle's deity took place in the cave ... In the 6th century BC the nymph Corycia lost the cave to Delphi, who then became the most important oracle. From then on, Pan was worshipped in the cave, as is evident in the rich archaeological findings. This can be seen as a tradition handed down from the Dionysus era ... The first oracle deity was Ge or Gaia (earth) and her prophet was Daphne; then came Demeter, Poseidon and Themis. They were followed by Python and Dionysus. As Apollo gained dominance, the older gods were pushed aside, though their temples were still to be found in the consecrated area.'

I want to get up onto the mountain, to the cave where the original oracle was. I seem to sense that Mary went there on her journey. On the map I have spotted a path up there that I manage to locate just north of the town. The first hundred meters go up across a small promontory and are more a climb than a walk. Today is going to be tough! As I get a little higher up, I can look down and see the stadium in the complex of ruins. Then something quite incredible happens. I suddenly find myself on a beautiful old path paved with stones. In some places the paving is well preserved with delicate small steps; in others the stones are uneven. The path zigzags up the mountainside. Down below, I see the ruins in their entirety and in the background the processional avenue coming from Kirra and the Bay of Corinth. This must be the most beautiful road I have ever walked, and it is not particularly strenuous. It obviously used to start in the temple square and even today it leads right up onto the plateau.

The ancient path to the Parnassos plateau

I am conscious that famous ancient people have very probably walked on these very stones. This thought transports me into a timeless state where I seem to meet heroes and gods.

Heracles, Athena, Artemis and Dionysus.

As the stone-paved path ends, I carry on up through a valley along a gravelly and stony one, and after a few kilometers I find myself at the foot of the mountain which holds the cave. On the map the final climb up to the cave looks fairly short, but it is in fact very steep. At first I go completely the wrong way and end up in a thicket. Have to go back again and a little further along the road before I find better signposting. The first 700–800 meters of the path are reasonably accessible; but for the last 200–300 meters I have to clamber up great stones. The path is well marked, but they seem to have finally given up building it and have simply climbed straight up. Several times the stones threaten to roll away under me. It is exhausting. At long last I reach the cave.

I take a breather. Have a drink of water and try to calm my nerves. This is where the great confrontation is to take place. There is no going back. I summon all my courage and approach the entrance to the cave. Mary stays outside. I ask permission from the guardians at the gate to enter the cave's realm of energy. Explain about Mary's pilgrimage. The gate slowly opens and I walk in and down. The cave is enormous and has a vaulted ceiling with the occasional stalactite hanging down. It may be 10–15 meters high and 20–30 meters across. It disappears in a funnel into the mountain. Over the centuries the ground has become leveled by earth sediments, so it is reasonably accessible, though cliffs stick up out the ground in several places.

I am tense; so tense that it takes all my energy to concentrate on the little ceremony I have prepared. As an introduction, I present gifts: first a small stone from Mount St. Gotthard. Then a little seawater from Kirra, as a reminder of the time when water covered the whole Earth and when Mount Parnassus was the first mountain to appear out of the salt water. For my third present I was going to whistle a pilgrim song which I have practiced for some days. But I have completely forgotten the tune. Not one note sounds right. After several attempts I give up and recite the text instead. This is bad.

I then ask the energy-beings in the cave, including Gaia, to accept the presents and to manifest them.

I sit down and wait for an answer. Nothing happens. The only answer I get is the distant, hoarse sound of screeching birds that seems to come from deep inside the cave. Probably bats. I again ask the energy-beings to show themselves and tell me who they are. Absolutely no reaction! Something tells me that I just have to wait. After some time I say, 'Dear Gaia, when I came here just under a year ago I sensed your presence, as I do now. I pray you, manifest yourself.'

I repeat these words three times, and finally a voice comes

through: '*Why do you wake us?*' snarls a cross voice. I answer, 'It is time to be awake, Gaia.' Slowly she becomes clearer but she is still annoyed. I ask her why I was so shaken the last time I was here. 'Is it something to do with me having been in your service?'

'*Lots of people have been in my service,*' she answers sullenly. I then ask about the Irish myth that a group of people were kept prisoners in the Cave of the Leather Sack in Greece. The name of this cave, CORYCION, means precisely that – 'leather sack'. 'Were they held prisoner here?' I ask. '*Lots of people were,*' she answers, still sulky. I am getting nowhere. Mary is still outside, and Michael does not want to get involved. I try to ease the situation with water, leaves and light, and suddenly the pilgrim song comes back to me. I whistle it several times.

I then perform a short ceremony, asking lost souls to ascend into Heaven.

The cave

The tune seems to have made the atmosphere a little less confrontational, and Gaia seemingly accedes to my request.

I pray that other shadow-beings may follow. I am surprised how few there are. On a mad whim, I ask all dark powers from the depths of the earth to come home to God. A torrent of shadows shoots up with indescribable force. As if a volcano has started to erupt. I quickly stop the explosion. Narrow it down and let the shadows stream quietly up in a column. They ebb out, and I pray that all my own shadowy sides may be sucked up by God.

The cave now feels very empty. So I pray that a new feminine power may take over. Nothing happens. No release. I finish, leave the cave and have a drink of water. I feel as if I have been in a tough battle. Relieved that it is over; but I have acted so much in accordance with my preconceived ideas and planned rites that I have not been able to use my intuition. I do not know if this is good or bad. I have not made use of my earlier conversations with Gaia. Quite the opposite. I have used presents to try to tempt her out, in order to get rid of her. Basically an old-fashioned male way of solving problems. I have been caught up in the web of a heroic expedition in spite of myself. As if I have switched onto male autopilot. In Thermo, Gaia told me that I would be tested. I have obviously failed.

I am afraid to clamber down the mountainside because of the danger of slipping on the many loose stones. So I take a small mountain road down. It is longer, but better. When I reach the road across the plateau, I aim straight for the first open café. Order a cup of coffee and sit down outside beside two ladies. We quickly begin to chat. They are sisters, one of whom lives in Canada. She tells me that they grew up in Arachova and that she has often been up in the cave with her father, before it was excavated. Their father was interested in archaeology and she wanted to dig too. Using a small spade, she once dug a hole at the entrance to the cave and found a small bone. Then one more, and soon she had found ten. Later, when the cave was excavated, they discovered that in the Stone Ages, people had made pilgrimages to the cave and that before entering they had thrown such small bones into it, and made a wish for something.

I have contact with the angel of the mountain. It will not pronounce on the result of my ceremony until tomorrow. I get the same reaction from Mary. Go down to the mountain town of Arachova.

Mary says that she went back to Delphi from here, so she cannot tell me anything about the route down to Arachova.

* * *

The next morning, tiredness weighs me down like a duvet. Consider whether to take a day off. Contact Mary, who does not say much about my conduct the day before, but she thinks that it is OK for me to spend another day in town. She also says that I am going to the convent 'Jerusalem' next – by road. That evening I go for a walk. Sense that Mary draws me up towards the church in the old quarter of the town. It turns out that there is going to be a wedding.

The ceremony starts with the bride and her father walking through town, led by a band. It is a long walk. At the church, the groom welcomes the bride with a wedding bouquet. They enter the church where there is room for only a few of the guests. The rest of us stroll about outside, chatting to each other. People wander in and out of the church. I poke my head in a couple of times and follow the proceedings. I see the priest using a crystal to make the sign of the cross over the groom's forehead chakra and then tap the bride's forehead chakra. As if to harmonize their intuitions. The ceremony lasts about an hour. Everyone is very smart, so at first I assume that they are all going to the wedding party afterwards. The bride and groom come out in front of the church and everybody crowds round to congratulate them. Pretty little white bags are handed out. I am given a couple and imagine them to hold rice for showering the newly-weds, as we do at home, but there is a small cake in one and sugared almonds in the other. Gifts from the wedding couple to their guests. After this, most people go home. A small group escorts the bride and groom on a new journey across town. I do not know where they go, presumably to some hotel or other. The couple has had to stand throughout the whole thing and the bride has had to walk all the way here and now back again. Pretty hard work getting married here!

Mary says she wanted to come up here because she saw a wedding at exactly the same place last time she came through.

The town of Arachova is next to a small pass between two valleys. The church stands exactly on the pass. Just behind the church, seven roads meet under an enormous tree.

There are several things I want to talk to Mary about, but she does not want to talk until we are underway.

* * *

Next morning I start by going up to the church at the pass. Mass is being said and I stay for part of it. I notice one nice little ritual. Just inside the vestry there is a bucket filled with flowers, lemon balm. Before entering the main church, one rubs a few of the flowers between one's fingers. Very fragrant and purifying.

At the crossroads behind the church, I take the road east.

I am on my way again and Mary is close. At last I can talk the whole thing through with her. She explains the whole course of events from Parga to Delphi. The whole thing has been one long test. Until you know your fears, you cannot know your strength!

This test has been planned for me all along. At home I was told, 'Greece will be a trial.' In Italy they said, 'Greece will be tough going'. 'At Parga I heard that 'the shadows passed on from the matriarchy might cling to you', that 'the bear from the car accident might well be in your area', that 'the cave might be full of snakes'. Worst of all was that my contact with Mary had not been clear, and that an 'imposter' gave me false messages.

'Learning to recognize your deepest fears is something you must do alone,' says Mary. The last ten days she has also told me not to drink alcohol. This was to deny me a possible way of escape.

There were in fact two tests.

The first was a test of manhood. To go out into the storm and scale a deserted mountain full of 'bears and snakes'. I shrank from this test at the last moment. That was acceptable. There was no reason to take on a pointless struggle.

It was also quite a trial walking 45 kilometers in the boiling hot sun. Even so, I feel that here I was not in danger of giving up. I did not have enough insight to give myself up to the Great Mother, but I could have given myself up to God.

The second test was in the Corycian Cave with Gaia.

I should have been suspicious when I got on the wrong path. It was hard going and I got very tired. I was running on male autopilot. My situation should have become completely obvious when I could not whistle the tune I had practiced. But I just plowed ahead. Tried to tempt Gaia out. My gifts were good and things loosened up. My prayer for all shadow-beings and lost souls was alright. But it all went wrong when I had the brainwave of including all dark shadows from the depths of the earth. I managed to contain the ensuing eruption, but only with help from others. The little scene trying to impose a new femininity was probably a question of my own inner femininity.

I may have discovered my own limits, but I had not understood nor passed the test.

Mary is now quite clear again, thank goodness. I am to go to the nunnery 'Jerusalem' – by road. Turn towards Dahlia and go up one of the gorges on the east side of Mount Parnassus. The last 5 kilometers are very steep, up through the mountain forest to an altitude of 800 meters. A Greek family and I arrive together and knock on the nunnery gate. We are let in and taken to the church. I stay there for a long time. Bless it.

When I come out, I sit down and look up the words for 'pilgrim' and 'stay the night' in my little Greek dictionary. Ask the nun if this is possible. She goes inside and asks her superior and returns with a definite no. So, crestfallen, I plod out of the nunnery. I expect I shall have to sleep in the open. Not far on, in the middle of the forest, there is a primitive camping area. I go down there. Some primitive shelters have been put up and there is clean water, so it is not a bad place to spend the night.

It is Sunday and groups of picnickers are sitting about the place. From one table a party waves to me and signs for me to join them. Two couples and their children. They invite me to eat with them. I cannot refuse and there certainly seems to be plenty of food. Christos and Tatjana speak a bit of English. They are both anesthetists. Petrus and Lucy are fishermen from Haldiki, where he also owns a flower shop. In spite of the language barrier we manage to have a good chat. They are very nice.

I tell them of my journey, and at one point Tatjana asks me why I am doing it. I explain about my vision of Mary and of my endeavor to find her route. Nobody says anything. Tatjana understands. Mary is very important in this country, but my story is just too far-fetched. After an embarrassing silence, Petrus changes the subject and brings us back down to earth with a question about the price of caravans in Denmark.

We discuss caravans for a bit and then we start looking at maps. Petrus knows the district and tells me which way to go. He is a regular here and shows me a simple plastic shelter where I can sleep.

Tatjana asks if I am not afraid of the wild animals. I do not want to start explaining about my bear and my snakes, so I ask, 'What sort of animals?' Petrus quickly says that there are only dogs. I have already made friends with a couple of dogs so this does not worry me.

The two families leave and I gather brushwood to sleep on. People are still wandering about and I assume that others are planning to sleep here. But one by one they slowly disappear and by nightfall I am the only one left.

Alone in the forest on Mount Parnassus. It is quite quiet and very dark. I know that it will be a long night, so I sit for a long time, breathing in the calm evening air. About eight or nine o'clock I settle down. I lie awake for ages. I can hear goats moving about in the mountains. Hear the sound of small stones rolling away down the mountainside, disturbed by animals. Although it is pitch-black I am not scared. I can actually enjoy the sounds and the fresh night air. Furthermore I seem to be in contact with the great Heart-angel of Mount Parnassus and that makes me feel safe.

I have two dreams:

First, I am standing in a pool holding the snout of a small crocodile. Wonder if it will be able to harm me if I let it go. Surprisingly enough, it seems to be talking to me: 'Do you not think I could have my food chewed before I get it served?'

Next I have a vision of two snakes. One is writhing on the ground. The other is poised for attack like a cobra. They are both whitish and not very big.

* * *

It was a long night. The sun did not rise until eight o'clock. Am not well rested; don't think I slept more than 20 minutes at a stretch. Nothing disturbed me. I heard only the goats. On the other hand it was really cold and I had to sleep in my fleece all night. I wash my face in cold water and shave. Dismantle everything I have set up, so that I leave the place as I found it.

Go down to Dahlia. Unfortunately there are no cafés open. I

was planning to head for the main road as Petrus advised, but when I reach a crossroads and see that to get to it I will have to take a dead-straight road across a very flat area, I begin to doubt. A very busy road out over flat land. It must be wrong. Consult the map and find another road. I ask Mary if she would mind if I choose this other road, and she does not object. As long as we get to Livadia.

However, after rounding a small promontory, the road turns back towards Mount Parnassus.

It is a beautiful sight but I cannot help wondering why I am being directed back again.

It seems I am to be confronted with the mountain once more. There must be something that I have not understood or learnt properly yet. As I puzzle over what this might be, Mary asks if I have understood my two dreams.

I am sure that they are dream versions of my worst fears. We consider them one at a time.

First dream: *'Where did the picture of the crocodile come from?'* Mary asks. I suppose it must be from TV and films as I have never met a real croc. *'So this is not about your fear of the animal then,'* she reasons. I say that I have had dreams of a crocodile snapping at my knees before. Mary says, *'And if it had managed to damage your knees, you would have found it difficult to make your way in life.'* This fits in quite well with my own interpretation, as I see my need for achievement as placed in my knees. *'Note that you are in contact with the crocodile. You can control it, and it even speaks to you. You can do things with it.'*

I ask myself how strong my need for achievement really is. Am I doing this journey for the sake of my own development, and is this development at all worth writing about? Because, of course, I am going to write a book, am I not? I now realize that the pilgrimage is becoming a personal achievement with the book as the goal. I try imagining that no book results from it all, and soon I can say to Mary that even without a book the pilgrimage has been a marvelous success. I am perfectly able to abstain from publishing anything about it. Mary suggests that I ask God to free me from the need to achieve.

I stand in the middle of the deserted, silent road facing Mount Parnassus. Pray that God will dissolve the angst-provoking image of the crocodile and the need for achievement that goes with it. *'Have you understood everything?'* I am asked. I state what I have grasped and am now ready to let go of. I expect to see the image somehow be drawn up skywards and disappear, but something else happens. The image is pulled downwards. Mary explains that things which belong exclusively in the lowest chakras become concrete matter again, returning to the earth-pole.

I conjure up the image of the crocodile again and then I consciously let go of it. The crocodile opens its jaws as if to bite me, but instead strokes my knees; and – hey presto – it is gone.

The second dream. Mary asks again, *'Where did the image of snakes come from?'* This image at least is based on something real. Once I had to wade through a nest of small snakes and I have often come upon snakes on my walks in the countryside. Mary concludes, *'This image belongs in the Hara chakra* [associated with sexuality]. *It has physical consequences and is controlled by sexual morals. In the religious ethos, sex is burdened with many taboos. Adam and Eve ate of the apple and discovered their sex, which they immediately covered up. This was the serpent's – or the devil's – doing. You have not been brought up to demonstrate freely that you desire somebody or to behave wantonly. In other words, this is a law-polarity where unrestricted, free and dangerous sexuality is tied to an idea that it is forbidden. It is a law-polarity which affects your physical existence. Remove the dirty and dangerous part and you are left with two clean snakes. The latent coiled snake and the poised attacking one. You can ask God to help you dissolve this law, for it is nonsense!'*

Again I position myself in the middle of the road and this time ask God to dissolve the law-polarity. The image of the moral pole dissolves and disappears upwards. The image of the physical pole moves downwards. Again I see the two white snakes, and instantly they alter character. They grow, take color and wind themselves into me. The power of the snakes is in me and it is up to me whether I want to use it or not.

We walk on. After a while Mary says that it would be a good thing to seal what has happened with a cleansing ceremony. So I cleanse myself with fire and water.

Through Grethe, I have since asked Mary about what happened in the cave on Mount Parnassus, and she answered:

'The feminine energy there is deeply connected with Gaia. In contacting that energy you are dealing with an extremely powerful authority. An angry authority that has been unacknowledged for nearly 2,000 years and has been sent into hiding. You turn up, the great wanderer, forgetting that she is understandably angry about the way she has been treated for so long and the way her power has been underrated.

'Your coming to the cave with the intention of meeting her awoke her power. But you awoke her anger too. It is not especially you she is angry with. She is angry with all the numerous conditions imposed on her. Once again you have disturbed a hornet's nest. There is a volcanic atmosphere in the cave just as there was in Disibodenberg [in Germany].There, it was a question of misused masculine power. Here it is about repressed femininity.

'You must not think that your mission was a failure. Whatever else, your presence there and your deep wish for change has altered the local energy. Things went as well as they could at that point in time. You had to learn what immense power Gaia possesses. You know what it is to experience the tension between Heaven and Earth, but meeting Gaia in her true nature is immensely more overwhelming. And Gaia cannot be altered, as she has her part to play in creation and she has by no means finished her task ... Obviously she will not be changed or transformed by anyone other

259

than her own inner being.

'We have reached a stage in Earth's development when it is time for man to learn a far more humble and respectful approach to Gaia. Gaia has been exposed to severe abuse the way man has worked with – and worked against her. Treated her creation grossly. So Gaia has a right to be angry about man's custody of nature. The first step is to embrace Gaia in a spirit of reconciliation ...

'Your mission will not be to change Gaia but to meet her respectfully, with great love in your heart. She does not need gifts – nor does she want any.'

The road to Livadia leads up through the mountains and is not very busy. A lovely stretch. As I reach the highest point, dark clouds start gathering again and I quickly put on my rain gear. Mary says that there is a small church further on, with a porch where I can shelter. And sure enough a very small church comes into view out in the middle of a field. Walk up to it along a small farm track. Quite unexpectedly I sense St. Michael's presence. The church is closed, but I can shelter in the porch and prepare myself for the ceremony which Michael's presence must surely indicate.

Michael and Mary stand before me, close together. First Michael says, *'You have been through a process of purification, and from now on, we are your true parents.'* I am rather taken aback, don't quite understand, and ask, 'But I am not nearly as pure as you.' Michael answers, *'That which is still lacking in you is so little as to be of no consequence. This is a consecration, Hans!'*

The consecration needs to be confirmed, and now something wonderful happens: a ray of light shines from above, down into Michael and, as if in a tilted mirror, it is reflected into me. The same thing happens from Mary. They then circle round me, forming a vertical halo. All the way round, except for a little V-shaped space arising from the gap between them. It seems quite deliberate that this V is left open.

'Your soul-polarities and your model-polarities are now one, Hans. We are your true parents, and we are one,' says Michael.

This was a beautiful and blessed experience and it makes a very deep impression on me. I sit in the porch for a long time, quietly rejoicing over what has happened.

'Now this stage of the pilgrimage is finished,' says Michael. *'You may choose the theme for the walk from here to Athens yourself,'* he continues. *'The stage from Aegina via Patmos to Ephesus is Mary's and John's.'*

I am surprised to be told that the stage is already finished here. In a way it feels right, but I do wonder, for it is still a long way to Athens. Soon I begin to speculate on the theme for the next stretch. The first thing that comes to mind is: 'Peace on Earth'.

'An appropriate choice,' says Michael.

I start out on the final 5 or 6 kilometers down to Livadia, asking questions as we walk. I learn that it is important to be certain of your soul-polarities before choosing your role models. They need not necessarily be the same.

If they are in accordance, so will there be accordance between thought and deed. Between what you in your heart of hearts want to do, what you think is ideal, and what you actually do.

Through Grethe, Michael later explained it more clearly:

'Once the soul is willing to be consecrated and to follow the spiritual path, trifles are no longer considered. The human mind wants to believe that you will be called to appear on some day of judgment, to account for what you have done – good and bad. This is an Old Testament idea, answering needs man no longer has. The very fact that you are willing to enter the melting pot is enough in itself. Certain trifles are thrown into the melting pot with you and help to form your experience of life. They are not to be considered sins or faults, but rather experiences that will teach you to follow your inner guidance instead of your own will. What is the

difference? Without knowing the difference you will not be able to decide when to listen to one voice rather than the other.

'It is vital that you have an ego and are not just governed from within, and that your ego possesses that willingness to serve which says: "I want to follow the path that will lead me to a merging with my soul's purpose."

'This is the consecration that you have been through.'

The first stage across the Alps taught me what it means TO BE CREATED. About understanding how each individual is formed and how they function.

The second stage through Italy was about what it means TO BE MAN. About how the energy of one individual connects with that of others, and about how everyone may enrich their environment by being a light.

This third stage through Greece seems to be about EMBRACING THE EARTH.

Understanding the basic conditions for life on this planet. Honoring the waters of the world.

There is something about Mother Earth I have not yet grasped. The trial on Mount Parnassus showed me that. I hope I may come to understand it later. On a personal level I think this stage was about dealing with my ego's fears and letting the path of my ego merge with that of my soul.

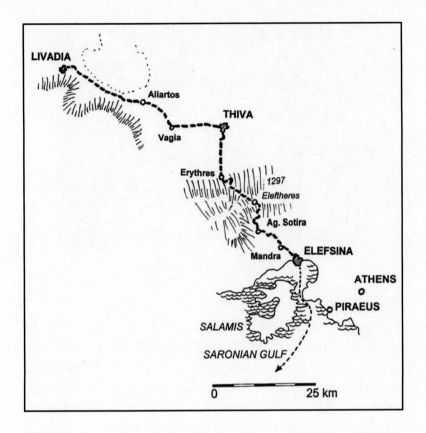

15

Peace on Earth

Attika

Livadia is a great surprise. It is situated in a gorge between two mountains, through which a small river runs. At the top end of town the river branches into a myriad of streams and waterfalls called Kria. This is truly the nerve of the town. Water bubbles and roars everywhere, giving a quite unique atmosphere.

The Kria waterfalls in Livadia

I dedicate this stage to 'Peace on Earth'.

Mary takes me along the road to Athens. A couple of kilometers out of Livadia, we turn up towards a small town. I notice a parked car on the other side of the road. An elderly man in a suit and tie gets out. He asks me a whole lot of things in Greek, which I do not understand. I explain, using gesticulation and place names, that I am on my way from Delphi to Athens. The man points to a mountain and tells me a long story which seems to be about 'the argonauts', but that is about all I understand. He says goodbye and drives into town. Soon he comes back with a passenger, stops and offers me a lift. As usual, I politely decline. Three hundred meters further on, he has again stopped and is waiting for me. He just wants to show me the direction to Athens. He points out two mountains on the southern horizon and further back between them, a third. Athens is just behind that one, he says. I also understand him to say that we are standing on the old road from Delphi to Athens and that I only have to follow the farm road beside us. I think he calls it the 'Royal Road to Delphi'. He is very helpful and I decide to do as he says. The farm track twists down through the hills, in places a sunken road. It becomes narrower, and I begin to wonder if it can be the right way. But suddenly I find half the road beautifully paved with stones. Ancient paving. So the old man was right. This really is the old main road from Athens to Delphi. The stone paving makes such a deep impression on me that I seem to see ancient Greeks in white tunics walking past me.

Shortly after, I am jolted back to the 21st century as the farm road merges with a motorway along the edge of a plain. The unending noise of cars ruins the tranquility. For most of the way, there is a wide verge to keep me from getting too close to them. It is still possible to talk.

Michael takes up my theme: 'Peace on Earth'.

'What is peace on Earth? The first thing that comes to mind is the absence of war. There are different types of war. Between nations, groups of people or individuals. War is often about exploitation, but can also be caused by cultural clashes. The background to all war is, paradoxically, man's recollection of being an angel – of having a divine existence. Through the fall from paradise, man entered the corporeal world in which finding food is a basic necessity. Physical effort and exhaustion is a new and surprising experience for many angels. It quickly leads to individuals attempting to get others to do their work for them. In the world of angels there is a divine hierarchy, an order which is partly remembered and now becomes distorted into a master–servant hierarchy. At its primitive stage the focus of this new hierarchy is on finding food. But their recollections of their divine world prompt the ruling classes to attempt to strengthen their privileged connection with the divine. They have a primitive notion of securing the future of their offspring by making this elevated, divine connection hereditary. The right to the throne becomes a question of bloodline. First comes the family, next the clan, then a population group which ultimately evolves into God's chosen people.

'Under the matriarchy, woman, in her role of life-giver, had the

closest connection to the divine. Under male dominance the balance of power became more and more abstract. Now there was both secular and religious power. It was in the interest of all powers to secure their privileges, and the more these could be tied to bloodlines, the stronger the power. Secular and religious powers each developed their own hierarchy. The basic doctrine was "We must abide by the dogmas for they are God-given."'

Michael goes on to say, *'Leaving hard physical work to others allows the individual time and energy to do what a person believes to be divine – to be better than others. This can be practiced in all sorts of ways. By eating and drinking as though life was a cornucopia. By having numerous women (or men) at your disposal for erotic entertainment. By moving to pleasanter climes. By taking revenge on others. By demonstrating wealth. By creating gardens of Eden. By building fairytale castles. By surrounding yourself with the finest art. By traveling all over the world. By going on pilgrimages.*

'Just let your thoughts run free. Imagine you had 100 years' wages and could use them freely.

This is basically a way of expressing a recollection of divinity. God is continually re-created. God creates continually. Man, a spark in God's sea of fire, does the same.

'God has defined his world of creation and each individual is free to do the same. More often than not, the individual simply accepts a contemporary idea of "paradise" which so far has usually been governed by the lower chakras. Securing one's own position and that of one's offspring and demonstrating to others that one has the power to do so.' Michael ends by saying, *'Every creator also defines the limits of his world. Most people forget that.'*

I try to imagine what I would do if I had a lot of money. I quickly get entangled in material creations and donations to worthy causes. I am no better than my predecessors. I too cannot avoid thinking that wealth would bring meaning to my life.

The antique road to Athens is apparently down underneath the tarmac, so I am still forced to walk along a busy road. The traffic is annoying and the weather keeps changing. First I put my waterproofs on and then I take them off again. And again. Heavy clouds seem to roll around the mountains. Whenever possible, I follow farm tracks beside the main road. Thirty kilometers later, I find a roadside hotel.

* * *

Next day Mary summarizes the lesson on war. The basis of all war is a misunderstood recollection of having once had divine status in the world of angels. When governed by the lower chakras, this misunderstood recollection leads to the selfish securing of privileges. Privileges are used to achieve ultimate happiness, which in itself is a misunderstood recollection of the divine world. In the lower chakras, ultimate happiness is most often interpreted as material values.

According to Mary, man must change his values.

If man continues to center his values in the lower chakras, he will wipe himself out.

Mary says, 'When Moses came down from Mount Sinai and saw his people worshipping the golden calf, he destroyed the first set of tablets. He went back up the mountain and was given new – far firmer – commandments with which to combat the dance of the Golden Calf. The Golden Calf is still worshipped. It is time for man to seek values higher up in the chakra system. Through the joy in Hara – of which we can learn much from so-called "primitive people" – up through the Solar Plexus into the Heart. There are no historical or evolutionary reasons to remain in the lower chakras.'

As we talk, it becomes clear to me: we must learn to understand that we are governed by a blind development-mechanism. A mechanism which chains us to the material. I think of our industrialized world. The market mechanism is blind.

Communism saw through some of the injustices of the free market and created a fairer division of goods, but not even communism could see beyond material values. We have to develop a way to organize society using other, higher values.

Mary makes quite clear that *'no angel – nor any one man – is of more worth than any other. None! No man is above another through a closer affinity with the divine. Each and every individual is a part of God, and God loves each and every one of them.*

'No one community is of more worth than any other community.

'No nation is of more worth than another nation and no nation has the right to rule over another.

'Nations are created through culture. Sometimes they coincide with an ethnic group or natural geographical demarcations. Nations can be redefined by mutual agreement.

'Religion is created through culture. No religion has the right to rule over another.'

Michael picks up from Mary: *'Peace on earth can only be achieved if man can reach a new understanding and a new view of the basic causes of discord. New values must be developed for your society. This is an absolute condition for peace.'*

South of Thiva I find my way onto a quiet track leading to Erythres. Honeydew melons and the last of the grapes are being harvested in the surrounding fields. From a distance I see farmers toiling on a hill. One of them walks towards me and is obviously intent on making contact. I have a choice: Do I worry that he might want money, or do I look forward to a chance for a chat? I choose the latter and go to meet him. He asks me a lot of questions but I do not understand a word. I manage to explain where I come from and that I am on a long journey. In the end I realize that he is simply curious, because normally nobody ever comes through here. He is kind and friendly and even offers me food. A positive encounter.

Shortly after, Mary continues our conversation on peace on earth:

'*On a personal level, world peace is a question of inner balance. More basically it is also a question of avoiding starvation and exploitation.*

'*It is imperative that all three energy-axes are well-functioning. You must be very clear on your law-polarities and your deepest fears.*

'*Go out into the world with joy and look upon other people as your equals. Rejoice in nature, in which you belong, and communicate with it.*'

Finally Mary asks: '*Do you know what peace at heart is?*' I fumble for a definition, but Mary gives me the answer: '*Room for love.*'

I was assured at my hotel in Thiva that there would a hotel in Agia Sotira, a walk of just under 40 kilometers. To my great disappointment it is closed for the winter. It looks as if it might not even have been open all summer. It is nearly six o'clock and the sun will set at about seven thirty. I do not want to sleep in the open tonight, so I plod on. Elefsina is another 15 kilometers, so I need to get going.

The going is downhill, which helps. I set a fair pace but feel somewhat at risk due to the large number of lorries hurtling along the relatively narrow road. I get buffeted and blown about quite dangerously and end up having to jump into the ditch every time one comes past. One driver gesticulates threateningly because I am too close for his liking; others wave encouragingly, as if I were a soldier on a march. I try and maintain a friendly attitude towards the lorry drivers while concentrating hard on the traffic and on keeping my footing. This may be the original antique highway, but it is definitely not suitable for pedestrians. It would be totally irresponsible to attempt to walk here in the dark. So I must hurry. Dusk is slowly but surely creeping across the sky. Colors are fading into the night. Just as darkness really sets in, I see the first street light. I made it. Seven kilometers an hour. I have done 52 kilometers altogether, which makes today my longest and hardest so far.

To my great surprise, there is only one hotel in Elefsina, and it is full. On hearing my tale, the porter takes pity on me and lets me sleep in the lounge.

* * *

I do not know anything about Elefsina. Next morning, Mary tells me to take time to study the town. I am puzzled. Though I saw signs to a museum and a couple of churches, I cannot imagine there being anything much worth seeing here. Mary tells me to walk south, and as the hotel porter directs me the same way to the museum, I guess there must be something to see after all.

I can see a mountain ridge towering up at the end of the street and head towards it .Suddenly I come upon the most amazing archaeological site. In the center, I can make out some sort of cave. It turns out that this is the site of the famous antique Eleusinian mysteries. Elefsina is Eleusis.

The site has just opened and I have the place more or less to myself.

Elefsina.

This is a fantastic conclusion to my journey over the Greek mainland. As far as I can see, nearly all the divine Greek mothers are represented here. The whole site is dedicated to Demeter and her daughter Kore. Artemis has her own temple at the main entrance. Athena is represented in a temple up on the mountain. Hecate – one of the oldest goddesses – has her own temple too.

DEMETER

Demeter is old – far older, for example, than Zeus, even though she is ranked as Zeus' sister in Greek mythology. Demeter, goddess of harvest and the fertility of the earth, was worshipped all over Greece and her festivals were very popular. She was worshipped as early as 1500 BC, maybe even earlier.

Her 'mysteries' were celebrated twice a year in Eleusis and were held in such awe that there is no record of any initiate ever breaking their vow of silence to reveal what the mysteries actually involved.

Mythology usually portrays Demeter as the grieving mother whose daughter Persephone was abducted and carried off to Hades, the realm of the dead, by Pluto, god of the underworld. Pluto wished to make her queen of the underworld. Persephone's original name was Kore – 'the virgin'. Demeter left Olympus and her fertility duties and went to search for her daughter, leaving the earth infertile.

Her search brought her to Eleusis where she rested, disguised as an old woman. She received a hospitable welcome from the king, who asked her to nurse his son. As a result she showed Eleusis great favor, declaring that it should be venerated henceforth and that she would initiate its people to the mysteries of the earth's fertility.

Much later, after many complications, Zeus managed to

---

persuade Pluto to release Kore. But by now, she had eaten of the food of the dead – pomegranates – and was therefore eternally chained to their world. It was finally agreed that Kore would spend four months of the year in Hades and the rest of the year with her mother.

ELEUSINIAN MYSTERIES

The Eleusinian mysteries were celebrated well into Roman times. There were 'the lesser mysteries', which were celebrated in March and served as preparation for 'the greater mysteries' which were held in September. The greater mysteries lasted nine days, starting with a procession along the sacred road from Eleusis into Athens where the festival was opened. Following purification and sacrificial ceremonies, the procession returned to Eleusis, stopping underway at the Kallichorun well, where the participants danced a whole night. More sacrificing and fasting led up to the actual initiation into the Mysteries, which took place in a special building called Telesterion. Initiates were strictly forbidden to reveal the secrets of the ceremonies. It is supposed that the participants worked up a sort of spiritual ecstasy. Perhaps the awaiting crowds, gathered outside the buildings, heard screams and screeches throughout the night, giving rise to juicy rumors of wild and unrestrained orgies.

Demeter-worship must have taken place over at least 1,800 years, maybe even longer.

The landscape here is very distinctive. A mountain ridge juts out into the bay, surrounded by water on three sides .The foot of the mountain stands in the water; its top reaches into the sky.

The most interesting feature is probably the cavern. Under an overhanging cliff, a bench is carved out of the rock and with it some ledges that may well have been steps, perhaps leading down to a now-obsolete pool. The place bears a strong resemblance to St. Michael's Mount near Strasbourg. According to the Orphic Hymn, the gateway to Hades lay right here. It fits in well with the idea that ceremonies were held here to contact the spiritual world and the ancestors. Halfway inside the cavern is a more recent temple to the god of the underworld, Pluto. This temple seems somehow intrusive, as though attempting to suppress the ancient mother-goddess.

Mary is very pleased with the whole temple site, which was fully functioning even in her time under the Romans. She told me later through Grethe:

'This was yet another haven. A lovely place to come to. A place of pilgrimage. People came to Eleusis from far away and started their journey to Delphi from here. It was a place of purification, where you confirmed your resolve to go to meet the gods. You also needed the feminine goddesses to bless and purify you, so there were baths here – a sort of waterfall – you could bathe in, so that you were prepared when you arrived in Delphi. The pool was used for purification.'

Water was an important aspect of the Goddess's temples. This becomes more and more clear to me, and I am certain it is a common characteristic in all the old temples from that time. As men gained influence and power and slowly took over religious ceremony, water gradually lost the significant part it had played in the Goddess's tradition.

Mary has tried to teach me about water. I wonder whether one can gain access to the knowledge of water through some special ceremony. That would be expedient, water being a crucial basic condition for the survival of man.

The first stage of my pilgrimage took me through the Alps

and taught me about BEING CREATED as a human being. The second stage was about BEING MAN among other men.

This third stage here in Greece has mainly been about the Earth, meeting Mother Earth, the Goddess and the Great Mother. The stage has reached a worthy end here in the Goddesses' Eleusis. Without earth to live on, man has no future. We must EMBRACE THE EARTH. We must learn to understand the feminine powers of the Earth and approach them with respect. If we do not, we will never achieve PEACE ON EARTH.

My tour of the site has brought me to the west gate, which overlooks the harbor. Mary tells me that she went down to the harbor and sailed to the island of Aegina. I walk down to the beach behind the ruins. A wonderfully peaceful place where a number of elderly men are enjoying a morning swim. Large harbors spread out on both sides of us. Here Mary bids me farewell.

PART IV

TO BE BORN AND BAPTIZED

Islands and Ephesus

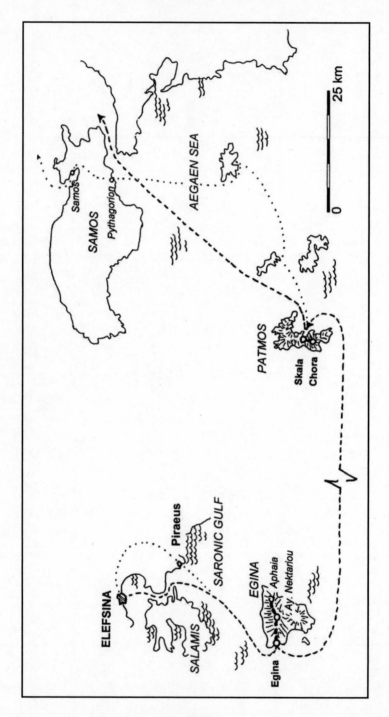

Islands in the Sea

Aegina and Patmos

I am sailing. A gentle breeze plays across the waves. The air, heavy with bow spray, washes away the dust of the road, leaving me thoroughly refreshed. It is blessed to be at sea. To be borne away on the waves.

The mainland lies behind me. Mary sailed the rest of the way, putting in at several islands, the most important being Aegina and Patmos.

AEGINA

Aegina soon comes into view. Less than an hour's sail from Piraeus. Mary tells me that she felt at home here and that it was a sort of base for her. She explains that the inhabitants were open-minded people who accepted her approach to the divine.

AEGINA

According to myth the Phoenicians named the island 'Aegina' due to the large number of doves that nest here. In Greek the prefix *ae* means 'island' and *gina* means 'dove' – Dove Island.

It has been inhabited for more than 7,000 years and has a turbulent history. In its golden era the Aegineans were the first people in the old world to strike coins in silver. And yet the island was often a subjugated pawn in high politics, and looting and plunder were everyday occurrences. The old capital was just north of today's harbor,

---

where ferries dock incessantly. The ruins of the ancient town have been excavated and are crowned by a solitary antique column. The remains of several Christian settlements from the first centuries AD have also been uncovered, indicating that refugee communities found a haven here in what was left of the old city.

One historical detail worth remembering is that it was here the church builder Julius lived before he traveled to northern Italy building churches as he went, his hundredth church being the one on the island Isola de Giulio, in Lake Orta.

Aegina may well have played a central role in early Christianity, and Mary's and John's story of their journey there may have been handed down through the centuries.

Mary crossed the Greek mainland alone. John apparently went by sea and probably waited more than a month for her to arrive. They were reunited here and I seem to sense their joy at being together again. It looks as if the family they stayed with were part of a fairly large Jewish colony. Mary says it was John who introduced Christianity here, sowing the seed for a Christian congregation during his month-long wait.

There is a long hike in front of me. Across the island from the town of Aegina on the west coast to the Temple of Aphaia on the east.

Halfway across, I pass through Nektariou, a small town with a convent and an enormous church which is said to be the largest in Greece. A place of pilgrimage. The earthly remains of the priest Nektarios are laid to rest in a sarcophagus at the convent.

NEKTARIOS

Nektarios (1846–1920) was canonized in 1962. It is not easy to be approved for canonization in the Orthodox Church and Nektarios was the first to achieve this in the 20th century.

He was at one stage appointed Bishop of Egypt but was subsequently suspended and expelled after being the object of false rumors. He was reduced to poverty while he struggled to become reinstated. But the church never acknowledged him again and it was not until the year 2000 that Nektarios received an official apology from the Patriarch in Alexandria.

Mary explains that the church still practices rituals very similar to those she and John followed nearly 2,000 years ago. At baptisms and weddings, for example. Mary is not advocating the upholding of old rituals, merely stating that these are a survival from her time.

The church is huge and impressive. But for me, the most powerful place is the inner courtyard of the convent next door. The moment I step into it, I feel a wonderful peace and harmony. A small church stands in the center and next to it the tiny chapel that houses Nektarios's sarcophagus. There are two doors to the chapel with an ancient pine tree growing between them, reaching out its branches to shade and cool the whole courtyard. In front of the tree is a well where pilgrims may draw holy water.

On a Sunday it is almost impossible to get through the throng of pilgrims as they flock around the well for water and queue to kiss the marble sarcophagus. I choose to visit the sarcophagus on a weekday when it is easier to find peace and quiet. I am not familiar with the Orthodox tradition and want to learn to understand what goes on here. As I sit quietly, I seem to make contact with Nektarios. He asks me, *'Do you believe in me?'* The question takes me by surprise. I hesitate. Answer that I find it difficult to understand all the kissing of his sarcophagus and his pictures – all this worshipping of his earthly remains. I hear myself speak to Nektarios.

'I can sense your presence here and now. I believe that much,' I concede. Nektarios helps me to understand. *'Believing in me can help the faithful get closer to God. Do not think of me as an idol. I am a helper on the path to God.'*

Nektarios came to Aegina very late in life. While teaching at Razarios Ecclesiastical School, he helped a group of young women start a convent on Aegina. On his retirement he came to live on the island himself. I cannot help comparing him with Padre Pio in Italy.

On my way out of the convent an insignificant mound opposite the main church catches my attention. Can this be a Michael-mound? I climb to the top and immediately sense St. Michael's presence. I prepare myself for a ceremony.

Michael asks, *'Will you honor all the religions of the world?'*

I do not need to consider my answer. 'Yes.'

Michaels then asks, *'Will you honor the different Christian denominations?'*

Again I answer, 'Yes.'

Finally Michael asks, *'Will you voice your own beliefs?'*

'Yes, I will.'

I continue my journey eastwards. An hour later I see the Temple of Aphaia towering up on the crest of a tree-covered mountain ridge. Its situation is quite exceptional, built on a mountaintop with water on three sides.

THE TEMPLE OF APHAIA

The temple is a well-preserved Dorian temple from the year 500 BC. There are, however, remains of much earlier temples here, dating as far back as 1300 BC. Aphaia, a local goddess, has been worshipped here for more than a thousand years. She has slowly been absorbed into the figure of Artemis, and perhaps even Athena.

I make contact with Aphaia before I even get to the temple. I decide not to hurry, though, and have a cup of coffee before entering the grounds.

Aphaia guides me through the temple while she explains that Aphaia, Artemis and Mary are three sides of the same Mother-of-Souls energy, each from her own era. She suddenly says that the temple is a 'gateway of souls'. Angels pass through this or other 'gateways', when they first become incarnate on Earth. Transforming souls to the physical environment on Earth takes a very special process. Apparently there are suitable conditions on Aegina at the moment. Aphaia/Mary assists at these 'rebirths', thereby fulfilling the role of Mother of Souls.

Through Grethe, Mary later talked of her role as World

Mother:

'Being World Mother is a position I hold. Just as you might take on a job. It does not mean that I will hold that position for ever. It all depends on the Earth's stage of development, and what is needed.

'When I take on the position of World Mother I become closely connected to one aspect of the feminine – motherhood. This means it is part of my responsibility to create the necessary magnetism to ensure that souls seeking to come down to Earth from the spiritual world, in order to be born, are whirled down to the right places. I cannot do this alone. I have, therefore, a group of assistants – Marian servants – who help me perform my World Mother duties.

'We are talking about a sort of magnetic power that draws souls to it. The souls who wish to be incarnate – and they must want this themselves – are drawn into the sphere of the Earth. Likewise, when you die you are helped out of Earth's sphere.

'This magnetism works through water. In some places the atmosphere is cleaner and therefore better suited. For example, you will often find a great influx of new souls in areas with dolphins.'

I ask Mary if she is present at all the other earthly gateways where souls are taken in and out. She hesitates.

'I cannot answer yes or no. If I say yes, I would be claiming to have colonized all the cultures in the world. If I say no, that would be wrong too, for I am present there. If you ask whether the underlying Mother of Souls energy is present at all the gateways, then the answer is definitely yes. Your concept of Mary belongs to Western culture, but it is just one of many ways to interpret this energy. In other places it is seen quite differently, even though the underlying energy is the same.'

Back in the town of Aegina, I make my way down to the beach, where the antique port must have been situated. Here I say goodbye to Mary as she boards a sailing boat.

From here, Mary sailed east. I must first go to Piraeus. Late that evening I go on board an enormous ferry. At first it looks as if my luck is in – a really nice two-berth cabin all to myself! But a moment later a woman comes in the door and is very upset at the prospect of having to share a cabin with a man. I really don't think I look all that terrifying, but I hurry off to find a steward.

The woman sits on the edge of the berth and tries to calm down while we sort out the misunderstanding. My luck slowly disappears out the porthole for it turns out I have been given the wrong cabin number and am now sent down to share a cabin with three other men. They are not that bad, though.

PATMOS

We arrive sleepily at Patmos early next morning. There is just room for the ferry to maneuver in the tiny natural harbor. We hurry ashore and the ferry sails straight off again. I meet Mary and John on a small fishing jetty. It is good to see them. We agree that the first thing is for me to find a hotel. Take the nearest one. Do a bit of washing and have a nap.

As usual there are a few chores to be done before I am ready to join Mary. At last, though, I don my hat and step outside. We are going up to the Cave of the Apocalypse.

PATMOS AND JOHN

According to legend, Patmos sank into the sea and Artemis and Apollo persuaded Zeus to raise it back up. The Romans used Patmos to house deportees. John was deported from Ephesus in 95 AD and spent 18 months on the island. It was during this stay that he received his revelations. Today the islands are a well-known place of pilgrimage.

John tells me that he was about 80 years old when he came here, and that his deportation to Patmos was no real punishment. He did miss his congregation in Ephesus, but Patmos was a lovely place to live. Mary agrees: *'Just feel the place.'*

I wander up to the Cave of the Apocalypse. Go in through the monastery and down the steps to the rock church. I can hear a priest saying mass and am lucky enough to catch a baptism.

I stay for the whole ceremony, fascinated by the way they use the water. First the child is undressed and the priest gently wipes his whole body with water. The child smiles.

He is then held under his arms and lowered down into the water three times. Every inch of his body is washed in the water to ensure that he is properly cleansed. He begins to cry. Not so much because of the water, but because of the wait for the long ritual that must be remembered and recited between each immersion. It is easy to see that the priest is tense and it seems to rub off on the child. Next a lock of hair is cut off and oil is rubbed on certain important parts of the body such as the soles of the

Baptism in the cave

feet. Finally the child is wrapped in a warm, white linen cloth.

Afterwards we are all given a little bow with a cross on it. The boy has been named Nicolas. His mother comes and offers us all cake. His father gives me a little framed picture of his son with a bag of sugared almonds hanging from it. He says: *'This is a present for you.'* The child looks straight at me and I hold his gaze for a long while. I feel almost as if I have become his godfather.

The service ends. I sit in the church and have a long talk with John. I imagine him sitting in the cave looking out over his bowl-shaped valley. This is one of the most inspiring places I have been to. It is the sort of place to write a book, or finish something off. John nods and says: *'Why don't you!'*

I go outside, sit down and enjoy the view. John asks me to slowly walk along the path home, read his Revelation, The Apocalypse, at the hotel and then come back again at about five o'clock.

Browse in the Book of Revelation, but am very sleepy and nod off. Wake up and read a bit more and nod off again. Can hardly shake off my weariness, but at five I get up and go back up to the church. A private Russian Orthodox service is in progress. It is very long drawn and the duty priest is obviously annoyed. At nearly six o'clock they are still not finished, but now the duty priest bluntly cuts in, douses the lights and tells them to leave.

As I sit through their service, I manage to ignore the Russians for quite a long time and concentrate on my contact with John. He shows himself to me wearing Orthodox black vestments and swinging a censer. I ask him if he prefers this denomination to other Christian denominations. He quickly protests that this is not the case, but that he wants me to understand the original tradition and the way he sometimes reacts. He tells me I must remember that his incarnation with Jesus and Mary has been crucial to his further spiritual development.

Then he stands beside me. Jesus appears in front of me and

says they wish to thank me for completing the journey. I wonder what is going to happen. I look into Jesus' eyes. He comes closer. His eyes grow larger and I can look through them like openings in a wall. I see an ocean of fire. I hear a voice in my head saying, *'The Apocalypse has begun. You see before you the purifying fire of love..'*

I am moved to tears, first of joy that Jesus has shown himself to me, and then of grief for what I believe the fire to mean. That all must be burnt.

Including all mankind. I leave the church without finding clarification and walk home weeping. Desolate that the great mankind-experiment has failed. I must stay here and try to gain a better understanding.

Entrance to the monastery at the Cave of the Apocalypse

* * *

Next morning I go straight back up to the church, weighed down by an enormous sadness. The church is shut. I look about and find the verger sweeping the grounds. He agrees to open up for me. Fetches a huge key and unlocks the door. He grants me ten minutes which is only just enough.

I sit down and re-envisage the fire I saw in Jesus' eyes. Today it seems to have almost burnt itself out. John explains to me that the fire in his revelation was the purifying fire of love. A fire that every man must pass through. Suddenly he asks, '*Are you ready to pass through the purifying fire?*' After a few moments' consideration I answer yes. I stand up. Now it is Jesus who stands in front of me; John stands on my right hand and Mary on my left. Michael is behind me. A hatch in the floor beneath opens. I do not fall through it, but remain hanging in mid-air. Flames dart upwards through the opening. I raise my arms in the shape of a cross and the fire encircles me.

In a glimpse I see myself without flesh. A pale skeleton shrouded in a veil.

The fire subsides and I am asked to step down into a hollow. I expect water to rise up around me immediately. And water does come, but stops a little way up over my ankles – as it did on Mount Michael in France. As I stand there, feeling the water, I realize that this is a baptism. Jesus Christ says, '*Your name is IO.*' I do not understand. 'Those are the letters for John,' I object. I am then told that as a child I too was baptized in that name, that my name, Hans, is derived from Johannes – John. The ceremony is over and I am filled with joy. My ten minutes are up and I must leave.

As I make my way up to Chora, the main town on the island, I ask Mary what happened in the rock church. '*Be joyful and proud. You have been baptized,*' she says. Again I object that I am not John, but a 'country bumpkin dropped from the sky'. '*John is also a simple fisherman "dropped from the sky",*' she answers smilingly.

'*Did you not some time ago promise to serve the new era?*' she continues. I recall my dedication from several years back, and have to answer yes. *'John is the heart of the new era. You are now a part of the John-energy,'* says Mary.

As I climb the steep path, something happens to my body. I become more and more dizzy and begin to wonder whether I am ill. For the first time on my journey I have forgotten my water bottle. Look for somewhere to sit down, and notice a small chapel a little further up, just above the rock church. I go inside. It is dark, but as my eyes adjust I see a painting of Mary with baby Jesus and a Michael-angel. Next to it is one of John and his disciple. I light a candle and can at last sit down and rest. The dizziness continues. In fact it gets worse. I need to lie down on the floor. Mary and John nod, and I stretch out on the floor with my feet towards the door and my head towards the altar.

Lying on the cold stone feels good. A sense that the earth and I are one seeps through me.

John comes to stand at my feet with his back to me. He becomes spirit and lets himself fall back and sinks into me. Mary does the same, and finally Jesus. At that moment I feel myself to be a giant, spreading myself out over an enormous area. The words *'I am Adam Kadmon'* come to me.

The moment is peaceful and I remain lying there for some time. Then I hear someone coming, so I get up, go outside and sit quietly on a bench under a tree. As far as I remember, *Adam Kadmon* is an ancient Jewish term meaning 'Primordial Man'. I have become man!

Like a small child I lie down on the bench and fall asleep.

Wake up after a while and continue up the mountain path to the monastery in Chora. The place is full of tourists and I have difficulty opening myself to it. I am still deeply affected by all that has happened today. One thing I do notice is a curtain in the iconostas picturing a dove flying vertically down into a grail. As if it is the Holy Spirit sent to bless the water in the grail.

* * *

Next day sees me back at the rock church. The door is open. A group of Japanese tourists are listening to a guide. I sit down and enjoy listening in.

THE CAVE OF THE APOCALYPSE

The guide explains about two hollows in the rock, fenced off and outlined in beaten silver. The largest one is the hollow, where John laid his head. The smaller one is where his hand lay. The guide says that after God revealed himself to John in the cave, it was shaken by an earthquake. Three cracks appeared in the rock, one long one and two short. These three cracks are said to symbolize the Holy Trinity. The guide moves on to the paintings and can even explain why John is depicted with a large bump in his forehead. I had been wondering about that. It seems that in the Eastern Church such a bump is a general symbol of an old and wise person. The painting of John the Baptist, on the other hand, does not have such a swelling. He is shown as a young man dressed in skins, for he lived in the wild and was considered something of a savage.

Presently a voice asks me if I wish to make an offering. I decide to make a sacrifice of my old, obstinate masculinity. I will attempt to reconcile myself with my femininity through a new form of masculinity.

My offering is accepted, and I sit still for a long time, meditating. Another man is here meditating, too. When he leaves I go and stand in front of a painting of the Revelation. Mary, Jesus and John are in front of me. First Mary gives me a kiss on each cheek and one on my forehead. John does the same. Then

Jesus places both hands on my shoulders and says, 'Old friend.' He laughs at my bewilderment. He is teasing me, I think. He now says more seriously and warmly, 'Love life. Love one another.' A beautiful sentence and, I believe, John's motto.

It took me a long time to realize what the teachings on Aegina and Patmos where about. At the start of my pilgrimage I learnt about what it was TO BE CREATED; then about TO BE MAN among other men; then on TO EMBRACE EARTH. Now I think I see the direction we are going in. The next heading must be TO BE BORN AND BAPTIZED. On Aegina I learnt mainly about coming down to Earth as a soul. Being born into the corporeal. But also about dying. About leaving the corporeal again. Here on Patmos I believed I had experienced a sort of death through the purifying fire. In fact, it was a cleansing, which led to a form of rebirth through baptism and being made man anew. Even though I saw it as something physical, it really happened on a spiritual level. As if my ego and my soul departed from an old way of living to be dedicated to a new life. It felt like an initiation. I was baptized IO into the new era. Thus I am 'a John'. I think there are going to be quite a number of 'Johns'.

This was perhaps the last and decisive initiation of the pilgrimage. I have walked a long way for Mary and have undergone many initiations, but maybe it was really all just a beginning.

* * *

Next morning there is a power cut. Sanitation is reduced to a minimum. I pack my things and buy a ticket for the ferry. Go out to the little fishing harbor outside the hotel. At the far end of the harbor, Mary and John are boarding a boat. Mary calls to me, 'See you in Ephesus.'

'Not at your house?' I ask. 'No, meet me at the harbor,' she smiles.

I had thought we would go directly from Kusadasi to her house but obviously she has to come ashore somewhere. Apparently in the great ancient harbor in Ephesus.

The little local ferry puts out from the quay and I leave Patmos. We put in at a few small islands before arriving at Samos where I disembark. The same evening I take another small ferry on to Kusadasi. The Turkish ferry had not seemed very welcome in the harbor on Samos, and in Kusadasi we seem to be suspect simply because we are arriving from Greece. Hatchets have been only superficially buried here. I hope the two countries can make genuine peace one day.

I have arrived in Turkey.

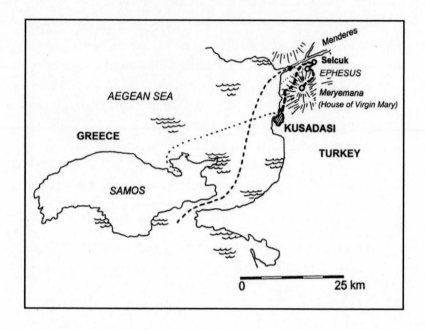

17

In Sight of the Goal

Ephesus and the House of the Virgin Mary

I am woken at six o'clock by the sounds of Kusadasi harbor. I get out of bed and settle down on the balcony to observe the comings and goings. My journey is almost over. Wonder whether I have done well enough by Mary. I know I will miss her. Remind myself to enjoy the last few kilometers.

Mary sailed directly to Ephesus so the 25 kilometers from Kusadasi to Ephesus are not really part of the route. But I need to stretch my legs and I am in no hurry. I want to savor every step of the way into the landscape where Mary spent the last years of her life.

I leave the port and go north along the coast and up into the wooded mountains.

Mary is delightfully lively and mischievous. She says today's walk can be counted as part of her pilgrimage route as she often used to come this way. The closer we get to Mary's home mountains, the happier she becomes. *'I'm almost floating!'* she says – but quite honestly, doesn't she always? She calls one of the mountains 'Big Brother'. The angel of this mountain appears. He is quick to recognize Mary and greets us warmly.

The road runs on down from the mountains to Ephesus, leading us, as we reach the plain, straight into the ruins of its great theater. In Mary's day you came by boat and the theater must have been visible to her from a long way off.

EPHESUS

Ephesus was one of the greatest towns in ancient history. Its situation and its harbor made it the natural connecting link between Asia and Europe. The harbor was originally at the bottom of a fjord, but this slowly silted up with sediments from the Meander River. In the time of Alexander the Great the harbor was moved further out to where Mary must have found it. But slowly the new harbor silted up too and this, together with the growing problem of a malaria plague in the swamps, spelled the beginning of the end for Ephesus. From a city of 200,000 inhabitants in Mary's time, it had shrunk to a small town by the year 1000. Today the town is called Selcuk.

The road from the theater to the old harbor

293

I go past the ruined town and up into modern-day Selcuk. Find the hostel where I have stayed before. A ten-year-old boy is at the reception desk and he shows me the rooms. He turns out to be an experienced haggler, and after a round of bargaining we agree on a price that suits us both.

Mary has been prodding me, saying that it would be nice to pop over to her house for a bit this evening – an informal visit before our official arrival tomorrow. I am very tired and need to rest a while first. At five o'clock, even after a nap, it takes all my energy to get on my feet. I ask Mary again if we have to go, and she insists it would be a good thing to do. She promises there will not be any ceremonies; all I have to do is take my small gift – a pine cone from Aegina.

I go into town to satisfy the worst of my hunger. I fall into conversation with Ibrahim, who claims to have sold some carpets to a Danish painter. He tells me it is 9 kilometers up to Mary's house, the only available transport being an expensive taxi. He offers to drive me up for an exorbitant fee. I turn him down, but Mary is pressuring me so I beat him down to a more reasonable fare.

We drive south up into the tree-clad mountains. We arrive a little after 6pm just as they are shutting up. I go past the café and the souvenir stands, up to the church they call 'The House of the Virgin Mary'. It is a humble place, built on a terrace among tall trees. You can hear the gentle trickling of a spring coming from below. The trees are bathed in gold from the setting sun. It is quite beautiful.

Look inside the church where mass is in progress. A priest and two nuns. Wander up a path. Sense I am getting close to where Mary's house actually stood. Here I offer Mary the pine cone from Aegina as a demonstration of my devotion to her and a token of my gratitude for the enormous experience she has given me. I sit down on a wall beside the church. Just sit there, taking in the evening glow. The dark silhouette of trees against a backdrop of distant, glinting ocean. A warm feeling of inner joy seeps through my body. Mary says that this is exactly what she wanted me to experience. Peaceful joy. The same feeling that gave her great support when she first lived here.

As mass ends, the priest approaches me and asks if there is anything I want, as they are going to close now. I tell him I have walked here from Hildegard of Bingen's convent in Germany. He passes this information on to the nuns and tells me he has several books about Hildegard. We arrange to meet here again the next morning to continue our talk. Ibrahim drives me back to town.

* * *

I am woken by the morning sun. Today is the day I must 'deliver' Mary. It can only pass too quickly.

First of all Mary needs 'picking up' at the ancient harbor in Ephesus.

I go out to the ruins. Walk down a path to the harbor front and find a landing place. However odd it may seem – seeing as how Mary and I have been traveling and talking together since Patmos – we have as warm a reunion as two who have not seen each other for a long while. We decide to walk through the town, as she would have done when she lived here. People greet her as we pass through the ruins, which in my imagination are now transformed into a busy, bustling city. Even the guards at the top gate greet her like an old acquaintance. We leave the town and aim south. As we start up the mountain, Mary tells me it will take a good hour to walk to her old house.

I sense a change. Mary becomes very straightforward; emphasizing that once I deliver her, she will be irrevocably *delivered*. The pilgrimage is finished and from now on I must trust to my own inner femininity. I am to expect no further instructions. I now have full responsibility for my own life – this is very clear.

Mary has protected me throughout the whole journey and she

assures me that this protection will continue until I reach home.

This all saddens me greatly. It is very hard to understand that this is goodbye.

At her site we walk quietly past all the souvenir stands and on up to the church. She tells me that this is where she held her ceremonies and services, but that her home was a little wooden hut further up the valley. She wants me to perform my ceremony in the church.

I go inside and am confused to find that the priest from the day before is already there. We exchange a few words and I decide it is time to make my delivery. I approach the altar. Bless the church as being part of 'The Virgin Mary's Pilgrimage Route'. The end goal. I go over the whole route, gathering the threads. Say that I hereby deliver the Virgin Mary at the conclusion of our journey. (Though it is really more a matter of her delivering me.) I give thanks for our fellowship and love. It has been a great joy to me. Ascertain that the route is now established – with the few alterations we agreed on underway. I hope I have been open and receptive enough to grasp the essential messages and lessons I have been given.

My 'delivery' is not quite over, but the solemnity of the situation paralyzes me and I am too unfocused to carry on. I break off the ceremony and go over to the café to write my diary.

Suddenly I am aware that Mary, John and my other friends from the spiritual world are standing in front of me, laughing. They tell me it is all over. Mary *is* delivered. I am to relax – and enjoy it all.

Through Grethe, Mary later told me:

'I lived in a hut where Mary's House now stands. There was another hut beside it which has not yet been found. That was where John lived when he was at home. When he was away I would use his hut myself or for visitors. We had great respect for each other. We were bound together by strong love and shared grief. And we were

able to help each other spiritually. It was he who had the huts erected, for they were not there when we arrived ... John traveled a lot but I did not mind. That was one of the reasons I had to cross the mainland on my own. I had to learn to be alone. So it would not matter when he was away. He was meant to spread the word abroad and I accepted that.'

The priest comes out and sits with me. He has brought three books by Hildegard which we discuss for a while. He then invites me to attend mass at 6pm. A Bulgarian bishop is expected. This leaves me with plenty of time. I fall into conversation with one of the nuns. When I tell her I have followed the route Mary walked from Germany, she exclaims, *'That's impossible! – Not that far. Mary only went as far as the Mediterranean.'* She accepts that there may have been an inner journey and inner experiences but no more than that.

I decide to explore the valley and make my way down to the bottom. Climb a bit further up, but Mary stops me. It is not necessary to go any further. The only place of importance here is where the sacred ceremonies were held. Her own wooden home is immaterial. The energy at her home can be compared with the energy I experienced last night. I seat myself under two tall pine trees. My 'friends' from the other world are still there laughing at me – and with me. *'There aren't any more initiations,'* they tease.

The House of the Virgin Mary

Well before six o'clock I go back up to the church. The bishop is very late and the nuns kindly advise me to go now if I want to make it back to town before nightfall. The sun has just gone down and I set a good pace. It takes me an hour and a half to walk the 9 kilometers.

I decide I have been meant to do this walk in the dark. On my own. Without Mary. The moon shines brightly and it is a beautiful evening. I can just glimpse the lights of the town in the distance.

In a way, I use this final walk to find my inner calm. Darkness envelops me. The road is deserted. Yet I feel completely safe and secure. As if the whole universe with its twinkling stars is smiling down on me.

It is strange to think that it is all over. But the fact remains. Mary stayed up in the mountain. My thoughts have changed color.

THE PILGRIMAGE IS OVER!

* * *

That evening I read a book on the discovery of the Holy Virgin's House. I lose myself in the story before falling asleep, and wake up next morning a little befuddled.

THE VISION OF THE HOUSE OF THE VIRGIN MARY

Anna Katharina Emmerich (1774–1824) was a German nun who bore the stigmata. She had numerous visions which were published in 1818–1824.

One vision she described tells us that Mary – after the death of Jesus – lived for three years on Mount Zion, then three years in Bethany and nine in Ephesus. Emmerich described in great detail the house where Mary lived. How

---

many rooms there were and what they each looked like. The view from the mountain behind the house and much more. The book tells of a group of French monks in Izmir who at first rejected these 'female fantasies' but later decided to examine the area, hoping to put an end to the rumors. To their enormous surprise they found the ruins of a house and mountain views corresponding exactly to Emmerich's descriptions. Later, archaeological studies verified that the house dated from the 1st century AD. Today the Roman Catholic Church recognizes the site and acknowledges Emmerich's vision.

An incredible story, but I cannot make sense of the number of years in the vision. Shrug it off and go off to visit St. John's basilica in town.

At the entrance to the basilica ruins, I read that Mary and John moved to Ephesus sometime between 37 and 48 AD.

Inside I tune in and ask John to come to me. He senses my questions and says, '*Just ask. This is a good opportunity.*' I ask, 'When did you move to Ephesus?' John answers:

'*Just as Emmerich writes. Six years after the death of Christ. But we had been here before. We decided to leave Palestine for a time the year after his death. We thought everything would die down after a while and that we would be able to go back to our old way of life and our work. We sailed to Ephesus – a number of us – and stayed for a while. Joseph of Arimathaea had been here several times and was very taken with the beautiful surroundings and the way of life here. We then sailed on to Marsala (Marseille). I won't tell you the next route. We separated and you found Mary and me in Bingen on our way home. Mary had had a number of revelations while we were at Mount Zion. Among others was an instruction that she was to make a long journey on foot from somewhere far north and that she was to settle in Ephesus. She fell for Ephesus and the mountains south of here right from the beginning. Especially "Big Brother". She felt at home with the female servants in the Temple of Artemis. I myself loved this hill.*

'*Our stay was unproblematic thanks to Mary's friends in the temple. And thanks to Mary we were not persecuted by the local inhabitants when we settled here. Neither here on the hill nor in the town itself. We were known and accepted.*'

This is the first time I have had such a long conversation with John. Things have changed. We seem more familiar with each other now.

* * *

The next day I do my washing in the little basin in my room. Just after ten o'clock I am back up at Mary's House, Meryemana. Sunday mass is just about to begin. My old friend the priest is presiding over the ceremony. In English, luckily. He is very focused and sincere. In his sermon he uses the parable of the Pharisee and the sinful tax collector praying together at the temple. The Pharisee boasts of all his good works and says he is glad that he is not like the sinful tax collector. The tax collector on the other hand is so ashamed that he dare not even turn his face towards God and prays only for forgiveness for a poor sinner.

The moral of Jesus' story is that it is the tax collector who will go to Heaven, not the Pharisee.

My priest's message is that we are all too busy taking exception to other religions – just like the Pharisee. We all believe our own religion to be the one true one. No – let us be like the tax collector, he concludes.

Afterwards I talk to the priest about his sermon. He invites me to visit him at his house later that day. That afternoon I knock on his door and he immediately invites me in for a cup of coffee in his kitchen. We sit there and have a long talk. His name is Tarcy and he comes originally from India. Has been here for six years. He gives repeated examples of the Hindu faith and their way of thinking. We talk of Western intellect and Eastern heart. He believes the two cultures are nearing each other and is glad of it. Openly admits that ecclesiastical formalities can create pointless barriers. *'We cannot meet in our brains. We can only meet in our hearts,'* he says. We talk about nature and how God is in nature. Very clearly. About Mary and water being connected. About Hindu architecture. About him wanting a new house of prayer to accommodate the many visitors here. The authorities, however, keep finding excuses to turn him down. We share half an Irish fruitcake. Finally he offers me the use of his tiny 'hermitage' in the garden. It turns out to be a sheltered corner with a statue of Christ standing on a tree trunk. On the end of a sawn-off branch he has painted the sign 'Oum'. The first word, according to the Indian way of thinking, to mean God. I sit there for an hour and a half taking in the magnificent view – a paradise on earth.

As I sit there, I suddenly sense the presence of Jesus and Mary. Jesus asks, *'Are you ready to return home?'* I have had plenty of time here so I am able to answer, 'Yes'. *'What have you learnt?'* is his next question. After some consideration I answer: 'To understand better what it means to be Man. The joy of living and the joy of being with the Virgin Mary.' After another question, Jesus says, *'Let us celebrate,'* after which he, Mary and John sit down on the ground. *'Will you slice us some bread?'* he asks me. I take an imaginary loaf, cut it and give them a slice each.

Jesus says, *'This is our body. Hallowed be it.'* We sit like this for a moment. *'I will pour the wine now,'* he continues. *'This is the holy blood of the Earth. The most pure water which, through the blessing, becomes spiritual wine.'*

This is the Last Supper of my journey.

* * *

As I traveled across Italy I was worried whether I would be able to complete the journey in the allotted time. I got confused and ended up going too fast. But this has given me nearly a week in Ephesus. Nearly a week to finish it all off properly.

There is time to deal with the unanswered questions, and Mary and I agree to spend the next four days working on four of them:

— What is the Soul of the Earth?
— More about the importance of water and our unde standing of it
— Understand thoroughly whether Mary actually walked the route
— What must I do next and how should I go about it?

We consider the first question during a couple of short outings in the area. Ephesus is built around a mountain called 'Ayasoulouk', which means 'holy water'. There seems to be an ancient mother-culture connected to it. The goddess Artemis Ephesia evolved from the fertile Mother Goddess who was worshipped here from the year 7000 BC. There is a lot to suggest that this mountain, this place, is one of the Mother Goddess's main abodes. I see this for myself when I visit the colossal cave vaults that are still to be found on the far side of the mountain. Even though many of them have collapsed, you can still see that it was originally an impressive system of very large caverns. There is an information board headed 'Cybele'.

CYBELE

Cybele was worshipped throughout most of the Roman Empire. She was regarded as the goddess of the Earth and of caverns. She originated from Phrygia, near Ankara.

At once I make contact with Cybele and I cannot help asking whether she is the Soul of the Earth. She answers, '*I have many names. The Great Goddess and Mother Earth among others, but I am not the Soul of the Earth. The Earth's soul cannot be compared to a human or angelic soul. I belong with man, but I have deep contact with the Earth.*'

There is something about the Soul of the Earth that I do not understand. I associate it with Mother Earth and the Goddess, but it is apparently not the same thing. There are goddesses galore in the area around Ephesus. Artemis, Cybele, why, even Athena is close at hand. She is said to have ruled in Troy and Smyrna (Izmir). Smyrna is less than 100 kilometers from here. She is characterized by the usual spear, helmet and shield – normally male attributes.

It is generally agreed that the names 'Smyrna' and 'Ephesus' stem from Amazon names. In fact there are several local town names that have Amazonian roots. These masculine women must therefore have had an important base here in east Turkey, and ancient contacts to the Mother Goddess must be tied in with the landscape.

I visit a museum where I find pictures of a series of female figures especially interesting. The oldest of them date back to about 5800 BC and portray the great, fat Mother Goddess. Through time, the figures change form completely. Cybele, for example, is narrow-hipped and broad-shouldered.

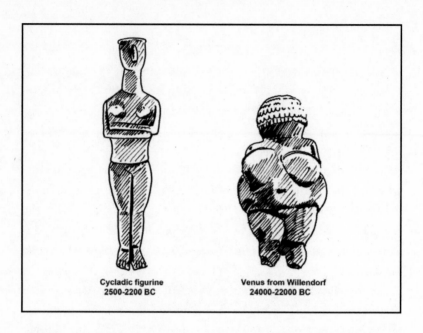

Cycladic figurine
2500-2200 BC

Venus from Willendorf
24000-22000 BC

This seems to be as far as I can go in my search for the essence of Mother Earth – the Soul of the Earth. I have done what I could. Several divine figures have been associated with Mother Earth, but none of them can be said to be the Soul of the Earth. I will just have to leave it at that.

Mary moves on to the next subject, the question of water. Again she explains that water is the basic condition for life. Water *is* life. Within its cycle it goes through all its states of existence. Water remembers. Water is the Earth's memory. Each individual molecule of water would be able to reveal the whole history of all cycles if we could decode it. Just as tree rings can mirror the life of a tree.

If we destroy the water, we destroy ourselves. Moreover, water is also the nature of femininity. Mary says, *'Look at the Earth from above. It is almost covered by a thin layer of water. This is a gift of God, and what you call life. All life began in water and thus also mankind. Therefore you have the whole of evolution in you. Your cells have this memory.*

'Water as an entity remembers – the deep sea of recollection. Everything you do to the waters of the Earth will be remembered and will need balancing energy-wise. Bless water as the fountain of life and you will be able to drink it as the elixir of life. As the best of all wine. Keep in mind how Jesus blessed the water yesterday. And keep in mind also that water can annihilate mankind. Respect and honor water as the most precious thing you have.'

We consider the third subject. The question of whether Mary actually walked the route herself. She assures me she did. *'As I told you before, your journey is taking place on two levels. One is your own personal level and yet there is another. Many of your experiences have been very personal – most obviously in the cave at Parnassus. What I have told you about my route is true. As if I, Mary, have been able to speak to you across the span of nearly 2,000 years. I am a soul-polarity within you, but I am also within you as the Mary who bore Jesus and lived almost 2,000 years ago. Remember, Hans, it is your faith that is most important.'*

I go back to Father Tarcy's. He invites me in again for tea. He asks me about the route I have walked and why. I tell him my story and he is intrigued with this new idea of Mary having made such a long journey, and he asks me to write about it in English. I also tell him that the journey has been a quest to balance the masculine and the feminine. Father Tarcy admits that the church favors the masculine, but adds that, to the catholic way of thinking, 'power' is feminine. The Holy Spirit is feminine and can be interpreted as the active divine power.

On my way back to town, I pass the car park where there seems to be some sort of disturbance. People are gathered round a horse-drawn vehicle. A man and woman are talking loudly in German. I ask if there is anything wrong. The couple say no, people are just curious. They have been recognized from a TV program about their journey from Germany to Jerusalem. I tell them briefly about my journey and ask about theirs. They have traveled through East Germany, the Czech Republic, Hungary, the Ukraine and Georgia. In Romania they were attacked and almost killed. The man still has a long cut across the top of his head and the left side of the woman's face is still paralyzed.

In spite of this, they managed to get back to Georgia where they put up for the winter. Later they went on to Bulgaria and now here to Turkey. They have been traveling for four years and have done about 5,000 kilometers. They expect to get to Jerusalem within the next two or three years! Some journey! My meager 2,300 kilometers are nothing to boast about.

* * *

The final day dawns. Visit Mary's place first thing. The custodian waves me through, as he has done the last couple of days. I go into the church and sit down. Mary comes through very quickly. Asks me to go into a side chapel known as Mary's bedroom. I am certain it has been a christening chapel and prayer room with water running gently through it. I stand against the back wall for a while. Mary looks me over from in front – my whole body. Then she asks me to turn round and looks me over from behind. She asks me to step into the middle of the room. All at once, water comes pouring down from above, as if I had stepped into a waterfall. A wonderfully purifying and beneficial experience.

Later, Grethe helped me to ask Mary whether I was correct in thinking there used to be water in that room:

'Yes. The water was collected in a large vat. Not like in baptisms today. It was more like a bathtub where John [and perhaps Mary herself] would baptize people who had listened to us and who wished for a ceremony through which they could be admitted to the Christian mystery. John knew of John the Baptist's rituals and carried on the tradition of being undressed and submerged in the cleansing water. One got in and bathed and was then dressed in a white robe to signify the ritualistic purification.

'And yes, the room was also used for meditation. Prayer mostly.'

The end is drawing close. There are a number of things that need doing. Mary becomes very direct: *'I want you to do two things. You have an object on you which I would like you to bury between the two pine trees in the valley. After that, I would like you to learn this prayer, and to say it up at Tracy's place: "Dear God, I beseech you, let the power of your mercy fall on all the homeless, the sick and the needy. Let them understand their situation and let the power of your mercy end their suffering. This I beseech you. Amen."'*

I know instantly that the object Mary refers to is the dove pendant I sewed onto my hat in Einsiedeln. I go straight down to my two trees in the valley. Dig a small hole and place the pendant in it.

'Dear God, I thank you that, when we were at the convent of Hildegard of Bingen, you granted me the power to give blessing. I thank you for blessing me with the presence of the Holy Spirit in the form of the dove above my head. This gift was dedicated to my pilgrimage and, to symbolize that, I now release the dove so that it may return home to you, I hereby bury this pendant. Amen.'

It feels right to return what I have been lent.

Next, I go up to the church. Ask Father Tracy's permission to go and sit in his garden, which he is only too pleased to grant. I walk up there. Settle down and say the prayer. Then I ask that any light I may have gathered along the route be directed through this prayer to the homeless, the sick and the needy.

It feels right that the energy does not rest in me, but flows on to others. Feels right to be part of a flow. Father Tracy joins me. We exchange addresses. He gives me a cup of tea to drink while I finish my meditations, which takes about an hour.

The fourth and final question presents itself: What must I do next? How should I go about it?

Mary asks me to write everything down and then compile it into a book. We talk about how I should set it out, and she announces: *'In two years the book will be published.'*

I sense that we are almost finished. The mood becomes very solemn. More figures seem to appear. They stand in front of me. There are five of them but I will only speak of the three in the middle.

To my right is John. He speaks first:

'You have promised to serve the new era. I am a part of the new era, which means you are a part of my energy. That is why I am here.'

In the middle is Jesus:

'I am here as the energy of Christ. You are a part of my heart-energy. That is why I am here.'

To my left is Mary:

'I am here as the human Virgin Mary, mother of Christ. I am here as the Mother of Souls. And I am here as the highest feminine energy.'

Symbolically we all hold hands and stand together for a moment. Then they all vanish. I give thanks for the grace of God throughout my journey. With all my heart.

* * *

I stand alone in the midst of God's wonderful nature. It is autumn. The air is sharp, clear and fragrant. The birds sing in beautiful dialogues. The trees of the valley stand around me, tall and erect, unfolding their magnificent foliage. Out on the horizon, between the walls of the valley, I can just glimpse the sea, blinking in the sunlight.

I am overjoyed to be alive, to exist, to be Man.

I suppose I could probably have come to the same realization at home. Maybe even in my own back garden. Sometimes it takes a long search to find the obvious. But I would not have missed this for the world.

18

Postscript

It is now a year since I came home from my pilgrimage. I have spent my time tending to my architect office and writing this book from my diary. This has in itself been a process of development. There are many events that I have not fully understood until now. Finally everything falls into place and I see the whole picture, though in the light of my understanding I discovered several blind spots. Some things were still unfinished, and certain stretches of the route needed correcting.

Even as I traveled, Mary made me aware of the fact that there were short stretches in Italy where I had gone wrong. In Greece there was a challenge I avoided and a test I did not pass. And it was still a puzzle to me how Mary and John had got from Marseilles all the way up to Bingen.

Through the invaluable help of Grethe, my clear-sighted friend, Mary has been able to confirm that there were things I could improve. But, as was always the case in our discussions, I did not get the answers handed to me on a silver platter. I was given further explanations of things that had already happened, or clues to led me in the right direction. That is why I had to go back.

On a new journey to Italy, I managed to correct several short stretches. The most important was the rediscovery of the Rieti valley, with the path through Francis of Assisi's sacred sites, and the understanding of the central role he played in my Italian pilgrimage. Everything that I was too busy to notice on my original journey. I have already added these corrections in their respective places in the book.

I had to return to Greece as well. Most importantly to Gaia. I clearly did not pass the test in the cave on Mount Parnassus. There was something I had not understood. All year, I have endeavored to understand Gaia and I have been in contact with her here at home through nature. I wanted to go back to the cave less prejudiced than before. So I returned to Delphi and Mount Parnassus. The following is an account of this new meeting with Gaia.

* * *

On a cold October evening I again arrive in Delphi. I check into the same hostel and even the same room as before. Last time, I enjoyed wandering about the temple site in the evening light, and I look forward to doing this again. When I get to the entrance it turns out that it shut at three o'clock. There are new opening hours. Very disappointing, but at least I can walk down to the springs in the Castalia gorge and get a sip of water. I do that, and deep in the gorge I lose myself in the gentle murmur of the water and the spectacle of the green banks along the stream. It hits me that this is Gaia's element. Trickling water and the power of green growth. This much at least I have learnt in the past months. As I think about Gaia, I realize that this place is the energy gateway to the whole temple area. If there is a gateway, there must be a gatekeeper. I ask the gatekeeper for permission to enter this energy realm. I have hardly concluded my request before an imaginary snake rises up in front of me. It is colossal. Between 1 and 2 meters in diameter. It rises up, ready to strike, and hisses: *'What do you want?'*

'Python!' I exclaim, and I just know that this is the fabled snake that guarded Gaia's mountain. It nods. All at once everything falls into place. Python is of course the gatekeeper of Gaia's temple mount, and one had to ask its permission to enter further into the realm. Though I have earlier been afraid of snakes, this giant one does not frighten me in the least.

I even experience a sort of intimacy with it. In fact it actually makes me glad, for Python must be the key to my reaching Gaia. I ask it to take on its old form from before Apollo's time, 700–800 years BC. *'In the 900s,'* it corrects me. Python becomes clearer and rises up even more threateningly. I ask permission to enter into Gaia's energy realm to speak with her. *'Come back tomorrow!'* it answers dismissively. Instead I ask about its work. I see an image of it snaking its way down from the mountain like a flowing river. The energy flow of life itself. Bringing life to plants, allowing them to grow and multiply. The snake bites its own tail, thus becoming a symbol of the great circle of life. Death included.

I take leave of Python and make my way down to the round temple, Athena Protania, which is still open. I get talking to the attendant, who happens to mention that it was at the Castallian springs that Apollo shot Python with his arrow. In other words it is completely in keeping with tradition that Python frequented the place where I have just met him.

* * *

The next morning I again present myself at the springs. Sense Python rising up. Suddenly it changes size. Becomes smaller and slithers its way towards me. It coils itself round my body, winding up round my neck and on up above my head. I can see the minute detail of its scales. Above my head, it rises up, faces forward and poises, ready to strike. *'Now you can go up to the cave,'* it says. *'I will sit here on your head. And beware! I will strike if needs be.'* I quickly promise to behave myself.

In my rental car I drive up to the plain and park at the foot of the mountain. I am dressed in my old pilgrim clothes, right down to my worn-out shoes. With Mary accompanying me, I climb the mountain, carrying the snake above my head.

Outside the cave I meet a German couple and their little boy.

They have spent the night here. By coincidence I had photographed them the evening before in Delphi. We talk for a bit. They start their breakfast, and I enter the cave.

This time, there is nothing to unnerve me. On the contrary. The cave seems completely neutral, and I am open and inquisitive.

At the base of the cave, I seat myself in front of the stone where I sense Gaia will appear. I have decided to be completely open but cannot stop myself apologizing for my behavior the year before. Gaia has actually been present from the moment I entered, and she seems not at all interested in my apologies. Quietly she tells me about her work. Her basic impulse is *the flow of life*. From birth to death. From sowing, through germination, flowering and production of fruit to harvest and withering. The cycle of life. Python is part of this energy. Suddenly Gaia becomes very direct, and asks me sharply, *'Will you serve me?'* I hesitate. Tell her I serve Mary and Michael and that I cannot desert them. Gaia seems to fade. I stay sitting there for a long time, but nothing happens. The German family come into the cave and for a while we talk and I watch them explore the deepest end of the cave. The boy is about four or five years old and digs away fearlessly, examining his findings under the stones. I realize I can learn a lot from him. If a snake appeared, I bet he would play with it.

After they leave, I contact Gaia again. We talk a bit until she once more breaks off, asking: *'Will you serve me?'* Again I have reservations, and Gaia fades away.

In the meantime, something has happened to the snake above my head. It has divided, becoming two. One on each side of my head. Almost like the Aesculapian staff.

Yet again I sit and try to establish contact, when a group of elderly Americans enter the cave, and they, of course, are not exactly quiet.

I tell myself that I have learnt all there is to learn in the cave and start up towards the exit. Halfway up, I turn. Gaia's question is still bothering me and I sense that it is me who is blocking the process. Ask Mary's advice and get a nod. Decide that as Gaia is the energy behind the flow of life, there cannot be any reason why I should not serve her, for I am also part of the flow of life.

I address Gaia for the third time and say that I am willing to serve her. Gaia slowly appears. Something is about to happen. I am standing on black ground but suddenly the floor seems to be torn out from under my feet. I float in the air over a deep and very dark hole. Slowly I am lowered down into the hole. Disappear into the darkness. For a long time. It is as if I am being lowered down to the center of the earth. There is a sea of fire that turns into light. A voice says, '*I am the Soul of the Earth. You are in the heart. This is where your physical form will be left. I am the Heart of the Earth.*' I ask if I can do anything for the Soul of the Earth, and am answered, '*Spread word of me.*'

Slowly I rise up again, am back in the cave and sense that I have fulfilled my task. I can happily take leave of Gaia and make my way down the mountain.

I drive back towards Athens, but Mary seems to want me to carry on along the pilgrimage route. I guess there are more stretches that need correcting. I drive to Dahlia and on along the small lanes I walked on my pilgrimage. There do not seem to be any corrections needed. I reach a main road, and consider turning on to it, but again Mary asks me to follow the old route. All right then, I think, I'll do that. A few kilometers further along, I reach the small chapel where Michael last initiated me and suddenly I realize why Mary wanted me to come this way. Something is to happen here again. I sense Michael's presence. I place myself on the spot where I was last shown that my role-models – my 'self' – were united with my soul.

Again I stand in front of Michael. On impulse I lift my arms outwards and upwards. Do it twice, as if to practice the movement. When I feel comfortable with it, I tell him I am ready.

Michael says, '*Feel the heart of the Earth beneath you.*' It feels so powerful that it physically pulls at my lower body. I feel the ball of fire at the center of the Earth and understand that this light is also God's light. The physical pole in the heart of the Earth pulls at my Root chakra while at the same time reaching right around my heart. *'Lift your arms,'* says Michael, and I slowly lift my arms, as a bird lifts its wings. I lift my arms – or wings – higher and now I feel the light pole above me. The Spirit. It pulls at my Crown chakra, reaching right down around my heart. As I lift my arms right up, it is clear that both poles are pulling at me, and they would pull me apart if they did not grasp onto each other in my heart. As my fingers meet and I form a vertical rod, fire consumes me from top to toe. It is as though I am 'de-fleshed'. From my heart down, my flesh – or matter – falls like discarded clothing and disappears down to the Earth pole. From my heart up, my flesh slides like clothes up to the Spiritual pole. Thus I am left standing, and the *'I'* experiencing this is my soul. Michael and Mary enter me. One on each side of my heart, inside the boundaries of my body. They turn and are now in place.

Mary laughs and says that this was the final – and missing – initiation. She ends with the words, *'The journey is now over.'*

And so everything fell into place after all. Gaia is all about one aspect of Mother Earth, the aspect of the flow of life on Earth. The Earth, as an entity, seems to have a soul rooted in its heart. If we wish to live a life well balanced between mind and matter, we must embrace the Earth. We must understand and respect it. It is a fundamental – and divine – part of our lives.

The final unresolved question was how Mary and John had got from Marseilles up to Bingen. They had come to the south of France – that much I had understood. But their journey from there on was hidden from me. I had an idea that the town of Vezelay might hold the key. Grethe confirmed this.

Once again Kirstin and I went camping in the German-French area. Let me close my story with an account of what happened there.

* * *

I am directed to Vezelay even as I reach the convent of Hildegard of Bingen. We drive there. In medieval times Vezelay was a very major place of pilgrimage. Mary Magdalene was worshipped here and it was the starting point for pilgrimages to Santiago. Today the town is dwindling, but is beautifully situated on a low mountain in an area of valleys. The church in Vezelay is wonderfully beautiful – an architectural masterpiece. Dedicated to Mary Magdalene.

I sense Mary Magdalene the moment I enter the church. I am guided down into the crypt, where I find a chair and settle down. The Virgin Mary is by my side. Mary Magdalene kneels just in front of me. She is so deeply intense and full of life that I find it quite overwhelming. She explains to me how she and other disciples sailed from Jaffa, the harbour of Jerusalem to Sicily. There they waited over a month for Mary and John to arrive from Ephesus, where Mary had been ill. Together they sailed to Marsala (Marseilles).

The group consisted of Mary, John, his brother James, Joseph of Arimathea, two others and Mary Magdalene. They traveled north. Whether they sailed up the Rhone or whether they walked I do not know, but they ended up in Vezelay. Jesus had told Mary Magdalene they were to go to Marsala and on up into the European continent if the persecution intensified. Jesus had added that this part of the world would accept his teachings. The group stayed in Vezelay for a long time. They were very unsure of how to proceed. After much deliberation they decided to separate and take various routes. James was in no doubt. He went southwest – towards Spain. Joseph of Arimathea went north-west with a few companions –to England. The Virgin Mary says that she felt drawn towards the north-east and that she and John went that way. Mary Magdalene stayed in Vezelay. They agreed that if they had not returned by a certain time – I think about three months – they should then make their own separate ways back to Palestine. I get the impression that Joseph of Arimathea came back and accompanied Mary Magdalene down to the south of France, where she probably remained the rest of her life. Mary, John and James never returned. They each established their own pilgrimage route.

I cannot tell you much about Mary and John's journey through France. But I sense that they crossed Johanniskreuz and continued east. It becomes clear to me that they boarded a boat in the ecclesiastical city of Speyer on the west bank of the Rhine and sailed with the current down river.

At Bingen they went ashore on the north side of the Rhine.

Through Grethe, Mary later told me about their whole journey:

'You are touching on a time that was one of the most painful parts of my life. It was an almost unbearable period of mourning. That is why it was a great joy for me to have company. Due to the perse-cution of Christ it was expedient to leave Palestine. I can confirm that we started by going to Ephesus as I needed to find somewhere I would not be recognized. At first I did not really feel I had to go very far. I just needed a new base. A safe place where I could feel secure. And Ephesus has always been a place where women are held in high esteem. There is a deep connection to what you were looking for at the prophetic goddess's cave on Mount Parnassus. Ephesus also honors the female contact with the deep. So it was a natural place for me to go to. There, I would be out of danger.

'First I stay in Ephesus where I find a humble dwelling. My physical body is worn out and I am grieving deeply, so I need to rest. It takes three months before I regain my strength and am ready to go on. It is not really me that feels driven to continue; it is rather John. There are rumors that we are in Ephesus. I feel safe enough here but John does not. He was of course one of the disciples and Jesus' followers are being searched for. So it is actually me who

accompanies John.

'In Sicily we meet up with Mary Magdalene and Joseph of Arimathea, who is by now an old man. Mary Magdalene is very weighed down by her loss. But it is in Sicily that we gather before going to Marseilles. Again we do not wish to leave here, nor have we a desire to see France, but it is necessary. We are being hunted.

'We are to go up into Europe because the Christian impulse, which as you know was born in the Middle East, has to be taken to Europe.'

In Vezelay they seem to have found sanctuary and help. Mary continues, through Grethe:

'We do not wish to separate. We just feel it is something we have to do. We have to walk the path that is laid out for us.

'Joseph of Arimathea goes to England with his men. James makes for Spain. He is physically strong and very determined. He is in no doubt as to his route. He knows where he wants to go. We leave something behind us in Vezelay – a secret – a special sort of energy to do with the meeting of differing ways. This can be Vezelay's task for the future.'

Talking of John's and her journey, Mary says:

'We aimed to go as far north as possible. Along the channel of light that runs through Europe. John and I travel to the place where Hildegard of Bingen came later. By then I was completely exhausted. I would not have been able to go any further. John is more robust and an immense help. Here we meet a humble man who takes us in. He tells us that there is a beautiful place we must see before turning back south. A place where God lives on Earth. He shows us the way. At that time it was a natural shrine. It was not possible to travel further north. Other powers ruled up there.'

Kristin and I drive back to the area of Hildegard's convent. I believe that the beautiful place Mary and John were shown lies a little to the west of the convent. There, the Rhine winds around a very distinctive mountain. The first thing you see is a vast memorial, the Niederwald Denkmal. A little further on in the woods, you find a so-called 'hermitage'. In the late Middle Ages it was inhabited by hermits. Looking southwards, we are presented with a quite exceptional view. The River Nahe, running into the Rhine right opposite us. The Nahe valley, bordered on both sides by sweeping mountains, behind which the landscape fades away into the horizon scene after scene. Here, the first stage of the pilgrimage is revealed, and in its own way this place becomes a powerful gateway to the whole journey. I get the impression that here Mary felt it was time to turn round and begin her journey home.

As I stand beside the hermitage, lost in the view, I suddenly feel that they are all here with me. Mary, John, Michael and Hildegard. We are to perform one final act.

I am to assist in driving a column of light into the ground. It happens. The column is full of inscriptions in a language I do not understand. It rises up high and reaches far down. I walk in a spiral out and in and round the column. Time passes. Then we drive a corresponding pole of light into the earth above the Virgin Mary's house in Ephesus.

The route is anchored.

May it shine.

Thank You

I may have made the actual journey and written this book, but neither journey nor book would have been possible without help from a lot of people. First and foremost I want to thank my wife, Kirstin Pinstrup Thomsen, who has given me invaluable support at home and with my research.

I also wish to thank my friends for backing me up with their cheerful indulgence.

It was the Englishman Peter Dawkins who taught me to communicate with angels. For several years I have taken part in Peter's seminars, visiting powerful landscapes where Peter has communicated with nature-beings and angels. After three or four years of following these seminars, to my great consternation, I myself was contacted by an angel and given a message to pass on. I did this and I have had open contact ever since. Without this 'apprenticeship' and further practice, I would never have been able to hear Mary's voice, find my way or have any of my communication with angels. For this I owe Peter an enormous debt of gratitude.

With Grethe Toftlund Nielsen's help, I have been able to have intimate conversations with Mary. Conversations which time after time have provided verification and clarification. My heartfelt thanks to Grethe for these wonderful opportunities.

While writing this book, I have received constructive criticism from good friends. Acute and well meant. I wish to thank Caspar Koch, Henrik Laier, Lars Bo Bojesen and Lise Burgaard for being there for me and helping me forward.

The translation of the book from Danish to English has been an admirable co-operation between my friend Philippa Steen and her mother Tove Angus. Thank you, both of you.

Finally – dear Mary: Thank you for asking me.

Fact Sources

1

Hildegard: *Hildegard von Bingen: En basun for Guds mund*, Kirsten Kjærulff, 1995

Convent of St. Hildegard: *Benediktinreinnenabtei St. Hildegard*, Rüdesheim/Eibingen, 2002

2

Mont St. Michel: *Les hauteurs du Mont Saint-Michel*, Jean Joseph Ring, Pays d'Alsace, 2000

Mont St. Odile: *Die Heidenmauer: Ein archäologisches Rätzel*, Francis Mantz, 1992

3

Sasbach: *Sasbach am Kaiserstuhl*, Kunstführer Nr. 2149, 1995, www.badische-seite.de

Endingen: *Die Wahlfahrt zur Weinenden Muttergottes von Endingen*, Katholisches Pharramt, St. Peter, 1991

Riegel: Board at the Chapel and www.riegel-amkaiserstuhl.de

4

St. Blasien: *St. Blasien/Schwarzwald*, Art Guide no. 555, 2001

5

Rapperswil: Homepage of the town

Einsiedeln: *Einsiedeln*, Art Guide no. 538, 2000

6

St. Gotthardt: *Göschenen, Kirchen und Kapellen*, Peda-Kunstführer 546, 2004. De.wikipedia.org/Wki/Gotthardmassiv

7

Orta San Giulio and Sacro Monte di Orta: Tourist brochures from Piemonte

8

Pisa: www.navipisa.it

Volterra: www.commune.volterra.pi.it and information from Ufficio Turistico

Siena: SIENA, Plurigraft, Casa Edice Perseus

9

Perugia: www.argoweb.it

Francis: *Den hellige Frans af Assisi*, Johannes Jørgensen, 1956

Templo di Clitunno: www.argoweb.it and www.umbriadagustare.it

Via Flaminia: www.wikipedia.org

Arrone: www.colorideellumbria.com

10

Piedeluce: www.comune.terni.it

The holy places of St. Francis in the Rieti Valley: *The Franciscan Sanctuaries of the Rieti Valley*, Massimo Fusarelli, 1999

The Song of the Sun: *Den hellige Frans af Assisi*, Johannes Jørgensen, 1956

Rieti: *Provencia di Rieti*, Instituto geografico d'Agostino, Rieti

Lanciano: *Lanciano*, Guida Visuale al Centro Storico, and *Sancturio del Miracolo Eucharistico*, Lanciano

11

San Giovanni in Rotondo and Padre Pio: *Saint Pio*, Angelo Giubelli, 2002

Monte Sant'Angelo: *Saint Michael Shrine on the Gargano*, P. Jan Bogacki, 2001

12

Korfu: www.corfuxenos.gr, www.culture.gr and *De græske øer*, Politiken, 2002
Necromantio near Acheron: www.culture.gr og www.greeklandscapes.com
Nicopolis: *Greek and Roman Mythology*, Michael Stapleton, 1982 and *The Gods of Olympos*, S. Brothers, 1997

13
Local booklets

14
Delphi: *Delphi*, Vanghelis Pendazos, former Director of the Museum in Delphi, 1984

15
Argonauts: *Greek mythology and Religion*, Maria Mavromataki, 1997
Eleusis: *Eleusis*, Kalliope Preka-Alexandri, 2003
Greek and Roman Mythology, Michael Stapleton, 1982
Athens between Legend and History, Maria Mavromataki, 1995
www.culture.gr

16
Aegina: *The Island of Aegina*, Flora Alifandi, 2002
Historic information in the ruins and Kolona
Saint Nektarios: The Saint of our Century, Sotos Chondropoulos
Patmos: *I was in the Isle of Patmos*, Archimandrite Theodoritos, 1968
What is Orthodoxy? Peter A. Botsis
Ceremonies of the Orthodox Church, Meliton-Richard Oakes, 2004

17
Ephesus: *Ephesus, Ruins and Museum*, Selahattin Erdemgil, 1986

The House of the Virgin Mary: *The Holy Virgin's House*, P. Eugine Poulin, 1999

The House of Virgin Mary, Egidio Picucci, 1999

Jungfrau Maria, Melih Öndün, 1995

Amazons: Information in the Archaeological Museum in Izmir

AXIS MUNDI
BOOKS

Axis Mundi Books, provide the most revealing and coherent explorations and investigations of the world of hidden or forbidden knowledge. Take a fascinating journey into the realm of Esoteric Mysteries, Magic, Mysticism, Angels, Cosmology, Alchemy, Gnosticism, Theosophy, Kabbalah, Secret Societies and Religions, Symbolism, Quantum Theory, Apocalyptic Mythology, Holy Grail and Alternative Views of Mainstream Religion.